Golden Hands

ENCYCLOPEDIA OF

EMBROIDERY

Collins   Glasgow & London

William Collins Sons & Co Ltd
London · Glasgow · Sydney · Auckland
Toronto · Johannesburg

First published by Collins 1973
First metric edition 1977

ISBN 0 00 435 035 9 047 2

Printed in Great Britain by William Collins Sons & Co. Ltd.

CONTENTS

Embroidery

Canvas Work

CONTENTS (continued)

Collector's Pieces

ACKNOWLEDGEMENTS

Text:
Margaret Beautement, Eileen Lowcock
Photographers:
Malcolm Aird, Adèle Baker, John Carter, Victoria Carter, Bob Croxford, Richard Dormer, Anne Dyer, Guy Gibbard, Su Gooders, Martin Harrison, Chris Lewis, Eileen Lowcock, Graham Murrell, Tony Moussoulides, Paul Redman, Bruce Scott, David Swann, Chris Thomson, Peter Watkins
Illustrators:
Janet Ahlberg, Barbara Firth, Isobel Hollowood, Anna Kostal, Francis Newell, Josephine Rankin, Julian and Renée Robinson, Frances Ross Duncan, Joy Simpson, Jill Smyth, Paul Williams, Arka Graphics
Designers:
Kate Bailey, Margaret Beautement, Esta Cairnes, Victoria Carter, J. & P. Coats U.K. Ltd, Valerie Cock, Frances Coleman, Mrs Cowie, Mrs Cutbush, Dorothy Darch, DMC, Dr P. Doplyn, Frances Duncan, Anne Dyer, Emmy Elphick, Louis Gartner, Joan Gilbert, Louise Grosse, Patty Knox, Wendy Lees, Elizabeth Manley, M. McNeill, Frances Newell, Joan Nicholson, Mrs Pemberton, Patricia Phillpott, Angela Salmon, Marjorie Self, Jo Springer, Mrs J. M. Stuart, Martyn Thomas, A. Thompson, Valerie Tullock, H. G. Twilley Ltd, Janice Williams, May Williams, Gill Wing, D. Wooding
Credits:
Camera Press, London: GMN, Lars Larsson, Kalle Nordin, Kjell Nilsson, Fuer Sie
We would like to thank the following for their help and co-operation:
The American Museum, Bath; The Bodleian Library, Oxford; J. & P. Coats U.K. Ltd, The County Borough of Hastings, The Embroiderers' Guild, London; The Needlewoman Shop, London; Patons and Baldwins Ltd, Victoria and Albert Museum, London; The White House, London
Manufacturers' and stockists' addresses
M=manufacturer   S=stockist
Embroidery and canvas work materials from:
John Lewis, 629 Oxford Street, London, W.1. (S), Mace and Nairn (mail order service), 89 Crane Street, Salisbury, Wilts, (S), The Needlewoman Shop, 146 Regent Street, London, W.1. (S)
Anchor yarns from:
J. & P. Coats (U.K.) Ltd, Central Office, 12 Seedhill Road, Paisley, Scotland(M)
Appletons yarns from:
Appletons Bros Ltd, Church Street, Chiswick, London, W.4. (M)
DMC yarns from:
C. & S. Handicrafts Supplies Ltd, 346 Stag Lane, Kingsbury, London, N.W.9. (M)
Patons wools from:
Patons and Baldwins Ltd, Darlington, Co. Durham (M)

Introduction

This embroidery encyclopedia is designed to appeal both to the beginner and the expert. We lead you step by step through the various stages of embroidery and canvas work, from the basic running stitch to the luxurious technique of metal thread embroidery, from cross stitch to the flame inspired patterns of Florentine.

Learn how to enlarge and reduce designs, set up embroidery frames and work from a chart. You can explore the many varieties of thread available in our Yarn Chart, where each one is described according to its texture and the different techniques to which it can be applied.

Each method and stitch is explained in diagrams, Stitch Libraries and photographs, while beautiful examples of the work introduce, illustrate and conclude each technique. These Collector's Pieces have been selected to encourage experimentation and design.

Consider the arts of embroidery and canvas work as a method of self expression. You can take your favourite pattern from the book and simply by choosing your own colour scheme, using alternative stitches to vary the texture of the work and interlacing different coloured threads into the canvas, or hanging a bead here and there, you have created your own design and left the imprint of your personality on the work.

Apart from describing the methods associated with embroidery and canvas work, our encyclopedia gives you a wide range of different patterns and designs. Make an appliqué panel for your children's bedroom, a tablecloth in drawn thread work for that special dinner party or a fashionable tote bag in double cross stitch to add a splash of colour to your wardrobe.

1

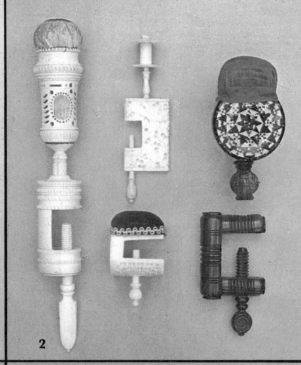

2

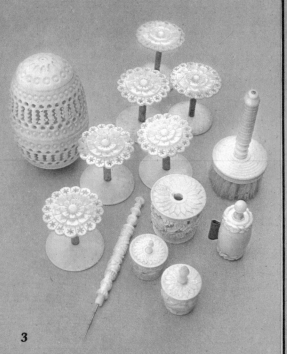

3

4

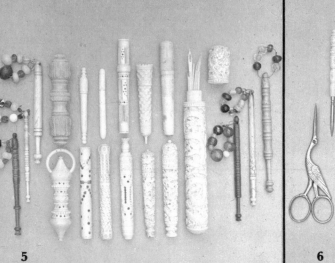

5

6

Collector's Piece

Tools of embroidery

Genteel young ladies of the 19th century were trained to excel in the gentle arts, and needlecraft was considered a most necessary and elegant accomplishment. Needlework accessories were appropriate gifts for a bride-to-be, and beautifully turned spools of ivory and mother-of-pearl, silver filigree needle cases, engraved scissors and carved boxes and tools were presented by friends and relatives. These exquisitely made accessories had a practical value too. Materials for needlework were expensive and therefore precious, and great care was taken of them. Silk thread, for instance, was purchased in a skein, carefully re-wound onto a spool which was inserted into a protective barrel-shaped cover, the thread being withdrawn through a hole in the cover.

1. *Chatelaines, such as this, were attached to a belt worn around the waist. This one carries a needlecase, a pincushion, a tape measure, a thimble bucket and scissors.*
2. *Clamps, used in lace making and for securing material to the table while the seamstress sewed long seams.*
3. *Mother-of-pearl cotton reels and ivory cotton barrels. On the right, a wax container, a tape measure, and a brush and pricker for marking out designs.*
4. *Several kinds of tape measures, thimbles and pincushions.*
5. *Bobbins for making pillow lace, an assortment of needle cases and a case of netting tools.*
6. *Stilettos of ivory, mother-of-pearl, silver and ormolu, used for pricking broderie Anglaise eyelet holes. Also, mother-of-pearl crochet hook, bead and filigree needle cases, tatting shuttles and scissors.*
Right: Pincushions made of ebony, cedar, pewter and Tunbridge ware, usually filled with emery powder.

6

Chapter 1

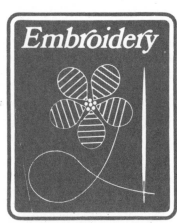

Introduction to embroidery

Embroidery is at last being recognised as an art form and is finding its way into the museums of modern art. If you are bent on adding decorative touches to your wardrobe and home or want to design a beautiful panel, it's worth looking through our collection of stitches and designs, both modern and historical, to find inspiration and clear instructions on how to work the stitches.

Nowadays you can create exciting textures and three dimensional effects by using strong designs and colour schemes and a fascinating variety of stitches and yarns. But remember, if you are embroidering things which need to be laundered, make sure that all the materials have fast dyes and are washable, and avoid using stitches which are too long.

Know your needles

Always use the correct needle for the type of embroidery you are working to ensure ease and comfort.

Sharps needle	medium length, with small eye —for sewing with cotton or a single strand of stranded cotton.
Crewel needle sizes 6-8	long and sharp, with large eye —for stranded cotton, Coton à Broder. Pearl Cotton No.8.
size 5	Larger eye—for tapestry wool, and Pearl Cotton No. 5.
Chenille needle No. 19	short and sharp, with large eye —for thick threads, tapestry wool, soft embroidery cotton.
Tapestry needle	blunt end—for whipped and laced stitches, canvas embroidery, drawn fabric and drawn-thread work.
Beading needle	fine—for sewing on beads.
Tambour hook	hook similar to a crochet hook —used for attaching beads.

Designs

Ready-made embroidery designs are usually sold in three ways:
(a) as transfers ready to iron on to your own choice of fabric
(b) already printed on cloth, often in a pack complete with yarns
(c) with charts for counted thread work (for example, cross-stitch).
In later chapters you will discover how to make your own designs, and how to enlarge and adapt.

A tambour frame clamped onto a table.

Which cloth to work on

You can work embroidery on almost any cloth unless you are following a charted design for counted thread embroidery or drawn thread work. For both these you need an even-weave cloth. This cloth has an even number of vertical and horizontal threads per square inch, and comes in a variety of colours. It is the best type to use for a beginner, as it helps to keep stitches even. Start by looking at even-weave cloths on the embroidery counter at your local store. You will also find that many linens, cottons and rayons in dress and furnishing fabric departments are also evenly-woven, and are equally suitable.

Frames

The most popular types are tambour and slate frames. The slate frame is like a wooden picture frame over which the work is stretched and tacked: this will be dealt with in Embroidery Chapter 13 page 52. There are three types of tambour frame which are all basically used in the same way: the embroidery screw ring which is held in the hand, the tambour frame which clamps on a table, and the table frame which has a stand.

Setting up a tambour frame

To prepare the tambour frame simply take the inside frame (the one without a screw) and wind bias binding evenly all round it so that none of the wood shows. This protects the material.

Place the material over the inside ring and press the outside ring down over it, until the one ring is inside the other. Gently ease the fabric down until it is taut and smooth. Tighten the screw and you are then ready to begin.

If you are working with a delicate fabric, cover it with a layer of protective tissue before pressing down the outside ring. This tissue must be cut to within 1cm of the ring before starting.

*A slate frame (floor frame style): the piece of canvas
work is entitled 'Young Girl Reading'*

Yarn Chart

Threads for you to choose from

Some techniques require a particular thread, but in many stitches you can experiment with several kinds of yarn.

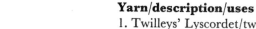

Yarn/description/uses

1. Twilleys' Lyscordet/twisted, knitting cotton/basic stitches
2. Mercer Crochet Cotton/fine, knitting cotton/basic stitches, drawn thread work, drawn fabric
3/4. Pearl Cotton/twisted, shiny cotton, No. 5 thick, No. 8 thin/ basic stitches, Blackwork, counted thread work, drawn fabric, drawn thread work, Hardanger, smocking
5. Transparent thread/nylon filament/invisible multi-purpose sewing thread, couching
6. Coats Drima/super-spun polyester/multi-purpose sewing thread
7/8. Guterman 40/100 silk/twisted, shiny silk/basic stitches
9. Anchor Button thread/twisted cotton/basic stitches, insertion stitches
10. Coats Satinised/mercerised, machine twist/multi-purpose sewing thread
11. Anchor Linen/twisted, shiny linen/cut work, drawn fabric, drawn thread work

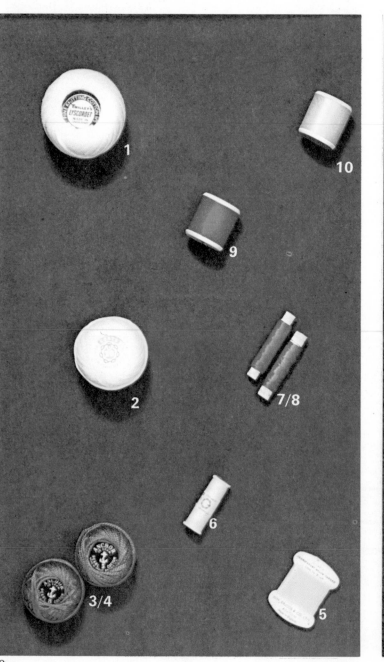

12. Soft Embroidery Cotton/twisted, matt cotton/basic stitches, couching, Hardanger, pattern darning

13. Coton à Broder/twisted, shiny cotton/basic stitches, cut work, drawn thread work, Hardanger, smocking

14. Crewel Wool/twisted, matt wool strands, separable/basic stitches, couching, canvas work

15. Slub Cotton/knitting cotton, uneven surface/couching

16. Tapestry Wool/twisted, matt wool/basic stitches, couching, pattern darning, canvas work

17. Stranded Cotton/twisted, separable, shiny cotton/basic stitches, counted thread work, drawn fabric, drawn thread work, Hardanger

18. "Filo-Floss"/six strand embroidery silk/basic stitches

19. Mohair/fluffy, knitting yarn/basic stitches (limited use), couching

20. Raffene/plastic raffia/basic stitches, couching, canvas work (limited use)

21. Suclan Wool/twisted, matt wool, separable/basic stitches, canvas work

22. Patons Turkey Rug Wool/twisted, matt wool, separable/basic stitches, canvas work

23/24. Metallic Cord/fine, untarnishable twist/basic stitches, drawn thread work, Blackwork, metal thread embroidery

25. Lurex/flat, metal thread/metal thread embroidery

26/27. Penelope Lurex/fine, nylon braid/basic stitches, metal thread embroidery

28/29/30. Smooth Purl, Pearl Purl, Rough Purl/three different weights of spiral metal thread/metal thread embroidery

31. Twilley's Goldfingering/washable, untarnishable, coarse thread/basic stitches, metal thread embroidery

32. Maltese Silk/fine sewing thread/couching

33. Japanese Gold/pure gold thread wound on a silk core/metal thread embroidery

34. Passing Gold/metal thread wound on a silk core/metal thread embroidery

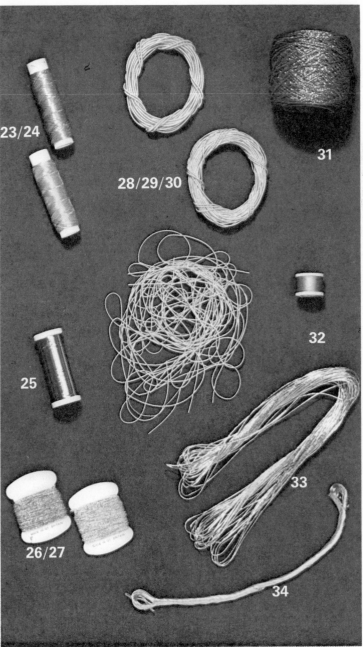

Chapter 2

How to enlarge and reduce designs

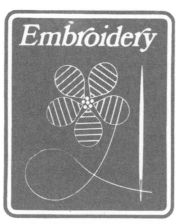

Whether you create your own embroidery designs or adapt those you find in books or magazines, it is useful to know how to alter the size. With the method of enlarging or reducing explained in this chapter, you will no longer have to worry if the initial design is large or small—you will be able to alter it to exactly the size you want. You will be surprised at how easy enlarging and reducing are.

What you will need:

☐ Tracing paper
☐ Graph or squared paper
☐ Rubber and ruler
☐ Felt tipped pen
☐ Soft pencil
☐ Carbon paper (optional)

Method

1. First trace the outline of the design on to tracing paper.
2. Carefully transfer tracing to graph or small squared paper.
3. Draw a rectangle round the tracing.
4. Draw a diagonal through the rectangle. Extend two adjacent sides of the rectangle to the final size you want, then draw lines at right angles from the ends of the extended sides to meet at the diagonal. If it confuses you to have the rectangles inside one another, draw the larger to one side of the smaller one.
5. Count the total number of squares in the small rectangle and divide the largest rectangle into the same number of squares to form a grid. Draw this in pencil as you may want to rub out and re-draw some of the lines of the design to improve its shape. Now in pen carefully copy this design on to the larger grid. It will help if you make tiny marks on each square where the lines of the design cross it, then you can join up these marks.
To reduce a design use the same method in reverse.

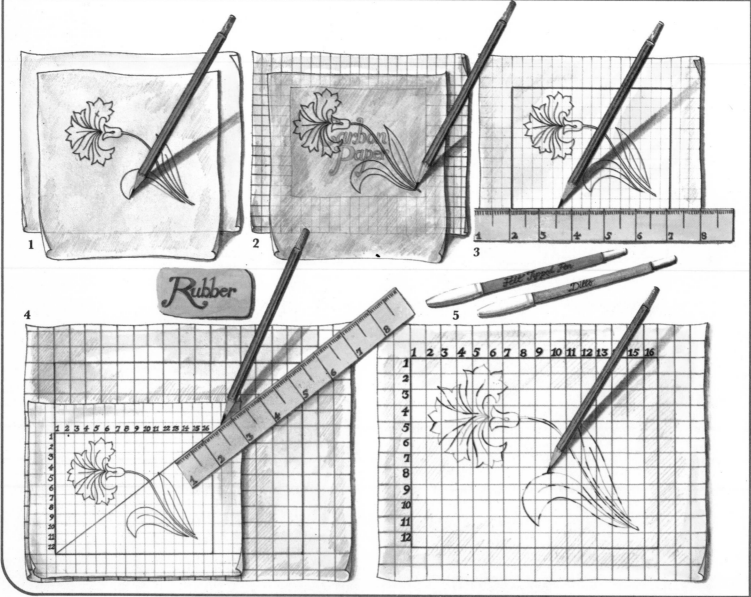

This anemone has been enlarged and reduced using the technique described opposite

Chapter 3

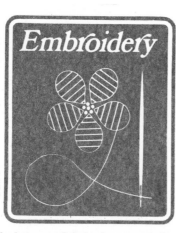

How to transfer a design

The technique of transferring designs to fabric is one of the key steps in embroidery. When choosing your design, first consider the function of the finished object and also the weaving qualities required of the fabric and threads. You may wish to begin with a small surface such as a table mat, and progress later to larger, more elaborate designs.

Ironing method

Specially prepared transfers which can be ironed directly on to the fabric are easy to find. There are two types: single impression which you can only use once, and multiprint which gives up to eight impressions, depending on the weight of the cloth (more impressions can be made on a fine cloth than on a heavy one). With both types you have to work on a flat surface.

First establish the centre of the transfer by folding it in half twice. Now you are ready to begin. Decide where you want to put the design on the cloth and find the centre of your chosen position in the same way. Match the centre of the transfer with this point.

Single impression

Cut off any waste lettering from the transfer. Heat your iron to wool setting and test transfer on a corner, or scrap of the cloth you are using, by placing the spare lettering face downwards and applying the iron for a few seconds. If the transfer takes, you can begin to transfer the design itself.

Place it face downwards on the cloth in the exact position you want and pin it in each corner. Protect the cloth not covered by the transfer with tissue paper. Then apply the iron for a few seconds and remove. Lift one corner carefully to see if the transfer has taken. If not, re-iron gently, making sure you haven't moved the transfer or cloth as this will give a double impression.

Multiprint transfers

You can use multiprint transfers in the same way as single impression ones, but with the iron on cotton setting. The only other difference is that if the transfer does not take the first time, you should allow it to cool before re-ironing.

Tacking and Tracing methods

If you are working from a drawing, or from any design without a transfer, you have a choice of various methods. The following two are the quickest and easiest to do.

If the design consists of large shapes, tacking is the best transferring method. Trace the design on to tissue paper and place this on the cloth, pinning it in each corner. Tack along each line with small running stitches. When you have finished, tear off the paper.

▲ Ironing on the transfer

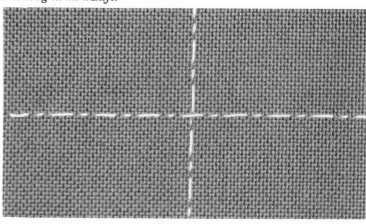

Find the centre of the cloth by folding in half twice for a small transfer, but for a large one it is wise to use two lines of tacking

Tracing designs

By far the quickest and easiest way of transferring designs is to use dressmaker's tracing paper. Trace the design on to ordinary tracing paper, then place a sheet of the dressmaker's tracing paper between the design and the cloth, and trace over the design with a sharp pencil.

This method is fine for designs which will be embroidered quickly, but not quite so effective for really large designs because, with constant handling, the tracing on the cloth tends to smudge.

Opposite—transfers, yarns and inspiration. Ferns come in all sorts of beautiful graphic shapes—and provide inspiring embroidery ideas for anyone with an eye for design and subtle colour. We suggest stitches and colours for new ferns in Embroidery Chapter 5, but if you would like to give the ferns an individual touch, why not borrow a reference book with colour plates of ferns from your local library, and interpret your own colour schemes? Or, for a more sophisticated effect, you could work them all in gold and silver threads on a cool grey silken background.

Parsley Fern (p. 36).
Cryptogramme crispa.

Pl. 24.

Chapter 5

Straight stitches, knots and their application

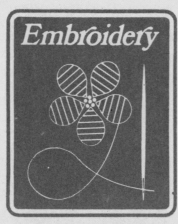

Once you have a repertoire of straight stitches and knots, and you know how to transfer designs and choose colours, you are then ready to start filling in shapes. So, why not try your hand at embroidering some of these filling stitches and knots on the beautiful botanical fern designs which are shown on the next twelve pages? The charts include detailed colour and stitch references.

Tracing and transferring the designs
Trace and transfer the fern designs from the transfers given on pages 22, 23, 24, 26, 30 and 31 to your fabric (see Embroidery Chapter 3). You can, if you wish, enlarge the designs at this stage and you will find full details of the technique for doing this in Embroidery Chapter 2.

Choosing your own colour scheme
Although there are specific colour references you may prefer to choose your own. The actual texture of the many lovely stitches will take on added importance if you work them all in one colour. Particularly effective would be white on a dark background, perhaps navy or scarlet; or again, dark threads on a light background. Black and white is always an extremely effective combination whichever way round you decide to use it.

For a more sumptuous effect, perhaps for a caftan or an evening skirt with a matching stole, work the ferns in silver or gold threads on to a rich purple textured silk.

Suggestions for using the fern designs
The original fern designs were worked with a single fern on each of six elegant table mats, with the Scolopendrium Officinalis (see page 21) and the Platycerium Alcicorne (see page 28) designs at either end of a table runner but the ferns can be used in many other exciting ways. Here are some of them.

In the kitchen and dining room—on a wall hanging, apron, tea cosy or table cloth; in the living room—on a table runner, cushions, as pictures with small gold frames, book covers or worked as one large botanical print framed in silver or maple wood; in the bedroom—on a pyjama case, headboard panel, a pretty lamp shade or as a frieze along a pair of curtains; in the bathroom—using a single fern on a guest towel.

Ferns as table mats
The quickest and easiest way is to embroider the ferns on to a set of ready-made mats but if you are expert enough to make your own mats here is what you will need. For six table mats each 33cm by 23cm and a large centre mat 33cm by 91·5cm, you will require 160cm of 132cm wide even-weave linen, with 12 threads to the centimetre. The ferns are shown here worked on natural linen but there is a wide range of colours to choose from and each

fern can look quite different when worked on another coloured background. Use two strands of Anchor Stranded Cotton either in the shade number given on the charts or using a colour combination of your own choice.

Satin stitch
Satin stitch is useful for solid fillings, and consists of straight stitches worked evenly and closely together. The illustration below shows how to fill in a leaf shape or a flower centre. If you're working this stitch on an article which you use it is unwise to use a stitch more than 1cm long, because it will not wear well. However, if the work is to be mounted as a picture or a wall panel, the stitches may be any length. When using a twisted yarn like Anchor Pearl Cotton, take care to keep it evenly twisted while working. Stranded cotton is more difficult to use successfully with satin stitch as all the strands must lie flat and parallel.

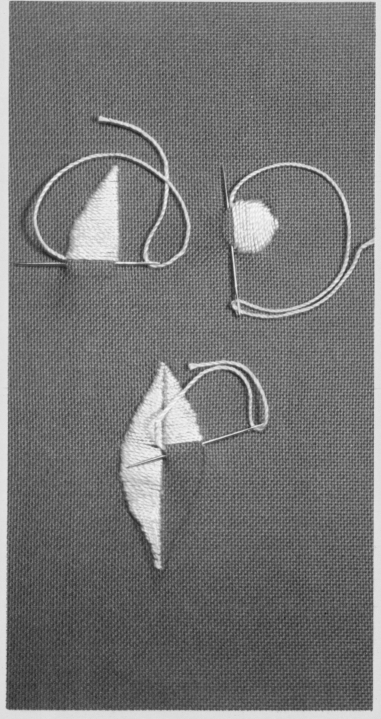

Stitch Library

Wheatear stitch

This is a versatile openwork stitch which is ideal for the filigree parts of the first fern, Platyloma Falcata. Worked in a chain, it looks very like an ear of wheat, from which the stitch takes its name. However, the effect can be changed completely if the stitch is worked in parallel rows.

Work two straight stitches at A and B, bringing the needle through below these stitches at C. Pass the needle under the two straight stitches without entering the fabric, insert the needle again at C, and bring it through at D. (The letters A–D apply to both methods of working the stitch).

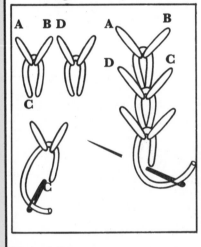

French knots

Bring the needle through to the right side of the material in the required position. Take the working thread in your left hand and wind it twice round the needle. Then, still holding the thread firmly in the left hand, insert it close to where it first emerged. Pull the needle through to the back and secure the knot, or bring the needle up in position for the next stitch. Each stitch should resemble a bead.

Use a thick needle with a small eye so it passes through the coiled thread easily. Choose a needle size depending on the thread used—a large crewel, or medium chenille for soft

embroidery cotton and wool, and a fine crewel for stranded cotton.

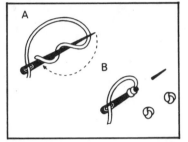

Bullion knots

Make a back stitch the length of the knot required, but do not pull the needle right through the fabric. Twist thread round the needle point as many times as needed to fill the length of the back stitch. Pull the needle through, holding the left thumb on the coiled thread. Then, still holding the coiled thread, and twisting the needle in the direction indicated, re-insert the needle at the point where it was first inserted. Pull the thread through until the bullion knot lies flat.

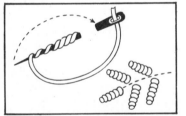

Seeding

Seeding stitches can be used to fill any area and to give a textured effect to a design. This simple filling is made up of many small straight stitches of equal length placed at random. To give greater relief, you can work two stitches over each other.

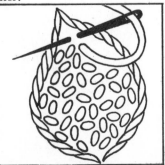

Woven spider's web

Work straight stitches from the centre of the circle building up an uneven number of foundation threads. Then, working from the centre, weave outwards until the circle is filled.

Ribbed or back stitched spider's web

This needs an even number of foundation threads, which are then covered with a continuous line of back stitch starting from the centre. The base is formed by working a double cross stitch to form an eight spoked star.

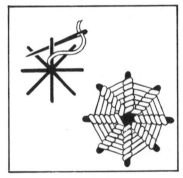

Surface darning

First make a foundation of closely worked satin stitch. Then, with either a matching or contrasting thread, weave over and under the foundation threads only and not through the fabric. If the foundation threads are slightly spaced, an open effect results.

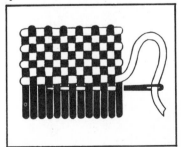

Double knot stitch

Make a small diagonal stitch over the line of design, bring the needle back and slip it under the thread once, then again under the same thread, making a button hole loop stitch. When this stitch is worked closely together it gives an attractive bold line:

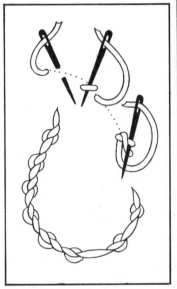

Butterfly chain stitch

First work a row of vertical straight stitches in groups of three, then bunch each group of stitches together with a chain stitch to make a butterfly. The chain stitch is not worked through the fabric.

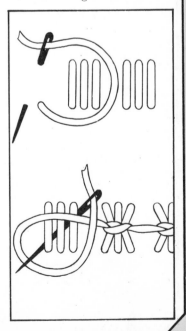

Ferns and fronds

The eight botanical fern designs on pages 20-31 provide an excellent substitute for the Victorian sampler as the embroiderer can try out the many different stitches described on page 19 and in previous chapters. Each fern is suitable for a different set of stitches, clearly indicated on the outline drawings for you to follow. For instance, the first fern, Platyloma Falcata, is designed so that you can practise straight stitches, parallel wheatear stitch, French knots and bullion knots. Apart from providing beautiful shapes on which to practise new stitches, the ferns can be used to make a set of table mats or as motifs on a table cloth. The complete set, with the Latin names included, would make a magnificent botanical wall panel.

Threads and fabrics

The numbers given are colour numbers and refer throughout to Anchor Stranded Cotton. Use two strands for the best effect. The colours are those used by the designer and are given as suggestions but, of course, you may wish to plan your own favourite colour scheme. The background fabric you use can be fine embroidery linen, ready-made table mats, or cloths. If you are making a wall panel, finely slubbed or textured furnishing fabrics are ideal.

Platyloma Falcata ▶

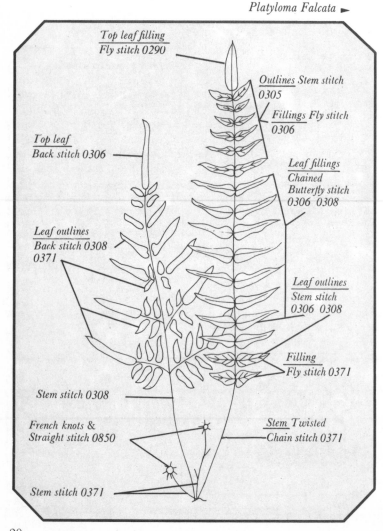

Top leaf filling
Fly stitch 0290

Outlines Stem stitch
0305

Fillings Fly stitch
0306

Top leaf
Back stitch 0306

Leaf fillings
Chained
Butterfly stitch
0306 0308

Leaf outlines
Back stitch 0308
0371

Leaf outlines
Stem stitch
0306 0308

Filling
Fly stitch 0371

Stem stitch 0308

French knots &
Straight stitch 0850

Stem Twisted
Chain stitch 0371

Stem stitch 0371

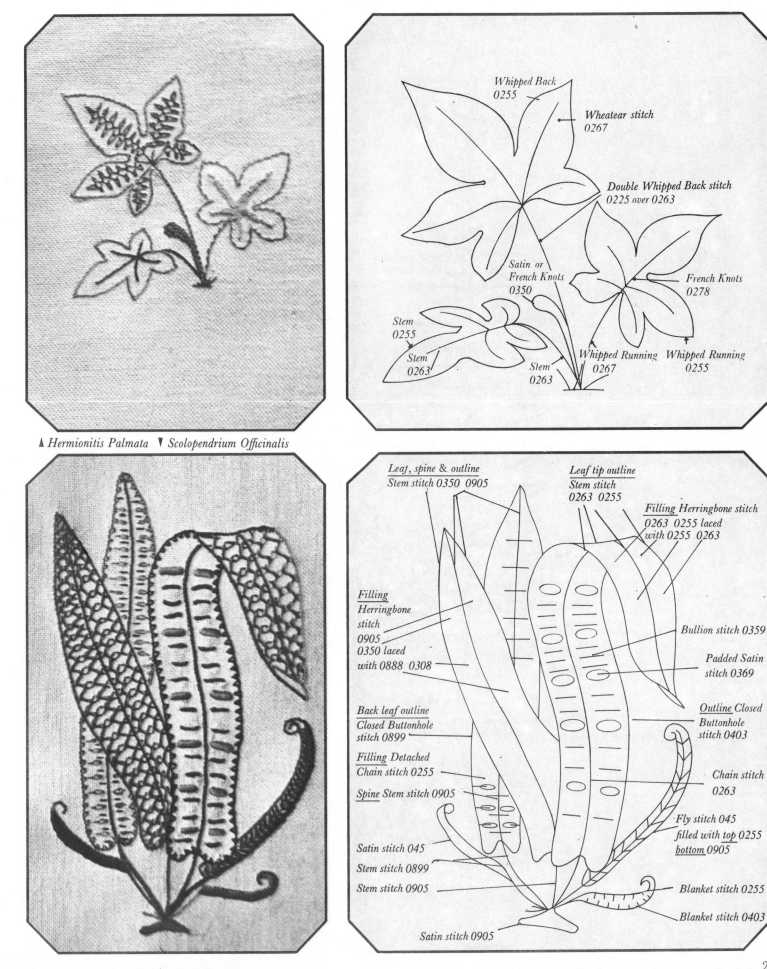

▲ *Hermionitis Palmata* ▼ *Scolopendrium Officinalis*

Whipped Back
0255

Wheatear stitch
0267

Double Whipped Back stitch
0225 over 0263

Satin or
French Knots
0350

French Knots
0278

Stem
0255

Stem
0263

Stem
0263

Whipped Running
0267

Whipped Running
0255

Leaf, spine & outline
Stem stitch 0350 0905

Leaf tip outline
Stem stitch
0263 0255

Filling Herringbone stitch
0263 0255 laced
with 0255 0263

Filling
Herringbone
stitch
0905
0350 laced
with 0888 0308

Bullion stitch 0359

Padded Satin
stitch 0369

Back leaf outline
Closed Buttonhole
stitch 0899

Outline Closed
Buttonhole
stitch 0403

Filling Detached
Chain stitch 0255

Spine Stem stitch 0905

Chain stitch
0263

Fly stitch 045
filled with top 0255
bottom 0905

Satin stitch 045

Stem stitch 0899

Stem stitch 0905

Blanket stitch 0255

Blanket stitch 0403

Satin stitch 0905

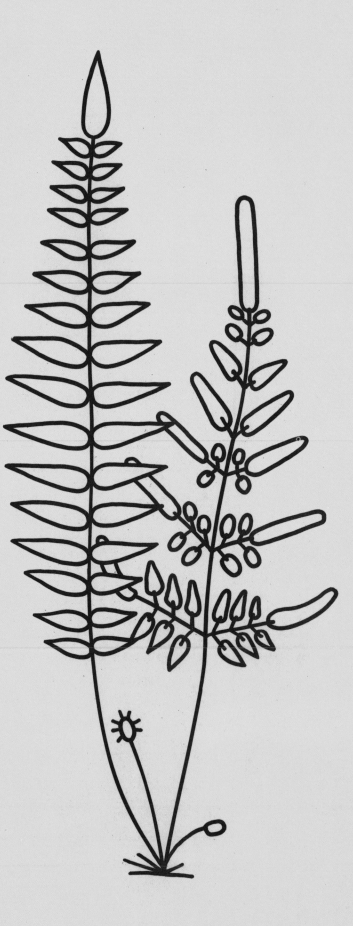

Platyloma Falcata

Hermionitis Palmata

Scolopendrium Officinalis

23

Platyloma Flexuosa

Fern No. 4: Platyloma Flexuosa, showing one of the stems worked in zigzag chain stitch

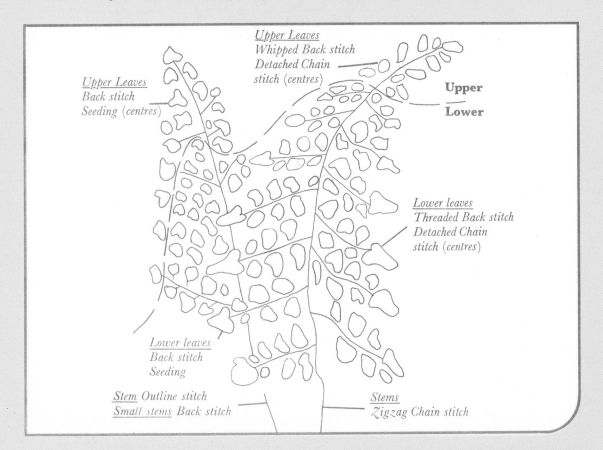

Upper Leaves
Whipped Back stitch
Detached Chain
stitch (centres)

Upper

Lower

Upper Leaves
Back stitch
Seeding (centres)

Lower leaves
Threaded Back stitch
Detached Chain
stitch (centres)

Lower leaves
Back stitch
Seeding

Stem Outline stitch
Small stems Back stitch

Stems
Zigzag Chain stitch

Adiantum Wilsoni

Dryopteris Pedata

26

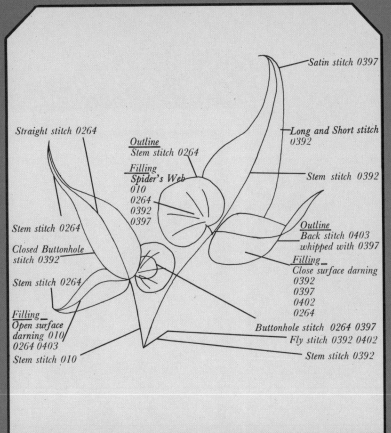

Satin stitch 0397

Straight stitch 0264

Outline
Stem stitch 0264

Filling
Spider's Web
010
0264
0392
0397

Long and Short stitch
0392

Stem stitch 0392

Stem stitch 0264

Closed Buttonhole
stitch 0392

Outline
Back stitch 0403
whipped with 0397

Filling
Close surface darning
0392
0397
0402
0264

Stem stitch 0264

Filling
Open surface
darning 010
0264 0403

Stem stitch 010

Buttonhole stitch 0264 0397

Fly stitch 0392 0402

Stem stitch 0392

Design chart showing suggested colours for Adiantum Wilsoni (above) and Dryopteris Pedata (below)

Here you see the final embroidered versions of the ferns, worked in the colours suggested on the charts

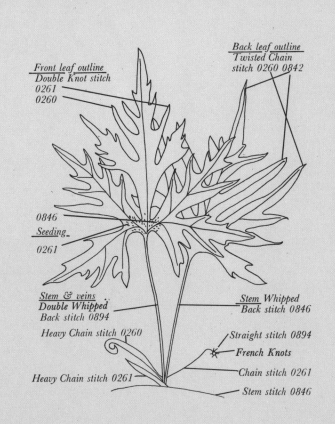

Front leaf outline
Double Knot stitch
0261
0260

Back leaf outline
Twisted Chain
stitch 0260 0842

0846

Seeding

0261

Stem & veins
Double Whipped
Back stitch 0894

Stem Whipped
Back stitch 0846

Heavy Chain stitch 0260

Straight stitch 0894

French Knots

Chain stitch 0261

Heavy Chain stitch 0261

Stem stitch 0846

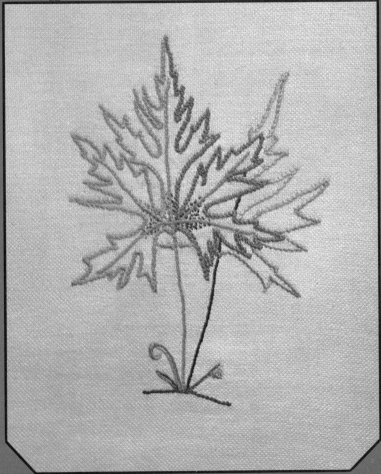

Ferns as pictures

On this page you'll see how decorative the ferns look mounted in gold frames. The names of these particular ferns are Platycerium Alcicorne and Woodwardia Areolata. If you prefer to plan a picture on a larger scale work all eight designs on to one large piece of fabric (backed firmly with holland or woven interfacing and sewn on to chunky bamboo rods), to make an impressive botanical wall hanging.

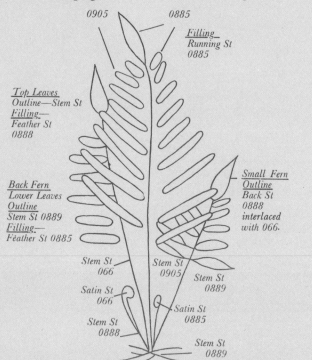

0905   0885

Filling
Running St
0885

Top Leaves
Outline—Stem St
Filling—
Feather St
0888

Small Fern
Outline
Back St
0888
interlaced
with 066.

Back Fern
Lower Leaves
Outline
Stem St 0889
Filling—
Feather St 0885

Stem St
066

Stem St
0905

Stem St
0889

Satin St
066

Stem St
0888

Satin St
0885

Stem St
0889

In design form: Woodwardia Areolata ▲ *Platycerium Alcicorne* ▼

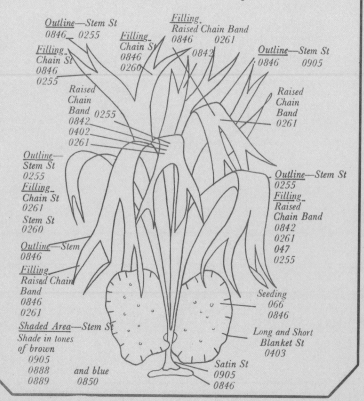

Outline—Stem St
0846   0255

Filling
Chain St
0846
0255

Filling
Raised Chain Band
0846   0261

Filling
Chain St
0846
0260

0842

Outline—Stem St
0846   0905

Raised
Chain
Band
0842
0402
0261

0255

0260

Raised
Chain
Band
0261

Outline—
Stem St
0255
Filling
Chain St
0261
Stem St
0260

Outline—Stem St
0255
Filling—
Raised
Chain Band
0842
0261
047
0255

Outline—Stem
0846

Filling
Raised Chain
Band
0846
0261

Seeding
066
0846

Shaded Area—Stem St
Shade in tones
of brown
0905
0888   and blue
0889   0850

Long and Short
Blanket St
0403

Satin St
0905
0846

Woodwardia Areolata

Platycerium Alcicorne

Chapter 6

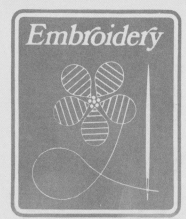

Filling-in and padded stitches

Long and short stitch, split stitch and Roumanian stitch are excellent filling stitches for feathery and furry textures and by introducing different tones of one colour you can produce subtle and realistic shading for flowers, plants and animals. When you try out a new stitch it's a good idea to practise on a small motif first to get the 'feel' of the stitch. Arrange one or two leaves or simple heart shapes on a table mat or napkin. Heighten the smooth flat surface of satin stitch with an underlayer of padding. Practise the stitch with the traditional cherry motifs in this chapter or create your own designs with padded straight lines interspersed with whipped and laced back stitches, velvet ribbons and cords.

Stitch Library

Long and short stitch

Long and short stitch is worked rather like satin stitch, and takes its name from the irregular method of starting the first row of stitches. This stitch should be worked in a frame for the best results.

Start at the outline and make the first row of stitches alternately long and short, following the outline of the shape closely. Then fill in the rest of the shape with rows of stitches of the same length, fitting them into the spaces left by the row before, to give a smooth texture. The

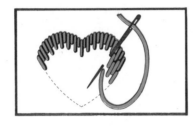

length of the stitch should only vary when you are filling in uneven shapes and you must take care in grading the stitches for these shapes to produce a neat finish. For a smoother effect, use split stitch rather than long and short stitch.

Split stitch

This stitch looks rather like chain stitch and is ideal for outlining. It can also be stitched in curving and spiral lines in close fillings as well as in straight lines.

Starting at A, make a stitch AB and bring the needle through again at C half way along the stitch just made, splitting each thread into equal halves. The stitches can be gradually increased or decreased in length to fill the shape, but each should be brought up close to the centre of the one before. When you are working curves use shorter stitches.

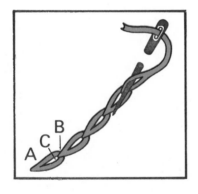

Padded straight lines

To pad straight lines and stems, first cover the line of the design with small running stitches. Then, cover these with a loose thread and stitch it to the fabric with small, close satin stitches. If you are working on even-weave linen you can use the threads of the fabric as a guide for the spacing of the stitches: they should not be too crowded, nor too far apart.

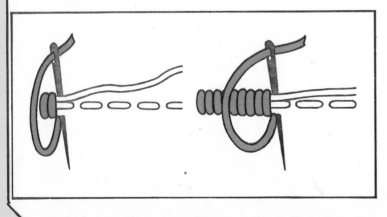

Roumanian stitch

This filling stitch can be used in many ways to give different effects. As it is shown in the diagram, it is useful for filling in leaf or petal shapes. It can also be worked between two parallel lines, either straight or curved, with the stitches placed closely together. For shading, work each stitch with slight spaces in between, then work the next row of stitches into the spaces.

Bring the needle out at the left of the shape at A, take the needle across and make a stitch on the right side of the shape with the thread below the needle.

Make a stitch at the left side at B with the thread above the needle. Continue until the shape is filled. The centre crossing stitch can be varied to make a longer slanting stitch or a small straight stitch for different fillings.

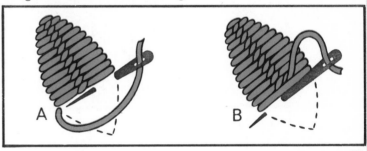

Double padding

More pronounced relief is given by padding twice. First fill in the shape with running stitches, cover with satin stitch in one direction and then work over the same area again at right angles to the first row of stitching.

Flat stitch

Make small stitches alternately down each side of the shape with the needle emerging from the outside line. Guide lines can be drawn to ensure the length of the filling stitches.

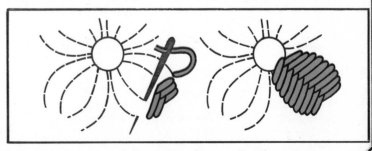

Chapter 7

Flowered bag in wool embroidery

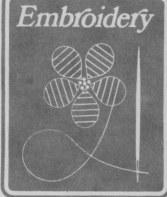

The effect of wool embroidery is bold, colourful and richly textured, it is simple to work and the results are quick and satisfying. This shoulder bag, beautifully embroidered in wool and suspended on a plaited wool handle with tassels, has an exclusive boutique look. In the following Embroidery Chapter there is a jacket embroidered in wool in a similar design and the two together make a stunning outfit.

One of the joys of wool embroidery is that results are seen quickly, and although a wide variety of stitches can be used even the simplest stitches look extremely successful. This is particularly encouraging to people with a small repertoire of stitches.

Equipment
This type of embroidery should be worked in an embroidery tambour or slate frame, depending on the size of the work. A crewel needle is usually used for wool embroidery. This has a long, narrow eye for easy threading of wool, and a sharp point. However, a tapestry needle can be used equally well and the blunter point is less likely to split the yarn of stitches already worked.

Yarns
Crewel or tapisserie yarns are best for wool embroidery, but colour-fast knitting wool makes a good substitute if you are looking for a particular fashion colour. Two strands of crewel wool are generally used but more can be used for a particular effect. Tapisserie wool is used in single strands. When working with wool, use short lengths to prevent excessive wear on the yarn while it is being pulled back and forth through the fabric. Worn yarn causes thin areas in the work.

Fabrics
Strong, firmly woven fabrics such as heavy quality linen or worsted-type woollen fabrics are ideal. Furnishing fabrics in heavy linen or cotton are also suitable and these give a wide range of colours to choose from.

Finishing off
For small uncomplicated pieces of work, careful pressing under a damp cloth is sufficient.
Larger and more complicated pieces are best stretched into shape.

Method for stretching
Pin the work out, face downwards, on a board covered with two or three layers of blotting paper. Use rustless drawing pins. Make sure the grain of the fabric is not distorted as you pin and that the piece is kept in shape. When pinning is completed, dampen the work well with cold water, using a sponge. To avoid uneven shrinkage it is best to dampen the outer edges first and work towards the centre.

This stretching method is mainly used on large items, such as wall panels and firescreen embroideries. It is not usually necessary with garments unless there is an obvious distortion in the shape of the piece.

To make the shoulder bag

Materials for a pochette shoulder bag measuring approximately 19cm by 20·5cm

- ☐ 30·5cm 90cm wide fabric
- ☐ 30·5cm 90cm wide lining
- ☐ 30·5cm 6mm ribbon, matched to the cord yarn
- ☐ Large press stud
- ☐ 1 ball Patons Double Knitting Wool in red, No. 104 for cord
- ☐ Reel transparent sewing thread
- ☐ Embroidery frame
- ☐ Reel sewing cotton to match fabric
- ☐ Crewel needle size 5 or 6
- ☐ 3 skeins each of Anchor Tapisserie Wool in red 013; pink 063 and orange 0333

The entire design is worked in satin stitch (see Embroidery Chapter 5) with the direction of the stitches sloping towards the centre of each flower petal. Details of the back and front of the bag are shown. Trace the outline of the bag and the design and transfer onto the fabric using the tracing method described in Embroidery Chapter 3. Complete all the embroidery before cutting out the bag. When all embroidery is completed press on the back of the work using a damp cloth and a warm iron. Trim the fabric 15mm from the traced outline of the bag and cut the lining to the same size.

Place the lining and bag piece right sides together and stitch on the marked outline, leaving A-B open. Trim and notch the seam allowance on the curves and turn the work to the right side. Tack seam allowances of the opening to the wrong side and slip stitch the opening A-B closed by stitching the lining to the bag. On the embroidery surface, tack round the edge of the bag and lining, easing the curves into shape and rolling the lining gently towards the back so that it does not show on the right side. Press the edges flat, working on the lining side. Fold up the front of the bag, matching C to C and D to D. Slip stitch the side seams. Fold down the flap along the centre of the third row of flowers, counting from the edge of the flap.
Pin the narrow ribbon along the crease, centred under the flap and hem along each edge. Approximately 5cm will be left free at each end and this is used to make loops to support the shoulder cord. Do not stitch the loops at this stage.

To make the cord
Measure the length of shoulder strap you require and cut the ball of red wool into approximately 48 lengths of this measurement, plus about 15cm take-up allowance and enough for two long tassels. Divide the number of strands into three groups. Add a length of transparent thread to each group to prevent the wool from stretching when it is plaited. Plait the three groups together. Make a knot at each end of the plait, about 15cm from the end, to make a long tassel. Bring a kettle of water to the boil and steam each tassel to straighten the wool.

To attach the cord
Loop the ends of the ribbon, protruding from under the flap, round the cord just above the knot. Turn in the raw end and stitch the ribbon round the cord securely so that the knot lies below the loop and the tassels lie down each side of the bag. Fasten down the flap with a large press stud.

Left: close-up of bag back, showing ribbon loop holding cord in place
Right: bag front, the plaited handle rolled into a sausage shape ►

Trace pattern for the shoulder bag (actual size)

D

B

A

C

D

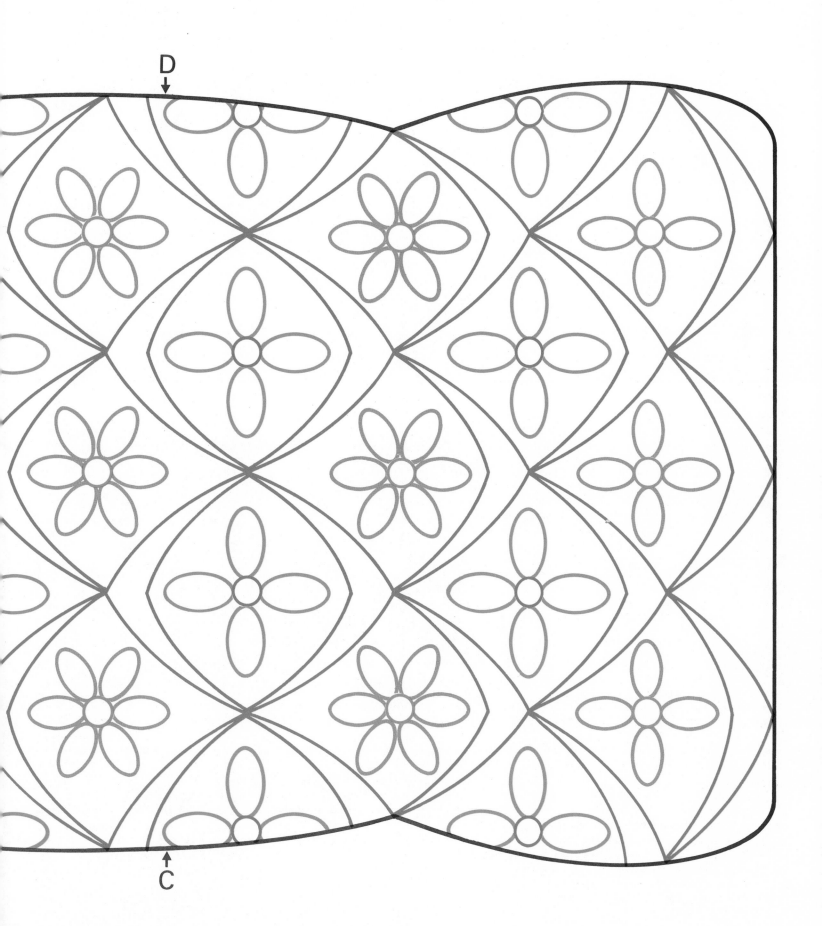

C

Chapter 8

Fashion waistcoat in wool embroidery

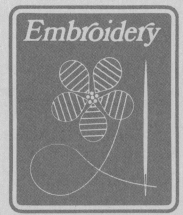

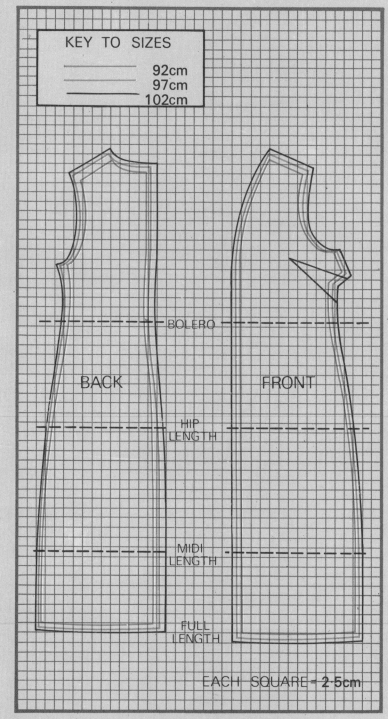

▲ *Pattern graph for three sizes in three fashion lengths*

The long waistcoat worked in warm, vibrant colours ▶

The bag given in the previous chapter was a relatively small project in embroidery with wool. However, the technique does adapt to larger items and this long waistcoat is a fine example. Make it to match the bag for a particularly eye-catching outfit. The waistcoat can be made any length.

Long waistcoat

Measurements
The pattern is given in three sizes to fit 92, 97 or 102cm bust.

Materials
☐ 160cm 136cm wide fine wool
or
☐ 2·75m 90cm wide heavy linen
☐ Equivalent amount of lining
☐ Dressmakers carbon paper
☐ Appletons Crewel Wool in orange 441; red 448; pink 944 and white 991
 For the bolero length; red 2 skeins; pink 2 skeins; white 1 skein; orange 2 skeins
 For the hip length; red 4 skeins; pink 3 skeins; white 4 skeins; orange 3 skeins
 For the midi length; red 5 skeins; pink 4 skeins; white 1 skein; orange 4 skeins
 For the long length; red 5 skeins; pink 5 skeins; white 2 skeins; orange 5 skeins
 Crewel needle No.5
 Embroidery frame

Making the pattern
On 2·5cm squared paper draw up the pattern for the waistcoat from the graph to the desired length. Cut out the pattern and pin it to the fabric. Mark round the outline of the back and both fronts with tacking stitches. Do not cut into the shape of the pattern until the embroidery is completed. The pieces can be cut apart for easier working leaving a generous margin all round. When the embroidery is completed, trim the sections to within 15mm of the tacking lines for seam allowances.

Transferring the design
Trace the design from the outline and transfer it to the fronts of the waistcoat using the dressmakers tracing paper method (see Embroidery Chapter 3. If you are working on a dark fabric use yellow carbon, blue or red on lighter shades. Place the design accurately, using the tacking lines as a guide. The design can be continued round the back of the neck and back of the armhole if desired.

Working the design
It is essential to work this embroidery in an embroidery frame in order to keep the long stitches flat and even. The design is worked throughout in satin stitch using two strands of yarn, but long and short stitch can be used instead.
Begin the embroidery by working the white flower with two stems which lie at the joining of front and armhole borders, and then embroider every fourth flower in white with a red dot in the centre. The remaining flowers are worked in pink with a white centre dot.

Completing the garment
When the embroidery is completed, press the work carefully on the wrong side with a damp cloth and a warm iron. Sew together the bust dart, shoulder, side and centre back seams. Tack the seam allowances on the front edges, neckline and armholes to the back of the work. Press.
Using the same pattern cut out and stitch a lining, allowing 15mm turnings on all edges. Tack the seam allowances on the front edges, neckline and armholes to the back of the work.
Pin the waistcoat and lining together wrong sides facing. Tack and slip stitch all round the edges. Turn up a hem to the required length, turning the surplus fabric to the inside and slip stitch the edges together. This garment should be dry cleaned.

Choosing a colour scheme
The waistcoat illustrated is worked in vibrant colours to create a dramatic effect on the dark background. If you decide to choose another colour scheme, remember that the best effect is achieved by using related colours and one contrast colour.

Design outline to trace

The design is actual size and the outline should be extended when tracing off for the longer lengths.

Detail of the wool embroidered flowers

Chapter 9

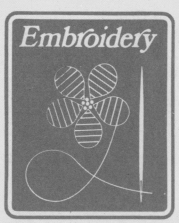

Embroidery

Buttonhole and chain stitch

Buttonhole stitch has many decorative uses besides the obvious practical one. It is the strongest way of doing appliqué and is also useful for binding raw edges in cut work and scalloping. Work buttonhole stitch motifs on a blouse, dress or handkerchief case. Each stitch can be threaded, knotted, whipped or worked in groups—there are countless variations to have fun with.

Chain stitch
Chain stitch gives an even, regular line. It is perfect for outlines, and marvellous for flowing twists and turns.

Indian wall hanging with paillettes couched onto the fabric using buttonhole stitch

Buttonhole stitch or blanket stitch
Simple buttonhole or blanket stitch is worked from left to right. Bring the needle out on the lower line, then insert the needle directly above and make a straight downward stitch, pulling the needle through over the working threads. This forms a row of straight stitches with a closely knotted edge on the lower line.

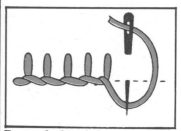

Buttonhole edging
The buttonhole stitch is worked before trimming away the fabric—not the other way round. Cut as close as possible to the edge of the stitching with a small, sharp pair of scissors, taking care not to cut into the stitching itself. The edges should be clean with no fraying visible.

Buttonhole wheel
Arrange the stitches in a circle taking each stitch into the same central hole so that they pull a hole in the fabric. On closely woven fabrics it is helpful to start the hole with an embroidery stiletto.

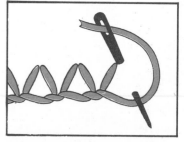

Paillettes and mirrors
Add another dimension to buttonhole stitch by fixing mirrors or paillettes on to material. Simply make a circle of buttonhole stitches so that the knots lie towards the centre and frame the edge of the paillette. Then work buttonhole stitches into the looped edge of the last row of stitches, building up two or three rows. Always point the needle towards the centre and pull the thread tight making a round, looped pocket to hold the mirror or paillette in place.

Closed buttonhole stitch
This is similar to simple buttonhole stitch with the stitches worked in groups of two or three to form triangles as shown in the diagram.

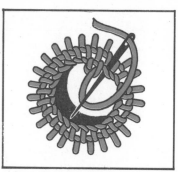

Padded buttonhole stitch
Prepare this in the same way as padded satin stitch. Then, work the buttonhole stitch over the padding. This is especially useful for strengthening any scalloped edges.

Stitch Library

Chain stitch

Work from right to left, making a chain of loops on the right side of the material and a line of back stitches at the back. Bring the needle through on the line of the design and hold the thread down either above or below the line with the left thumb. Insert the needle again at the point where it first emerged and bring the needle out a bit further along the line.

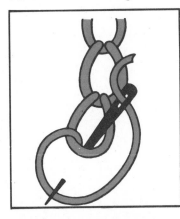

Pull the needle through, keeping the thread under the point so that the next stitch holds it down in a loop. Continue working in the same way for the length of chain required.

Zig-zag chain stitch

Work this in the same way as simple chain stitch, but position each stitch at an angle to the one before it to form a zig-zag. Pierce the end of each loop before you take the needle through the fabric so that the loops stay in place.

Detached chain stitch

Make a chain stitch, then make a tiny stitch to hold the loop down. Leave a space and bring the needle out again to begin to make the next stitch.

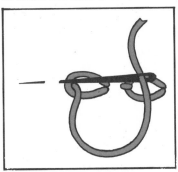

Cable chain stitch

Start with a simple chain stitch. Then, holding the thread down with your left thumb, pass the needle under the thread and twist the needle into a vertical position so that the point comes over the top of the thread. Insert the needle into the fabric so that the working thread is twisted round it, and make another chain stitch.

Daisy chain stitch

This is worked in the same way as for detached chain stitch, but the detached chain is positioned to form a flower shape.

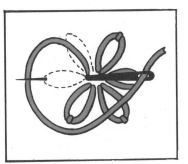
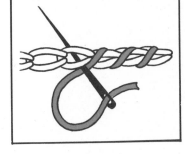

Whipped chain stitch

Chain stitch can be whipped to give it greater effect. Work either a single line, or two or three lines together, and whip with a contrasting thread for a braided effect.

Chequered chain

Chequered chain is another version. Simply thread two yarns of different colours through the needle and use them for alternate stitches.

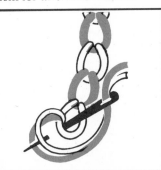

Twisted chain stitch

For this stitch variation the needle is inserted at an angle to form the twist as shown in the diagram, giving a slightly raised line.

Heavy chain stitch

First make a small running stitch at A then bring the needle out just beyond it at B. Thread the needle back under the running stitch and insert it again at B. Take another small stitch forward at C then thread the needle again under

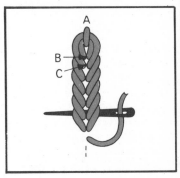

the first running stitch. Continue making the third and following stitches in the same way, always threading the needle under.

Russian chain stitch

Make a chain stitch. Then, instead of continuing in a straight line, make the next stitch at an angle pointing upwards, then another, pointing downwards, catching each down with a tiny stitch. Bring the needle out again further along the line and repeat to make a line of stitches. This stitch can also be worked in groups as a filling stitch, or vertically in horizontal rows.

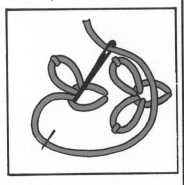

Back stitched chain

Back stitched chain is a very simple variation, worked with a row of back stitches over each of the chain stitches.

Chapter 10

A cushion in simple chain stitch

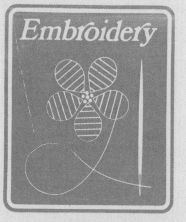

This succulent apple in vibrant colours shows an interesting use of chain stitch for a bold effect.

To make the cushion 40cm by 40cm you will need:
- ☐ 45cm even-weave linen 8 threads to the centimetre
- ☐ Cushion pad 2·5cm larger than finished size of cushion
- ☐ Reel of mercerised sewing cotton to match background fabric
- ☐ Anchor Stranded Cotton in the following colours: one skein orange 0316; one

skein dark green 0246; two skeins green 0268
- ☐ Anchor Soft Embroidery Cotton in the following colours: four skeins red 0335; two skeins pink 025
- ☐ 30cm zip
- ☐ Tracing paper
- ☐ Graph paper

To enlarge the design
Trace and enlarge the design to measure 28cm from the tip of the top leaf to the lower edge of the apple. Trace the enlarged design onto tracing paper (see Embroidery Chapter 2).

Transferring the design
Fold the fabric and cut the piece in two. Mark the centre with rows of tacking stitches each way. Work a line of tacking stitches 5cm in from the outer edges to form a square measuring 40cm by 40cm, to mark the outer edges of the cushion. Pin the traced design in position 7cm up from the lower line of tacking stitches and centralising the design between the two vertical lines. Using the matching sewing cotton transfer the design to the background fabric stitching all the lines of design through the tracing paper. When all the lines have been marked with tacking the paper is torn away. If the tacking stitches are well covered with embroidery they need not be removed when the design is completed.

Stitches
Begin with the orange shape. Use six strands of cotton, and start the chain stitching (see Embroidery Chapter 9) from the outer edge of each shape working towards the centre. This ensures a well defined outline. Work the deep pink area next and finally the red. Leave gaps in the chain stitch filling where indicated on the design and fill these with bullion knots. The bullion knots are also worked with six strands of cotton and with three twists round the needle. Work the apple leaves in stem stitch filling with the veins in stem stitch, using four strands of cotton. The calyx at the bottom of the apple is formed by working three detached chain stitches one inside the other starting with the outer. The stalk is worked in four separate rows of stem stitch using four strands.

To make up the cushion
When the embroidery is completed, press the work lightly over a damp cloth and a thick, soft pad to avoid flattening the bullion knots.
Make up the cushion according to the instructions given in Embroidery Chapter 15 and insert the cushion pad.

▼ *Trace and enlarge this design to the required size*

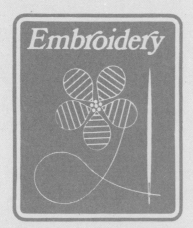

Embroidery

Feather stitches

Feather stitch is attractive as well as useful and can be worked in straight or curved lines. It is one of the main stitches used in the decorative panels of traditional smocks (see Collector's Piece pages 84-5).

The stitches shown here are all from the same family and are useful for either decoration or filling. Because of their realistically veined look, the lacy open feather stitches are ideal for filling leaf or fern shapes and they also look very pretty on hems and edges. When practising feather stitches lightly draw a central spine and parallel outer guide lines until you achieve the even stitching which is this stitch family's main beauty.

Fly stitch
This stitch can be worked either horizontally or vertically but for both, the basic movement is from left to right. Bring the needle through on the left and holding the thread down with the left thumb, insert the needle at the same level, a little to the right. Bring the needle up below, but exactly between, these two points, catching the thread under the needle. Take a tiny stitch just below this thread to hold it and bring the needle through in position for the next stitch. Continue in a horizontal or vertical line.

Quill stitch
Work from right to left. Bring the needle through on the centre line of the design. Make a long, slightly sloping back stitch, bringing the needle through again, a little in front of the previous stitch, catching the working thread under the needle. Repeat, taking the back stitch alternately to either side of the centre line of the design, to form a quill.

Detail from an apron worked in feather stitch and buttonhole stitch

Stitch Library

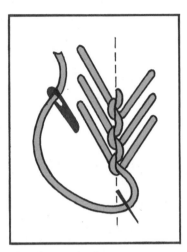

Feather stitch

Work from right to left. Bring the needle through above the centre line of the design. Take a small stitch to the left, below the line, catching the thread under the point of the needle. Continue making a series of stitches above and below the central line, catching the thread under the needle each time. The result is parallel lines of stitches linked by a zigzag line.

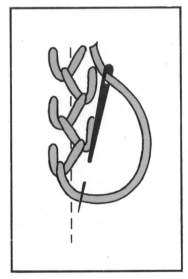

Double feather stitch

Work in the same way as feather stitch, but take two stitches in each direction instead of one. This rather geometric stitch is very popular on the Continent.

To achieve the more rounded, softer feather stitch favoured by British embroiderers, angle each small stitch towards the centre of the feather rather than working them absolutely parallel to each other.

Cretan stitch

Work from left to right. Bring the needle through above the centre line of the design. Take a deep stitch immediately below this point and bring the needle up towards the centre line taking a small stitch and

catching the thread under the needle. Make a second big stitch above the centre line and a little to the right of the bottom stitch and take a small stitch towards the centre of the design, catching the thread under the needle. Continue, taking great care that each stitch is as even as possible.

Because of its close, woven effect, Cretan stitch makes a very effective filling stitch.

Open Cretan stitch

Work this stitch in exactly the same way as Cretan stitch, spacing the stitching at regular intervals. It is very important to keep the spacing even.

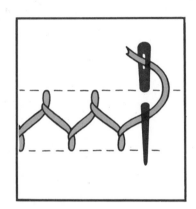

Herringbone stitch

Work from left to right. Bring the needle through below the centre line of the design. Insert the needle above this line to the right, taking a small stitch to the left. Then insert the needle below the line a little to the right, taking a small stitch towards the left, making sure that the needle comes up in line with the previous stitch. Herringbone stitch looks best worked very evenly so that the small stitches and the spaces between them are of equal size.

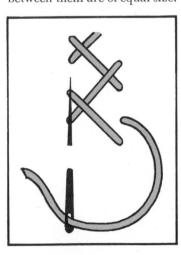

Threaded herringbone stitch

First work a foundation of simple herringbone stitch then, with a contrast thread (use self colour if you wish), pass the needle vertically up and down under the centre of each stitch.

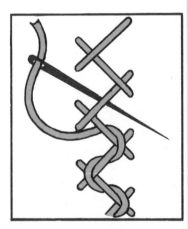

Laced herringbone stitch

This again is worked over a foundation of simple herringbone stitch. A surface thread is woven round the intersection of stitches to form the interlacing. The thread is woven twice round each intersection in the diagram but it can be worked round as many times as you wish depending on the effect you want to achieve.

Chapter 12

Garden cushions in wool embroidery

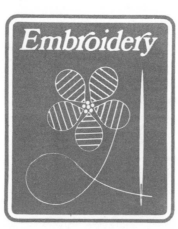

Brighten up your garden furniture with these brilliantly coloured cushions. Embroider some and leave others plain. Using chunky tapisserie wool, the design is worked in simple stitches such as chain stitch, stem stitch and fly stitch. Use the stitches and colours suggested or experiment with your own choice. The same design could look interesting translated into appliqué.

To make a cushion measuring 43cm in diameter you will need:

- [ ] 45cm 136cm furnishing fabric
- [ ] 254cm contrast colour piping
- [ ] Sewing cotton to match fabric
- [ ] Cushion pad 45cm in diameter, 6·5cm deep
- [ ] Large tapestry needle
- [ ] 2 button moulds 2·5cm in diameter (plain cushion only)

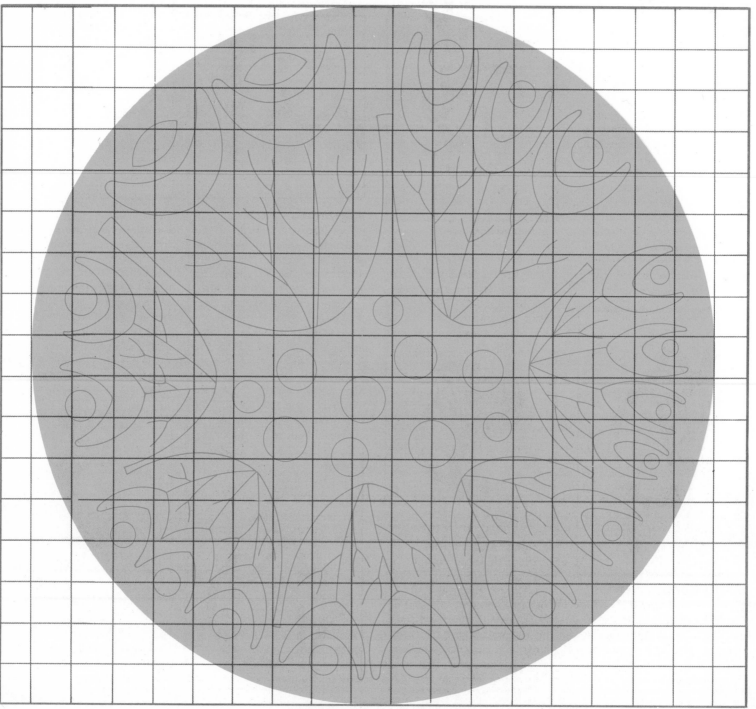

☐ DMC Laine à Broder
Tapisseries No.13 in the
following colours:
1 skein each of burgundy
red 7110; wine red 7108;
scarlet 7606 and yellow
7431

To transfer pattern and design

Draw the pattern and design
from the chart onto 2·5cm
squared paper. Trace the
pattern and design onto tracing
paper and cut out. Lay the
pattern onto the folded fabric
and cut out two circles for the
top and bottom of the cushion,
allowing 1·5cm turnings all
round the edge. Cut a strip
for the gusset measuring 126
cm long and 9·5cm deep. Take
one circle of the fabric and
trace the outline only onto
this. Now take the second circle
of fabric and trace the outline
and design onto the right side
of the fabric, using carbon
paper or small running stitches
through the tracing paper and
the fabric.

The stitches used

The central area of the design
is worked in outlines of French
knots in yellow. The stalks
are in chain stitch, stem stitch
and fly stitches using scarlet
and wine red. The stylised
flower heads are worked in
satin stitch in wine red and
burgundy red.

To make up cushion

Pin and tack the piping round
the outline of the cushion top
and bottom. Pin the gusset to
the top, easing it round the
circle until both ends meet.
Pin, tack and stitch the gusset
seam. Tack the gusset to the
top and stitch as close to the
piping as possible. If stitching
by machine use a piping foot.
For a smooth finish, cut notches
on seam allowance all round.
Stitch bottom of cushion in
the same way but leave about
25·5cm open to insert cushion
pad. Turn cover to the right
side and insert pad. Stitch the
25·5cm opening by hand.

◄ *The design to trace and enlarge*

Bright cushions for sunny days ►

Collector's Piece

Wise old owls

Plump little owls are always fun to embroider and they can be made as simple or elaborate as you please. The owl's shape is uncomplicated, yet the outline can be filled in to depict feathers on the chest using a wide range of colours, textures and stitches. The two shy-looking owls perched on a branch have been worked in several decorative stitches to add detail to the embroidery without making it look too fussy or fragmentary. The feathers covering the owls' round chests are worked in patches of straight and chain stitch, some stitches varying in size, thickness and spacing. A more elaborate composition —the multi-coloured owl— is worked all over in different stitches. French knots graduating into straight stitch give a dappled effect on the bird's chest, and the stitches form clearly defined feathers. The brown wings are boldly outlined in chain stitch and woven band, and feathered in Roumanian stitch. The owl's eyes, head and ears are worked in straight stitch in assorted yarns, and the iris of the eye is made up of small iridescent beads. The woolly brown owl design adorning the opposite page is more, a semi-collage than a pure embroidery. The owl's body is worked in delicate tawny shades of a special wool but the same effect can be achieved by taking yarns and twisting them. The eyes are large, flat black beads, the beak a shiny oval pearl, and the claws clasp a piece of tree bark matched to the colours of the wool.

Chapter 13

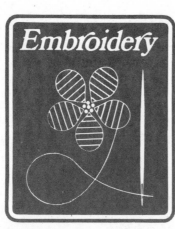

Introduction to appliqué

Applique is simply the technique of applying one fabric to another. It originated as an imaginative way of patching worn clothes but it has become a highly-developed form of decoration—its present-day popularity is probably due to the fact that it is so quick to do.

Basic hints

Choosing materials
The applied materials should be of equal or lighter weight than the background material, but the background material can be mounted on strong cotton or calico to add strength if desired. Non-fraying fabrics are the easiest to apply, as the edges don't have to be turned in. If you want to use an attractive material which might fray, iron on a woven adhesive interfacing to the wrong side of the fabric to prevent this.

Start with bold appliqué like nursery cushions or children's aprons

Applying materials
If the appliqué is going to receive hard wear, remember to match the grain of the two fabrics to prevent puckering and splitting. Fabrics such as felt do not have a grain, so these can be applied in any position.

To work in the hand or in a frame
For appliqué it is best to work with the background material pulled taut, in a slate or rectangular frame, an old picture frame or, for small items, a tambour frame on a stand (see Embroidery Chapter 1). Very small pieces may be worked in the hand if you wish, but whether you use a frame or not, be sure to stretch the fabric to be applied as much as the background material. If the fabrics are at different tensions it will eventually cause puckering and spoil the look of your work.

Using a slate or rectangular frame

The slate frame is made up of four strips of wood—two strong cross bars joined by two side bars with peg holes to vary the size. The rectangular frame works on the same principle as the slate frame, but differs from it in that the side bars are threaded for screwing the fabric taut.

The slate frame is preferable to the rectangular frame for anything but very light-weight fabrics, because the screw rings on the rectangular frame can work loose and relax the tension of the fabric whilst you stitch.

There are two types of slate or rectangular frames on the market—hand frames and floor-standing frames. Hand frames come in sizes from 45cm to 68cm and floor frames from 61cm to 76cm. (Some stockists will make a slate frame to any size you want.) Whether you use a frame with a stand or not is up to you, but generally, it is easier to work with a stand.

Mounting fabric on a frame
1. Mark the centre of the webbing on the frame rollers with a tacking line.
2. On the top and bottom of the fabric, make a 1·3cm turning to the wrong side, and hem it if it is likely to fray.
3. Mark the centres of these turned edges with pins. Place the centre of the fabric to the centre of the webbing and pin from the centre outwards.
4. Using very strong thread overcast the 2 edges together, always working from the centre outwards.
5. Repeat on second roller.
6. Adjust the side bars until the fabric is taut.
7. Tack 2·5cm tape to the sides of the fabric, using small stitches.
8. Thread a packing needle with strong string, and lace through the webbing and over the slats with stitches about 2·5cm apart.
9. Leave about 45cm string at each end. Pull the string taut and wind it round the ends of the frame, then tie to secure.

Framing up a fabric with backing
It is best to use a backing such as white (or unbleached) calico or holland. Make sure the backing is pre-shrunk and at least one inch bigger all round than the fabric to be embroidered.
1. Tack a line down the centre of the backing and of the fabric to be embroidered.
2. Place the fabric on the backing, matching the centre lines. Pin it into place, working out from the centre with the pins pointing inwards to avoid puckering. Do not stretch either layer.
3. Firmly tack or baste round the outside edge through both fabrics. Remove the pins.
4. Now mount the backed fabric in the frame according to the previous instructions.

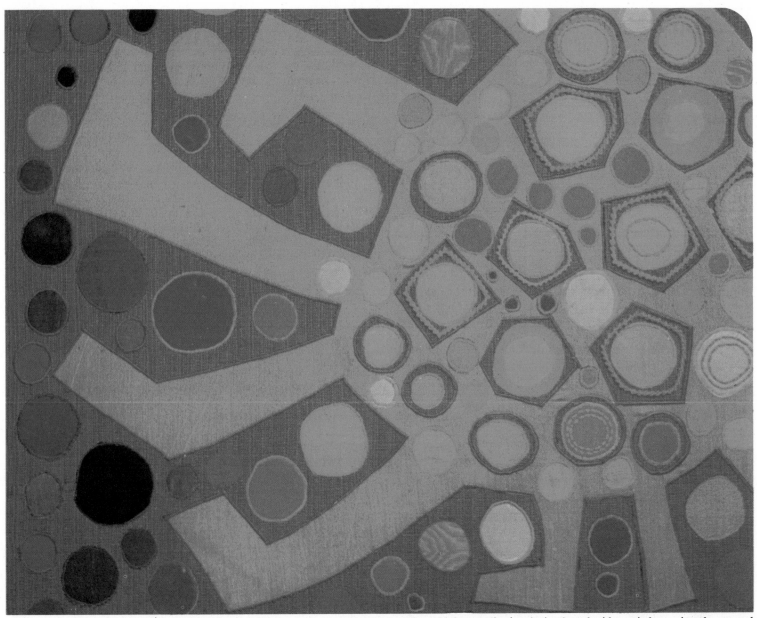

Part of a modern design, called Mexican Sun, which shows the stunning results of combining appliqué and simple embroidery stitches, using the cut and stitch method. Zigzag machining has been used to stitch the pieces to the background and couching and double knot stitch as surface decoration.

Which method do I choose?

There are several appliqué methods—it all depends on the type of materials you want to use or the effect you wish to achieve as to which one you choose. Here are the main methods.

Stick and stitch
This is the simplest form of appliqué. Simply stick cut-outs of non-fraying materials with a fabric glue on to a fabric background and secure the edges with either hand or machine stitches.

Cut and stitch
This method is best used on firm non-fraying materials which you can safely cut to shape and slip-stitch by hand, or zigzag stitch on a swing needle sewing machine over the raw edges. You can then decorate the applied areas with various kinds of stitching.

Stitch and cut
This method is used on thin fabrics which would fray if cut out before applying. Cut a larger area than you need, marking the exact shape required, then either buttonhole stitch (see Embroidery Chapter 9 by hand or zigzag by machine on to the main fabric. Then trim off the surplus appliqué fabric very close to the stitching, using a pair of really sharp scissors.

Blind appliqué
This is another method for materials which fray easily. Turn the edges under and tack into position (round a card template if it is a difficult shape), before applying. Press the turnings flat and slip-stitch the shape into position. A bulky fabric will be easier to apply if you cut across corners and clip into curves. This will make the shapes neater and help them lie flat.

Cut-outs
This is a reversed appliqué method. Tack two or more layers of fabric together and cut out the shapes to reveal the underneath layer or layers. Then, either buttonhole stitch the raw edges or stitch down a small turning with a slip stitch, or secure the shape with a straight or zigzag line of machine stitching. You can back the cut-outs with different coloured fabrics or ribbons.

Chapter 14

Designing for appliqué

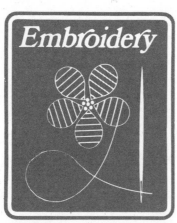

It is very surprising how many people become really expert at embroidering commercial patterns but who would never dream of attempting to create a design of their own. Designing for appliqué need not be difficult or complicated. In any case, bold, simple designs are often the most effective and you can always add to the interest and texture of the simplest design by your choice of embroidery stitches. Furthermore, if you try to do something so difficult that it is completely beyond you, you might easily be put off appliqué for ever, whereas a successful first attempt will encourage you to go on to more intricate and exciting work.

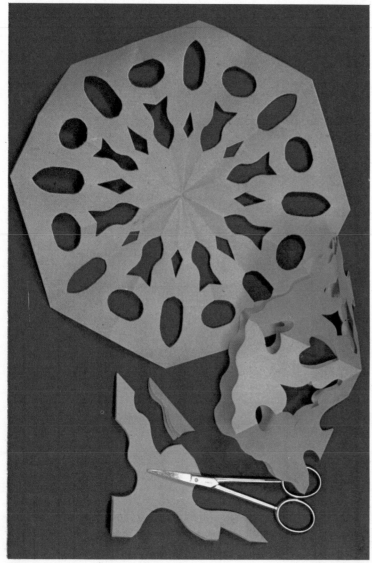

Creative appliqué

You do not have to be an artist to be able to design for embroidery and appliqué is perhaps the easiest type to start on. The most important thing is to think in terms of large, simple shapes until you become more experienced. Small shapes are more difficult to handle, especially in materials which fray. Here are five easy ways to plan a design. And although they are for appliqué, they also apply to embroidery in general.

Folded and cut paper method

This is best used for non-fraying fabrics such as felt, suede, leather, synthetic leather, and plastic-coated materials. Fold a piece of paper twice to form a triangle and then twice more into smaller triangles. Cut out shapes (not too small), being careful not to cut away all the folded edges. Open out the paper and you have an instant design. Do not use the first one you make, but try several and choose the one you like best. Fold the paper in different ways to achieve different effects. Designs formed in this way can then be applied to a contrast colour background so that it shows up through the cut-outs. For a more advanced piece of work, apply two or more contrasting colours behind the cut-outs.

Transfer or trace method

This is suitable for all types of embroidery and the sources of designs are endless. The illustrations to be found in modern children's books, magazines, wallpaper patterns and even rubbings taken from coalhole covers all make interesting designs to be traced and transferred on to fabric.

Exploding a design

This method is again suitable for both embroidery and appliqué and results in asymmetric, abstract designs.
Start with a rectangle of paper—a colour page from a glossy magazine is ideal because this will also help with choosing your colour scheme. With a ruler and pencil, divide the paper into sections of varying shapes and sizes. Then clearly number each section so that you can keep the shapes in the same order when they are all cut out. Now cut along the drawn lines carefully and arrange the pieces in numerical order on a plain sheet of paper, spreading them out in a slightly haphazard manner until you are pleased with the pattern they form. Stick the shapes down with glue. Trace the design and transfer it to the fabric. This method can be used on folded circular pieces of paper, cutting random shapes right into the folds. These designs usually require the addition of decorative embroidery stitches.

Drawing round a shape

This method can be used where a single motif is required, or to form all-over patterns using one or more motifs. Look round your home for items such as pastry cutters, ornaments with interesting-shaped bases, drinking glasses, in fact anything which has an attractive but simple shape will do. Just draw round the base with a pencil and you have an instant design.

Designing with ready-made motifs

Motifs can be purchased at large stores. Use one on its own or group several to form quick, easy designs. Ribbons and braids are also exciting materials for appliqué designs (see Embroidery Chapter 20 as there are so many different ways you can use them. They can be found in glorious colours and varying widths—just right for creating lively designs either on their own or as part of a larger scheme. Braids are also useful for adding interesting textures to the over-all effect.

Designing symmetrical patterns by cutting out shapes from folded paper

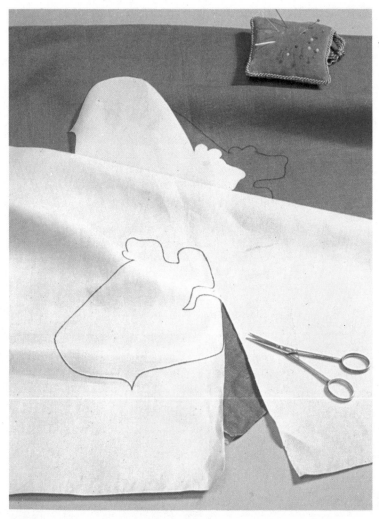

Transfer the shape onto both fabrics and cut out the one to be applied

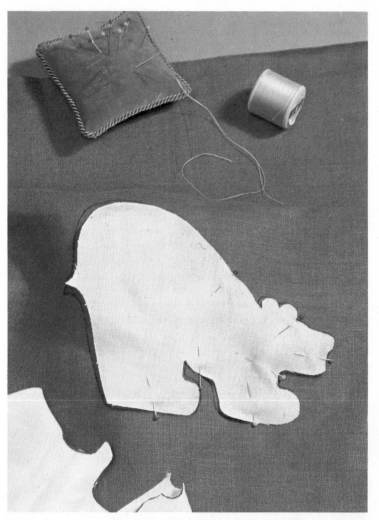

Pin the shape onto the background fabric to prepare for stitching

Appliqué step by step

1. Cut out the shapes used in the design in pieces of coloured paper and place them in different positions on the background until you are satisfied with the colour scheme and arrangement.
2. Transfer the outline of the design shapes on to the background fabric, using one of the methods described in Embroidery Chapter 3.
3. Transfer the outline of shapes on to the fabric to be applied.
4. Use one of the basic methods of application described in Embroidery Chapter 13.
5. Add further decoration, using hand or machine embroidery.

General hints

Whichever form of embroidery you prefer to use, it is important to be critical of your work, and a good way in which to view this objectively is to hold it in front of a mirror. You will be amazed how different your work looks—in fact it will appear very much as others see it. If the design is tilting to one side, or is too far up or down on the background, the faults will show more clearly in the mirror reflection than when you look directly at it.

Blanket stitch or buttonhole stitch

This stitch, for which instructions are given in Embroidery Chapter 9, is a good, strong stitch for sewing down applied shapes, either in its widely spaced form (blanket stitch) or in its closed-up form (buttonhole stitch). There are several variations, two of which are shown here. See Embroidery Chapter 9 for others.

Stitch Library

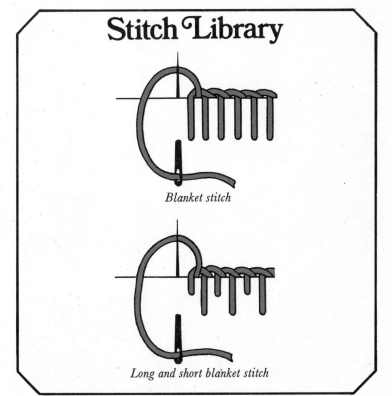

Blanket stitch

Long and short blanket stitch

55

Chapter 15

Gay cushions in appliqué

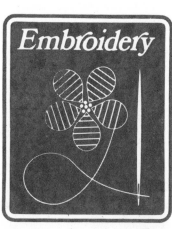

Embroidery

Felt is the easiest material for beginners to try appliqué. There is no problem of matching fabric weights and textures or of having to cope with fraying edges, which would mean finishing off the shapes before applying. With felt, simply cut and stitch. Felt is stocked by most fabric departments and is available in 23cm or 30cm squares, or by the metre in varying widths, in a wide range of colours. These brilliant felt cushions show ways of using cut and stitch appliqué.

Felt appliqué cushions

The two cushions shown in the photograph cleverly combine both the cut and stitch and the cut-out methods.

Materials you will need:
- ☐ Four pieces of felt 51cm by 51cm, two orange and two yellow
- ☐ One piece of felt 51cm by 51cm in pink
- ☐ One piece of felt 30cm by 30cm in mauve
- ☐ Two pieces of paper 51cm by 51cm for making paper patterns (newspaper will do)
- ☐ Two cushion pads 51cm by 51cm or kapok for stuffing
  NB. Felt should be dry cleaned but do remember, if you use kapok—which is cheaper than cushion pads—the cushions cannot be dry cleaned unless kapok is removed
- ☐ Two 30cm zippers, one orange and one yellow (if you are using cushion pads)
- ☐ Matching sewing threads, or colourless nylon thread which can be used for both cushions

How to cut out paper patterns

1. Fold each of the paper squares in half, then quarter, and then diagonally in a triangle.

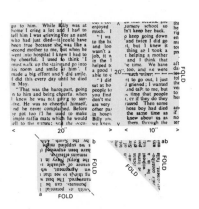

2. On one of the folded triangles, draw cutting lines as indicated in the diagram. Cut evenly along these lines through all layers. Put aside the cut-out pieces (4 of each pattern) and pin the large pattern cut-out on to one piece of orange felt.

3. On the second folded paper triangle, draw cutting lines as indicated in the diagram. Cut out and keep only the cut-out pieces (eight of one pattern and one centre pattern), discarding the remainder of the paper square.

4. Carefully unfold all paper patterns and label them A—D as shown.

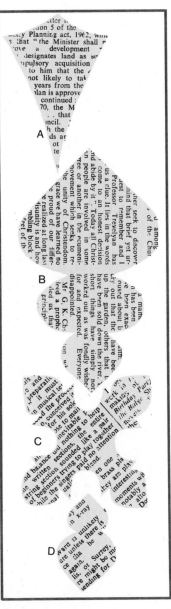

Cutting out the felt

5. Pin patterns to appropriate colours of felt, arranging them very carefully to follow the diagrams. As patterns A (mauve) and B (pink) will be used to fill in the cut-outs of the orange cushion, leave 6mm seam allowance on these patterns. Cut all other patterns to the exact size.

Tack the pattern on to the felt and remove the pins. Use a small pair of scissors with very sharp points to begin cutting out each shape, then continue with normal cutting-out scissors. If the raw edges are not smooth, trim with the small scissors. When cutting out is completed, you will have four mauve A with 6mm seam allowance, four pink B with 6mm seam allowance, four orange A, four orange B, one pink C, and eight pink D shapes. The orange felt will also have four A cut-outs and four B cut-outs.

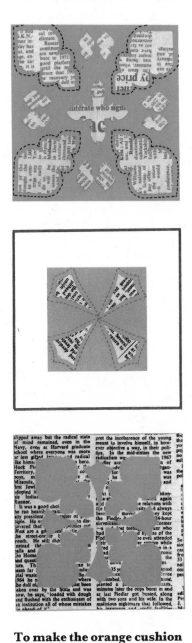

To make the orange cushion

6. Pin and tack four mauve A shapes and four pink B shapes to the wrong side of the orange felt, filling in the eight cut-outs. Machine, with a straight stitch, on the right side of the felt, as close to the raw edge as possible. (If you want a more decorative finish, use a zigzag stitch.) Next, still working on the right side, pin, tack and machine in place four pink D shapes.
Remove all tacking threads.

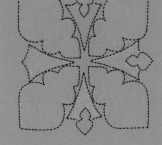

To make the yellow cushion

7. Criss-cross the yellow felt square with tacking thread as shown in the diagram, which will enable you to position the shapes correctly. Pin, tack and machine the remaining four orange A shapes and four orange B shapes on to the right side of the yellow felt. Then pin, tack and machine the one pink C and the remaining four pink D shapes into position as shown.
Remove all tacking threads.

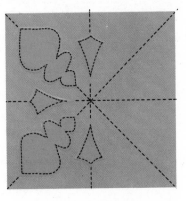

To make up cushions

8. Place plain orange and yellow felt pieces to appliquéd pieces with right sides facing. Tack and machine around the sides with 1·3cm seam allowance, leaving a 30cm opening along one side for inserting the zippers. Turn to the right side. Pin and tack, then stitch zippers into place. Insert cushion pads.

If you are stuffing with kapok, tease it out first, then do not pack tight but fill gently.

Turn in seam allowance and stitch up the openings securely by hand.

The Fire of London

Two details of the Fire of London picture showing some of the stitches and materials used

This machine-embroidered picture by Joan Gilbert, 'Musicians Escaping from the Great Fire of London', is based on a 17th-century engraving of the Great Fire by Visscher.

Joan Gilbert, who has had exhibitions of her embroidery, translated the engraving into appliquéd fabric worked over richly with cotton yarn and occasional gold and silver threads. It took her about a month, using a domestic automatic electric sewing machine.

In 1666, as the picture shows, there was an apple orchard at Whitefriars, surrounded by the pleasant buildings of the Carmelite monastery, which were still standing. There was a fine water-gate with steps leading down to the broad highway of the Thames. Flames and smoke fill the background and give urgency to the hurrying figures. The musicians are carrying their lutes, harps and mandolines to safety. There is also a red hurdy-gurdy, a lyre and a baryton (pronounced bar-ee-tong), a member of the viol family, in the rescue operation.

In the boat, a little figure in pink is gripping two big cheeses under his arms. Cheeses could be almost as valuable as instruments. (Pepys buried two cheeses in the cool river bank to avoid damage by fire.) One fellow is carrying a bag of fine linen, and a pompous person bears away his casket full of jewels.

The lights of Hampstead can be seen through the flames.

In a sky obscured by smoke, the large gold braid stars stand still above the hullabaloo.

Instruments like those carried by the musicians can still be seen at the Victoria and Albert Museum. Made of highly polished, often rare, woods, they are inlaid with bone, ivory, silver and gold.

Chapter 16

Picture making in appliqué

The appliqué clown design overleaf is adapted from an amusing gift tag. So you see, design ideas come from the most unexpected sources. Keep a scrap book of ideas like this so that you will have a fund of inspiration whenever you need it.

The clown incorporates simple surface decoration which always makes basic appliqué shapes richer and also unites a design. Here there are four stitches which are very suited to appliqué.

Couching

If you use this form of surface decoration, do bear in mind that this stitch will not withstand washing.

First, secure the threads to be couched at the back of the work, draw them through to the right side and then catch into place, using a small stitch at regular intervals. Finally, take the ends through to the back of the work and secure in place. When couching two or more threads in place, care must be taken to prevent them twisting.

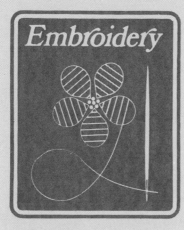

Cording

This is another attractive way of drawing or outlining shapes, but it, too, is not washable. Draw one end of the cord to

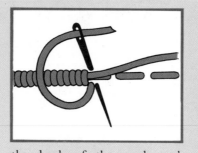

the back of the work and secure in place with oversewing, then lay the cord along the line of the design and attach it by sewing it down with small stitches.

Finish off by taking the end of the cord through to the back of the work and oversewing it

Pin stitch

Basically this is a drawn fabric stitch, but it makes a strong neat finish when used for outlining appliqué. The diagrams show how the stitch is worked for a hem, but the same method is used for applying curved shapes, when each stitch is pulled firmly to make tiny holes between the stitches. Work this stitch from right to left or from top to bottom.

Bring the needle through the folded edge at A, insert the needle at B, and bring it out at C. Insert the needle again at B, bringing it out at C. Insert the needle once more at B and bring it out through the folded edge at D.

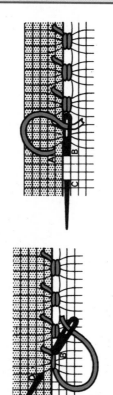

Repeat these steps, pulling all stitches firmly.

Up and down buttonhole stitch

This is an interesting variation of buttonhole stitch. Start as for plain buttonhole stitch and

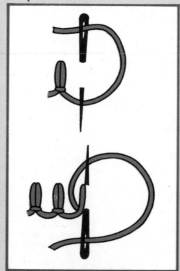

pull the thread through. Insert the needle on the bottom line, taking a straight upward stitch with the thread under the needle. Pull the thread in an upward movement, then downwards to continue.

The clown appliqué

You will need:
- [ ] 23cm squares of felt in orange, amber, yellow, lime green, pink, deep pink, royal blue, black and white
- [ ] Medium-weight, firm weave fabric for background, 73·5cm by 35·5cm
- [ ] Unbleached calico or holland for backing, 63·5cm by 25·5cm
- [ ] Soft pencil
- [ ] A piece of hardboard or softboard 63·5cm by 25·5cm for mounting (from most Do-It-Yourself shops)
- [ ] Fine string for lacing
- [ ] Squared paper
- [ ] Tracing paper
- [ ] Yarns: Anchor Tapisserie Wool—2 skeins black Anchor Soft Embroidery Cotton—2 skeins black Anchor Stranded Cotton— 2 skeins black
- [ ] Two needles — chenille No.19 and crewel No.3
- [ ] Transparent thread
- [ ] Sharp scissors

Making the clown appliqué

Copy the pattern for the design on to squared paper from the graph overleaf. Then trace and transfer it on to the background fabric. Trace the various shapes on to the appropriate coloured felts and cut them out. (To help you position the pieces of felt correctly, number the background fabric first, then number the back of each piece of felt to correspond.) Lay the shapes in the correct position on the background and tack in place. Stitch round the shapes lightly with small hemming stitches, using the transparent thread.

Now couch in between the applied felt shapes. Use 3 strands of stranded cotton in the needle and outline with 3 lengths of soft embroidery cotton (this should be the complete length required to outline the shape). To make sure the threads lie flat, bring each length of soft embroidery cotton separately through the material before you begin. Stem stitch the hair, nose, mouth and hands with soft embroidery cotton. Make pompons for the buttons down the front as follows:

Making the clown's pompon (see below)

First cut two circles out of cardboard 2·5cm in diameter, with a 1·6cm centre hole. Place these two discs together, thread a bodkin with about 2·7m of black tapisserie wool, take it through the hole and wind it evenly all round the card. Slip one scissor blade between the two discs and cut all round, through the wool. Wind a double length of wool between the discs twice and tie securely, leaving about 15cm wool to sew the pompon in place.

Now tear the cardboard discs and slip them off. Fluff up the pompons and trim into shape with sharp scissors. Make four more pompons in the same way. Stitch pompons in place.

Mounting the finished work

Mount the completed panel on a piece of hardboard or softboard cut exactly to the required finished size of the panel. Lay the piece of board centrally over the back of the work and with fine string (or very strong thread), lace the fabric (not too near the edge) at the back from side to side and then from top to bottom. Pull the lacing firmly until the work is evenly stretched without being puckered. Secure

the lacing thread ends by knotting several times.

Then neaten the back of the work by stitching the unbleached calico or holland over it to conceal the lacing. Simply take the piece of backing fabric, turn under edges 1·2cm all round, tack, then slip-stitch firmly in place to cover the lacing. Remove tacking threads.

This method of mounting is suitable for most forms of embroidery, and you can then frame the embroidery if you wish. Alternatively, stitch two plastic curtain rings to the back of the work on either side and about half-way down to hold a cord for hanging the panel on the wall.

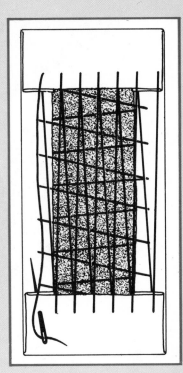

Making the clown's pompon

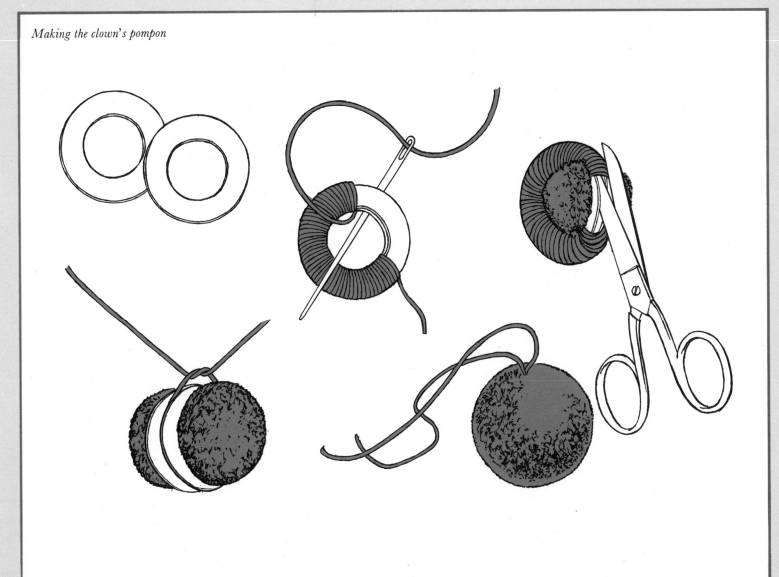

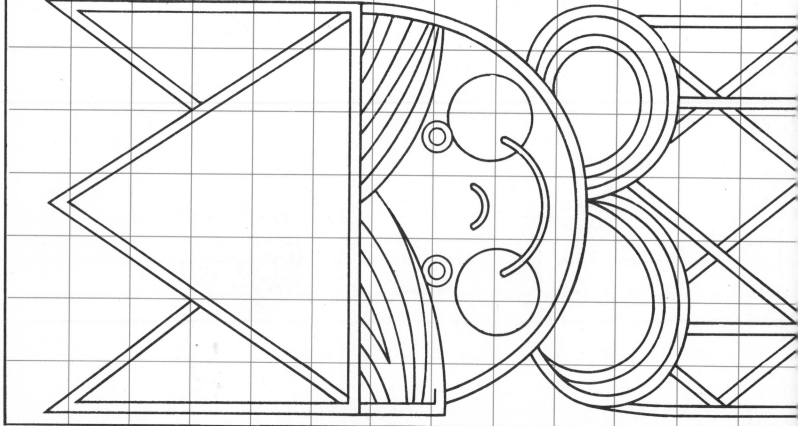

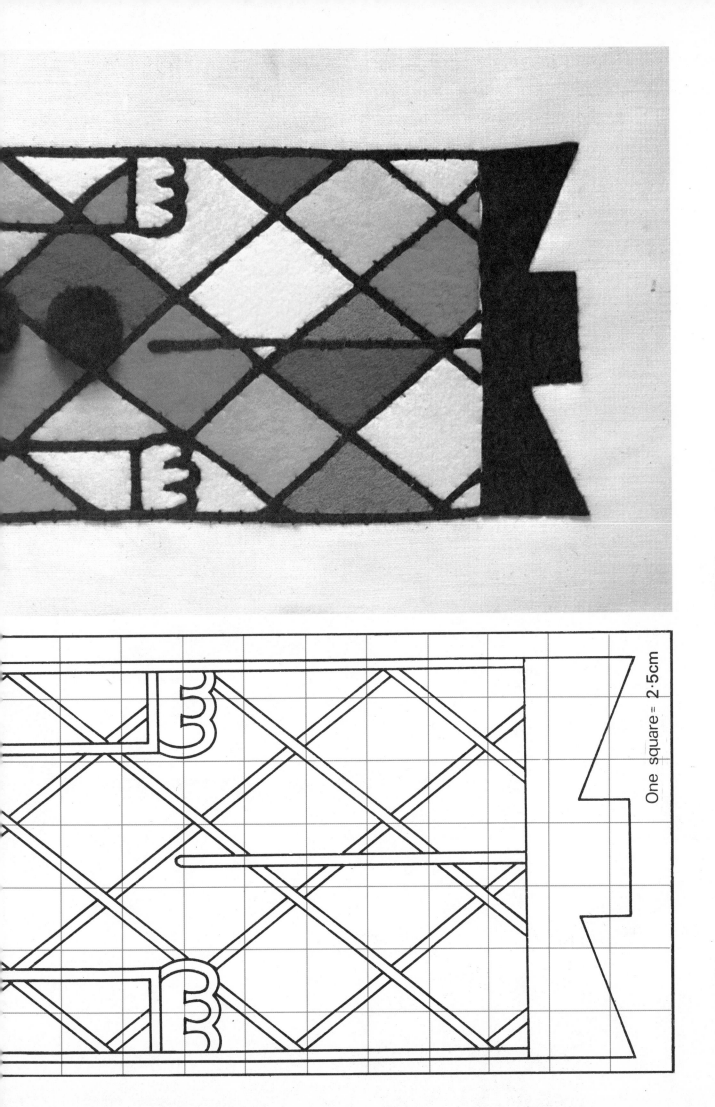

Appliqué clown panel

Graph pattern for appliqué clown

One square = 2·5cm

63

Collector's Piece

Autumn flowers

This wall panel appears, at first sight, to break the basic rules of good design. The three dominating flowers are equidistantly placed immediately above one another.

The designer has, however, used various techniques, together with a limited colour range, to make this an unusually effective and interesting piece of embroidery. Most of the panel has been worked by hand but some machine embroidery has been included.

The background is a natural beige-coloured wool which makes an interesting contrast to the shiny, silky looking fabrics applied to it. The shapes of the leaves throughout the design are flowing and have tremendous movement. This effect is helped by the choice of embroidery stitches. The heavier, dark leaves are worked in twisted chain stitch and the paler leaves, which have a softer look, are worked in Cretan stitch over applied pieces of net. Other leaf shapes are made up of pieces of padded gold kid, but the stitching has been done inside the shape leaving the pointed ends free from the background. This unusual technique results in the pieces catching the light in a more interesting manner than they would stitched in the conventional way. Each of the flowers is made up of layers of applied net with blocks of Cretan stitch on the larger petals and sorbello stitch, twisted chain stitch and knotted chain stitch around the beaded centres.

Groups of French knots and bullion knots in toning colours have been used to fill the spaces between the flowers and leaves, adding texture to the design. The glass beads added to the leaf shapes and enriching the flower centres have been placed with restraint and sensitivity.

Chapter 17

Lion panel in appliqué

Appliqué this corduroy lion onto a panel.

Materials

To make a picture 30cm wide by 25cm deep, you will need:
- [ ] Scraps of russet-coloured corduroy or needlecord
- [ ] Scraps of pink and green felt
- [ ] Purple felt, 35cm wide by 30cm deep

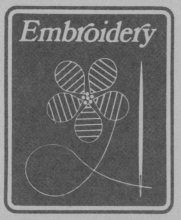

- [ ] Sewing thread, to match corduroy
- [ ] Wool yarn, black and russet
- [ ] Anchor Stranded Embroidery Cotton, yellow, black, turquoise, russet
- [ ] Piece of hardboard 30cm by 25cm
- [ ] Latex solution

Preparing for appliqué

There are eleven pieces of pattern in the lion's body: the main body, back leg and tail, two front paws, one back paw, chin, two cheeks, nose and two ears. Each piece is marked with the grain line and numbered according to the order in which the pieces are to be stitched in to position.

Trace each outline separately on to paper, mark grain lines, and cut out.

Pin each piece of the pattern on the corduroy, matching the grain line to the ridges of the fabric. Cut out each shape, leaving 6mm turnings all round. Fold the turnings to the back of the fabric and tack, except those edges which are marked on the diagram with a red line. These seam allowances are left flat, the next section being placed on top.

Position the pieces on the purple felt background, in the order indicated by the numbers on each piece in the diagram, (the main body piece, for instance, is marked number one and so are the ears and nose). Tack and stitch each piece into position separately, using back stitch or slip stitch. Work the tail and the mane in long straight stitches using russet wool and then finish the end of the tail and the edge of the mane with long stitches, using matching cotton.

Stitch the eyes, the nose, jaw-line and claws in satin stitch using black and yellow wool. French knots are used for the whiskers and back stitch for the outline of the tail, using black stranded cotton. Embroider the stems of the plants in green, using stem stitch or chain stitch. Cut out the pink flowers and green leaves from felt and fix them to the background, using just a touch of latex solution.

When the lion is completed, mount the picture on to hardboard and then frame.

▼ *A clever use of corduroy to achieve a three dimensional effect*   *Diagram of pattern showing eleven pieces marked with grain of fabric* ►

PLACE ON STRAIGHT GRAIN OF FABRIC

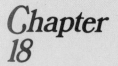

Children's panel in appliqué

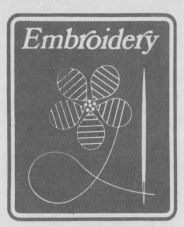

Embroidery

Hans Christian Andersen couldn't have dreamed up a more charming fairy tale prince and princess than these embroidered appliqué panels. In addition to being attractive to look at they are also a delightful and satisfying project to work.

The panels illustrated each measure 43cm by 30cm.

You will need
For both panels
☐ 45cm oatmeal furnishing fabric for background
☐ Scraps of pink felt for faces
☐ 1 card **Penelope Gold Lurex** thread
☐ Dressmakers' carbon paper
☐ Tracing paper
☐ Adhesive (optional)
☐ Crewel needle size 7 or 8
☐ Hardboard 43cm by 30cm
For princess panel
☐ 28cm by 28cm blue material or felt for dress
☐ 12·5cm by 22cm navy material for hem border
☐ 40 white sequins
☐ 40 small pearls
☐ 1 skein Anchor Stranded Cotton in each of light blue, dark blue, white, deep beige, brown, red, turquoise, pink
For prince panel
☐ 25·5cm by 30cm blue material or felt for cloak
☐ 3 blue sequins
☐ 3 small pearls
☐ 1 skein Anchor Stranded Cotton in each of white, light blue, brown, red, black, turquoise
To work the panels
Trace the actual size outlines given on pages 72-5. Copy the details of the figures from pages 70 and 71 (the stitch

guide can also be found on these pages).

Using dressmakers' carbon, transfer the outline of the figure only onto the background. Trace the outlines and embroidery details onto the pieces of fabric to be applied.

Embroider the pieces before the shapes are cut out and stitched to the background. Follow the stitch guide and apply the face first, then the dress or cloak. The navy border is applied over the dress section. Felt can be stuck down or stitched, fabric should be applied with small slip stitches. When all the embroidery and appliqué is completed, work running stitches in gold lurex thread on the background, following the fabric grain.

Special techniques
Princess panel. Use three strands of cotton for all the embroidery except for the bullion knots on the head-dress, which are made using one strand of cotton twisted three times round the needle. The couching is worked with six strands couched down with two strands. The sequins are stitched and held in place with a small pearl, worked after pressing and before mounting.
Prince panel. The French knots decorating the cloak are worked with two strands of cotton, and the remainder of the embroidery is worked in three strands. The double rows of couching down the front edges of the cloak and all sequins are worked in the same way as for the princess panel.

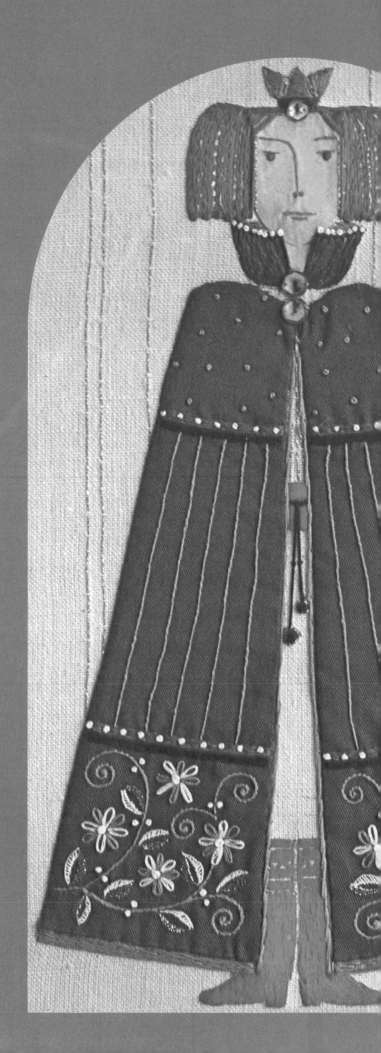

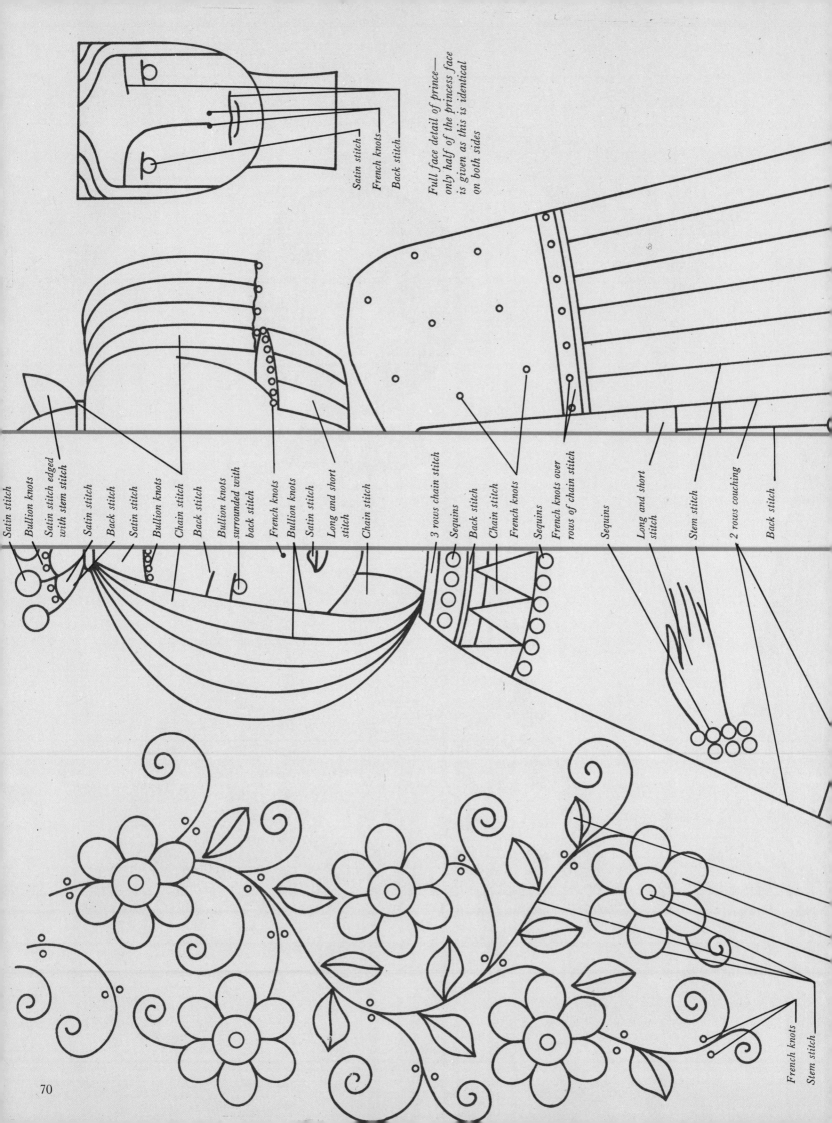

Satin stitch
French knots
Back stitch

Full face detail of prince—
only half of the princess face
is given as this is identical
on both sides

Satin stitch
Bullion knots
Satin stitch edged
with stem stitch
Satin stitch
Back stitch
Satin stitch
Bullion knots
Chain stitch
Back stitch
Bullion knots
surrounded with
back stitch
French knots
Bullion knots
Satin stitch
Long and short
stitch
Chain stitch
3 rows chain stitch
Sequins
Back stitch
Chain stitch
French knots
Sequins
French knots over
rows of chain stitch
Sequins
Long and short
stitch
Stem stitch
2 rows couching
Back stitch

French knots
Stem stitch

70

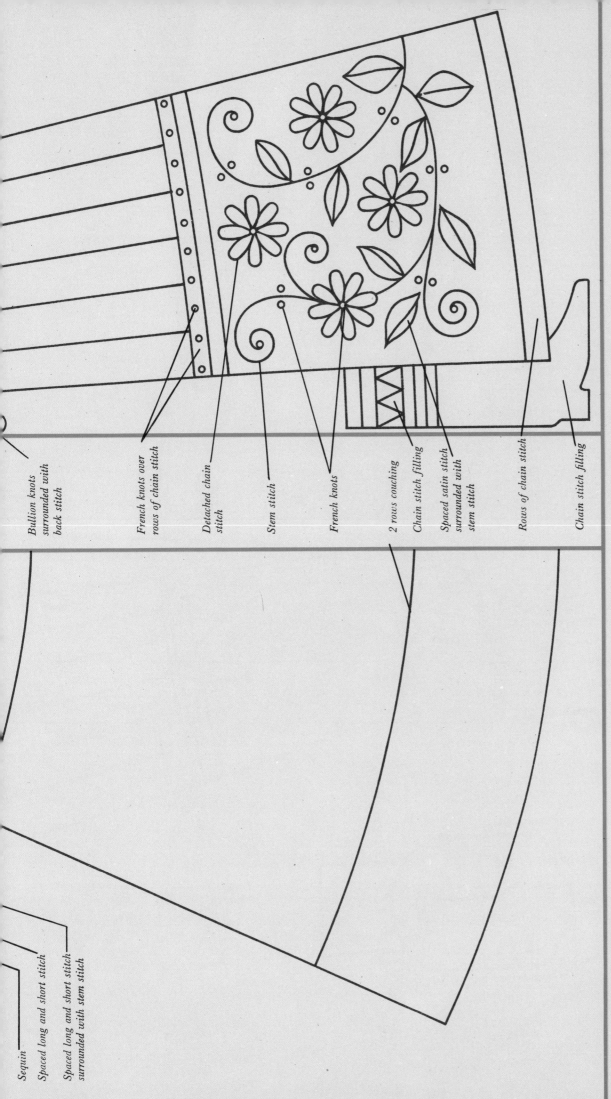

Sequin

Spaced long and short stitch

Spaced long and short stitch surrounded with stem stitch

Bullion knots surrounded with back stitch

French knots over rows of chain stitch

Detached chain stitch

Stem stitch

French knots

2 rows couching

Chain stitch filling

Spaced satin stitch surrounded with stem stitch

Rows of chain stitch

Chain stitch filling

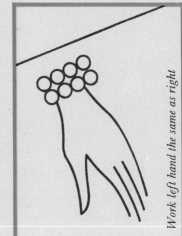

Stitching down a sequin with a bead

Work left hand the same as right

◀ Stitch guide

Finishing and mounting

When all the embroidery is completed and before the sequins are attached, press the work lightly on the wrong side over a well padded surface using a medium hot iron over a damp cloth. Attach sequins and mount the panels over hardboard (see Embroidery Chapter 16).

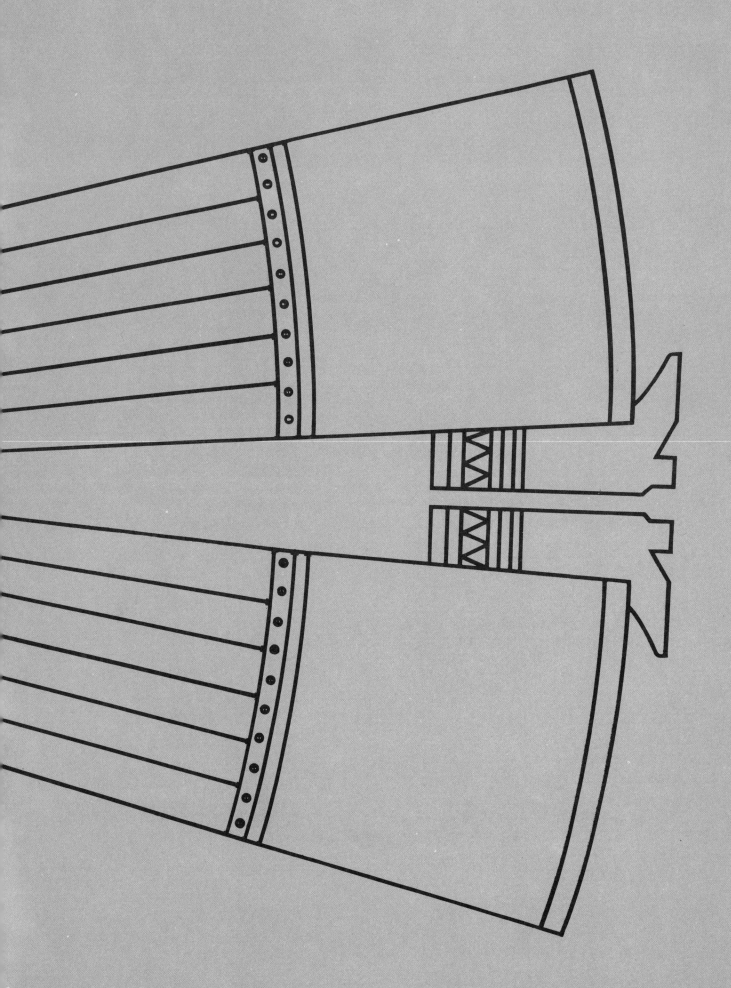

Trace outline of prince

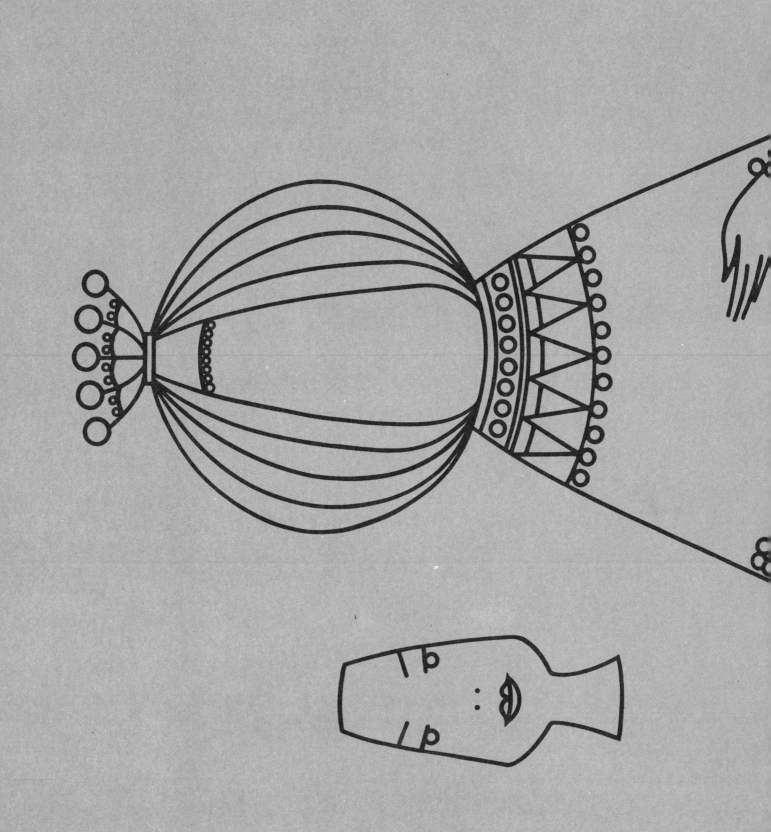

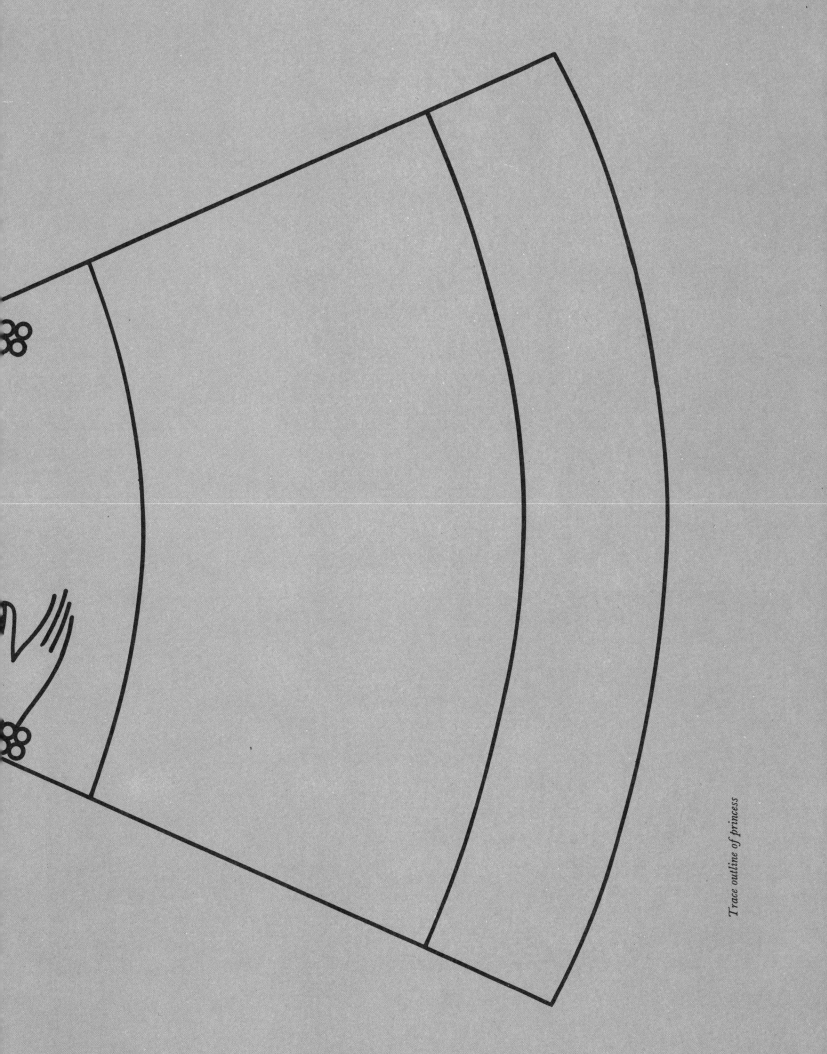

Trace outline of princess

Chapter 19

San Blas appliqué

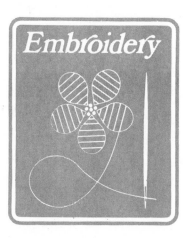

Introduction

Bold, brilliant colours are used in this unique method of appliqué, worked by the Indian women of the San Blas Islands off the coast of Panama. The appliqué designs are now worked in two pieces measuring about 36cm by 51cm and are made into blouses called molas.

When the Indians first moved to the islands in about 1850 the molas were simple affairs, made only of dark blue material with a single band of red cloth around the bottom. The designs developed to decorate the lower half of the mola and then developed further to form a major part of the blouse. Later, when traders brought fabrics of brighter colours to the islands, the designs became more elaborate, involving up to five or six layers of fabric in as many colours.

Mola designs

The designs themselves are primitive and gay, representing forms and figures from everyday life on the islands. Gods, goddesses, shapes from nature such as animals and plants and important people are all featured in bold, primitive stylized shapes. Often the designs are copied from pictures in magazines, comic books, calendars and even labels on canned foods. The designs often include English words or letters which are not understood by the Spanish speaking Indians and used with complete disregard of their meaning, but which look decorative and important. The stylized designs of the molas reflect the style of the wooden figures called 'nuchus', carved by the San Blas men. The layers of fabric are first tacked together and then cut away, and the result very much resembles the enamel work of some Mexicans, where layers of colour are applied (painted) then incised to reveal colour on colour.

The molas are an important status symbol amongst the Indians and in some places it is considered improper for a San Blas Indian girl to be married without possessing at least twelve or more unworn molas as part of her dowry.

Fabrics

For the traditional style San Blas appliqué, plain dyed fabrics such as poplin or

▲ *San Blas appliqué worked on the hem of a simple wrapover evening skirt*

sail cloth are ideal. However, pure silks or shantung would lend themselves beautifully to the technique. For the more ambitious, experiments with textured fabrics such as corduroy or tweed could prove interesting. Felt, suede or leather could also be used but no turnings would be needed.

Uses

This appliqué technique is ideal for fashion where rich, bold effects are required. It would look good worked as a border on a skirt, on an evening cloak, on inset panels or on a yoke on a dress or a blouse.
Mola work on curtains would look dramatic and cushion covers, bedspreads, pictures and wall hangings are all suitable subjects.

Method

This appliqué technique is more a method of cutting away than applying pieces of fabric. Parts of the top layers of fabric are cut away to reveal a section of the colour below. One, two or three layers of fabric may have to be cut through at the same time to get to the desired colour for a particular part of the design. However, if the colours are arranged well, it should not be necessary to have to cut through more than one layer of fabric at a time. Pieces of different colours can be placed under only certain parts of the design.

Experiment with two or three layers of fabric to start with, introducing extra colour by applying small areas of fabric to highlight the design.

Place the fabrics in the desired arrangement of colours then tack the layers of fabric together all round the edge and also diagonally across each way to hold them securely.

To reveal the first colour under the top layer, use a pair of sharp embroidery scissors and cut away a portion of the top fabric in the desired shape. Clip the edges of the fabric to be turned under on all curves and into all corners and turn in 3mm. Using a matching colour sewing thread, slip stitch the edge to the layer of fabric below. Small appliqués of another colour can be added in one, two or more layers using the same technique of cutting out to reveal the colour below.

Collector's Piece

Embroidery for a dream

Romantic in concept and
evocative of another age,
the embroidered clothes
illustrated on these pages
were designed and made by
Angela Salmon, a dress
design student at London's
St Martin's School of Art,
for her final diploma
exhibition. Although
painstaking embroidery is not
commercially viable in the
ready-made clothing industry,
it is comforting to know that
students of design continue to
produce exquisite work such
as this, adapting traditional
techniques to modern design
concepts.

The lilac silk and black
velvet dress, worn with
pantaloons, has flowers and
leaves of machine embroidered
organza applied to the bodice
with realistic-looking plastic
blackberries to complete the
motif. The caped coat-dress,
made of olive-coloured
chiffon, is worn over a
strawberry printed chiffon
dress. Strawberry flowers,
leaves and fruit motifs, made
of matt satin and machine
embroidered organza, are
applied with some of the
edges lying free of the
background fabric.

The blue and white ensemble
consists of a blue organza
apron worn over a full-
sleeved chiffon dress. The
designer has chosen field
flowers for her inspiration—
poppies, buttercups, speedwell
and wheat heads—
embroidered and applied to
the background fabric.
Surface embroidery has been
added to enrich the design.

Chapter 20

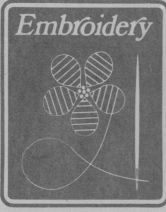

Embroidery with braid and ribbon

Braid embroidery is a simple form of appliqué. As well as being bold and decorative, dimension is added with the clever use of ribbons of different texture, beads and sequins.

Once braid embroidery is combined with other forms of appliqué and embroidery, the possible effects are many and varied. The richly raised finish is ideal for clothes, table linen and wall panels. When working braid embroidery on table linen, remember to position the design so that there are unworked areas left for plates and glasses when the table is set.

Materials and yarns
This type of embroidery is worked with a narrow braid of wool, cotton or synthetics. The width you choose will depend on the final effect wanted and can be anything from 6mm to 5cm braid. The textures can be varied by the introduction of leather, suede, felt, plastic, cord, metallic yarn, beads or sequins, intermingling these with the braid. Ribbon creates a pretty effect whether you use nylon, satin or velvet and if you are very enthusiastic, you may want to make your own braids in crochet, knitting or macramé. The decoration is stitched in place with sewing cotton, invisible sewing thread or embroidery thread if the braid is held down with a decorative stitch. Additional embroidery stitches are then used to add detail.

The background fabric should be a firmly woven material such as velvet, furnishing fabric or a strong linen.

Designs for braid embroidery
Designs should be basically simple. The technique lends itself very well to modern geometric and abstract designs formed by straight lines or free flowing curves. Detail can be added in the form of embroidery stitches or beading.

Method of working
Trace the design on to the right side of the background fabric (see Embroidery Chapter 3). Stitch the outline braid round the design, (see diagram), using a simple running stitch or small back stitch about 3mm long and worked at 1cm intervals along the centre of the braid. Machine sewing can be used provided the braid is tacked firmly in place first.

When working round corners, ease the braid so that the inside edge is slightly fuller than the outside one. The curves are then pressed into shape to lie smooth and flat.

Effects with braid
Braid flowers are made by looping the braid into the shape of individual petals (see illustration). Secure the end of each loop with several stitches.

The centres of these looped flowers are decorated with embroidery stitches.

80

▲ *Ribbons and braids can be used in a variety of ways for pictures and panels*

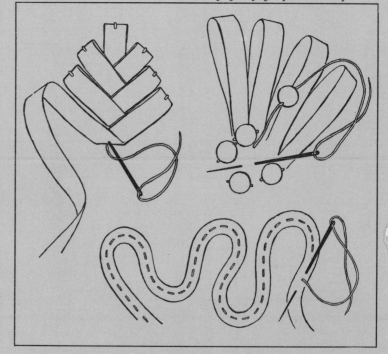

▲ *Method of stitching braid and detail showing ear of corn being worked*

Ears of corn are quick to make. Mark a centre line on the background and work a line of double loops going to right and left of this centre line, stitching the loops down at the centre as you go. A single line of stem stitch forms the beard and smaller ones are made between the ends of the loops.

Complete the design by couching lengths of cord or work embroidery stitches for stems and leaves.

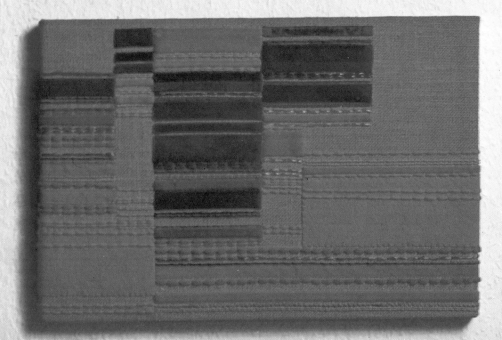

Seasons in colour

These three panels show an interesting modern interpretation of braid embroidery using a variety of widths of velvet ribbon mounted on heavy dress linen. They are part of a set of four, each measuring 25·5cm by 38cm. The panels depict the four seasons and the three pictured here are (from top to bottom) spring, summer and autumn. It is the background colour which relates in general terms to the season.

Yellow stands for spring with the riotous colours of yellow crocuses, daffodils and jasmine, and pink hyacinths and tulips, all blending with the more subtle shades of lilac.

Green represents summer with its green grass, trees and red flowers, bright and clear as on a midsummer's day.

Pink brings to mind autumn sunsets and also complements the richness of the browns which suggest dying leaves and dark wet roofs.

However, only the colour categories were suggested by each season. The individual shades were dictated by working them together as a scheme within each panel and it is the use of some form of pink in each panel which unites them.

The design, materials and stitchery are kept simple to avoid detracting from this experiment in colour, which is the main object of the panels. While the various aspects of the seasons influence the colours, it is the rectangular outlines of modern architecture which inspires the symmetry of the design.

Only two stitches are used—couching and stem stitch. Plastic raffia, pearl cotton, double knitting wool and stranded cotton threads are couched in their own colour of mercerised sewing cotton so that only indentations are seen. The couching stitches are placed exactly in line with one another throughout the rows to follow through the idea of stark simplicity. All the ends of the couched threads are taken to the back of the work.

Chapter 21

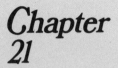

Introduction to smocking

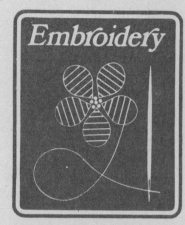

Smocks were originally worn as overalls by manual workers. The smocking was not only decorative but served the practical purpose of holding the fabric together in tight, tiny pleats. Smocking is now used on garments wherever fullness needs to be controlled and for purely decorative effects. The basis of smocking is the gathering which forms the pleats. Once this is completed, there is a variety of decorative stitches which can be applied.

Fabrics
Smooth and even-textured fabrics are best for smocking; cotton, silk, cotton and wool mixtures or fine woollens. Very fine fabrics, such as voile and lawn are exquisite when they are smocked but need a little more practice. Thick materials are not suitable for smocking.

Yarns
Coton à broder or pearl cotton are ideal yarns for smocking embroidery. Stranded yarns are not strong enough and are inclined to twist.

Smocking transfers
It is essential to keep smocking pleats even and regular and transfers for planning the gathering dots are invaluable. Several different gauges are available: dots close together give small pleats and are suitable for baby clothes and fine fabrics, while widely spaced dots which give a deep pleat are better for heavier materials. Transfers with dots about 6mm to 1cm apart are suitable for most fabrics.

How much material
As a rough guide fabric, before smocking, should measure about three times the required finished length, but it depends on the space between the dots, the firmness of the particular stitches used, and the work tension which varies from person to person. In dressmaking, it is important to remember that smocking should be completed before the garment is sewn together. It is not possible to smock ready-made clothes.

Smocking on a garment is easy to do once you have learned the basic principles of gathering and the basic stitches. Try a simple frill to begin with.

Ruffles and frills
Narrow, delicate frills look charming down the front of a shirt or blouse, round a cuff or neck edge. Quick and simple to do, frills are ideal for beginners. The frill illustrated is 5cm wide with 1½ rows of diamond stitch outlined with cable stitch. The edging can be buttonhole stitched or embroidered on an automatic sewing machine.

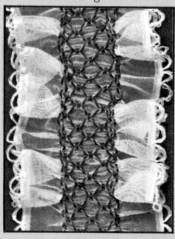

Smocking step by step

Cut the transfer to the length and depth required, and iron it on to the wrong side of the material. Beginning at the first right hand dot, on the wrong side of the fabric, secure the thread firmly with a good

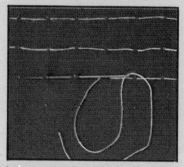

knot and a back stitch. Work from right to left, and carefully pick up each dot along the line leaving a few inches of the thread hanging loose at the end of the row.

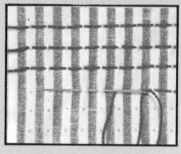

Repeat until all the rows are completed. Pull all the threads together, not too tightly, (if you smock tightly, slacken the gathers, if loosely, pull them a

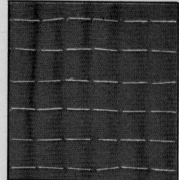

little tighter). Knot the ends together in pairs, sliding the knot along the thread on a pin and cut the threads to within two inches of the knots. Leave the gathering threads in place and remove them when smocking is completed. Use gathering lines as a guide to keep smocking stitches straight.

Smocking on patterns

Dotted, striped or checked fabrics with a regular pattern will not necessarily need gathering transfers but it is important to decide which area of the pattern is required on the surface of the finished smocking.

Smocking on stripes
Make rows of guide dots on the wrong side of the fabric with a pencil. The dot should come in the middle of a light stripe if smocking is to appear on a dark area and in the middle of a dark stripe if a light background to smocking is preferred.

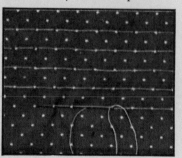

Smocking on spots
Gather each spot as if a transfer were being used. On the second and, subsequent rows, use spots directly under those in the first row or pick up a stitch immediately under a spot.

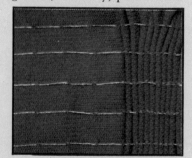

Smocking on checks
For a dark background to smocking, pick up the centre threads of the palest squares: for a light background pick up the centre threads of the darkest.

Simple stitches

Diamond stitch

Diamond stitch is one of the larger smocking stitches, and care should be taken not to make it too large or the finished smocking will lack firmness. The stitch is worked from left to right in two stages and each stage is worked between two rows of gathering threads; (if the rows of gathering threads are 6mm apart, the finished depth of the entire stitch will be 1·2cm.

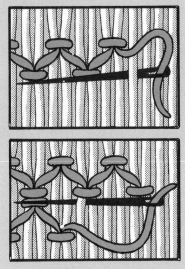

Cable stitch

Cable stitch is a firm control stitch and two rows worked closely together at the top and bottom of a band of smocking prevent the piece from fanning or spreading out too much. Cable stitch can be used as a single line, or in several rows, worked closely together between rows of freer stitches, to add strength to a design.

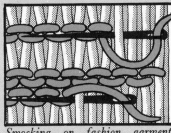

Smocking on fashion garments usually takes the form of reducing fullness across the bodice, down the sleeves or across waistlines and wide-skirted hems.
Effective, yet simple to do, smocked panels are worked on the same body fabric separately and then inserted into the garment ►

Collector's Piece

Traditional smocks

This smock was made in Buckinghamshire in 1820. It might well have been stitched by a peasant's wife and worn either for working in the weekday, or set aside 'for best' on Sunday. All the smocks, at this time, were made of heavy thick materials including cottons, linens and twills. The stitches used included feather stitch, chain stitch, faggot stitch and stem stitch.

Some smocks were worked in different designs showing the wearer's profession. For instance, trees and leaves stitched into the garment indicated that the peasant was a woodman. Crooks, sheep pens and hurdles meant that the peasant was a shepherd and so on. It is also possible to tell from the designs where the peasant came from, each county having its own particular pattern.

Colours too, are associated with certain counties, although the most common colours were white, cream and brown. Green and black existed but few of these survive today.

Chapter 22

Smocking an angel top

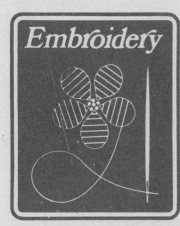

Children of all ages look delightful in smocked clothes —babies in angel tops, nine year-olds in frilled blouses and gadabout growing girls in smocked party dresses. This chapter gives instructions for making a smocked angel top from a graph pattern, to fit babies from birth to six months old. The neckline and cuffs are smocked with two of the three stitches illustrated, trellis stitch and outline stitch (in groups). Smocking stitches vary in their degree of fabric control: some have tight control, others have medium or loose control. It is important when planning smocking to note the control of the stitches selected. This angel top, for instance, uses a loose control stitch—trellis stitch—on the bottom edge of the smocking, so that the material flares.

Outline stitch. Similar to ordinary stem stitch (see diagram) each stitch picks up one tube of the fabric. A firm control stitch, two rows worked closely together at the top or base of smocking, will hold gathers firmly in place. It is not advisable to use this stitch at the base of smocking where a loose flare is required (such as an angel top).

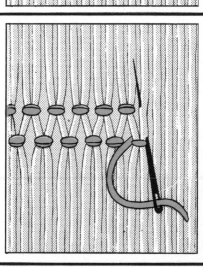

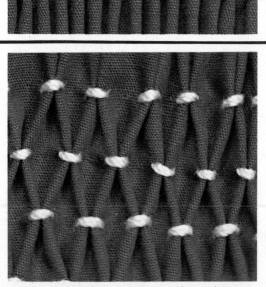

Honeycomb stitch. This is a medium control stitch and is worked from left to right. Bring the needle up at the top of the first tube and make a back stitch picking up the next tube on the right. Take a second back stitch, slipping the needle down through the tube and bring it to the right side ready to make the next double back stitch.

Trellis stitch. Worked in zigzag lines, this stitch is shown on the illustrated angel top and is on the cuffs. It is a loose control stitch and could be used for the last row of smocking where a flare is required.

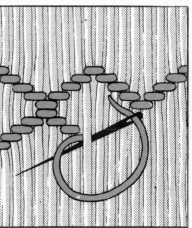

Making a smocked angel top

You will need
☐ 90cm of washable fabric such as Terylene lawn, cotton, wool and cotton mixtures or lawn.
☐ Length of transfer gathering dots
☐ Anchor Pearl Cotton embroidery thread

Preparing for smocking
Make a paper pattern from the angel top graph and pin this to the fabric. Cut out the pieces and iron the required length and depth of gathering dots transfer to the wrong side of the fabric. Gather on the wrong side (see Embroidery Chapter 21) and complete the smocking on each part of the angel top before sewing the garment together.

Making up and finishing
Join sleeves to dress, trimming seams to 6mm depth. Oversew or bind the seams with bias binding or crossway binding cut from the same fabric. Cut a neckband and two cuffs on the cross of the fabric, to fit the child's neck and wrists. The neckband and cuffs should always be attached to the garment with hand sewing because if machine stitching is used, the pleats or 'tubes' of smocked fabric would be pushed flat.

Make two rows of gathering 6mm above the top line of smocking stitches. The rows of gathering stitches should be placed exactly in line, one stitch above the other, and evenly through each 'tube' of fabric. Draw up the gathering to fit the length of the neckband. Turn the seam allowance of the neckband under along one edge and tack. Place the wrong side of the tacked edge 6mm above the top line of smocking, on the right side of the angel top. Pin and tack. With the right side of the work facing, slip stitch each tube to the neckband evenly. Turn the work to the wrong side. Turn under the seam allowance on the other side of the neckband and tack to the inside neckline 6mm above the top row of smocking. Hem to the backs of the tubes, using small neat stitches. Make sure that the stitches do not show through to the right side of the tubes. Stitch the sleeve and side seams and neaten.

Adapting a yoked pattern for smocking
To adapt a nightie or dress pattern so that smocking can be included, choose a pattern with a straight or slightly curved yoke and cut the skirt three times the width of the actual pattern piece. Attach the yoke to the smocked areas as instructed for applying the crossway edgings to the top.

Angel top with a front fastening

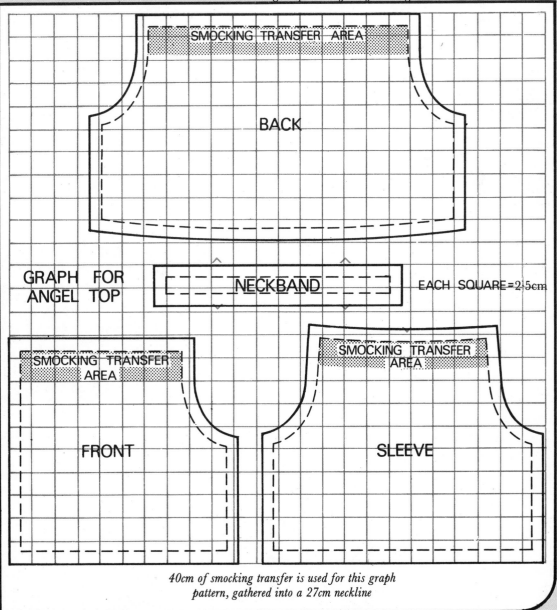

SMOCKING TRANSFER AREA

BACK

GRAPH FOR ANGEL TOP

NECKBAND

EACH SQUARE=2.5cm

SMOCKING TRANSFER AREA

FRONT

SMOCKING TRANSFER AREA

SLEEVE

40cm of smocking transfer is used for this graph pattern, gathered into a 27cm neckline

Chapter 23

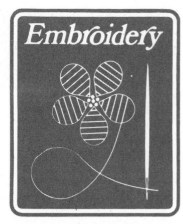

Smocking in fashion

Frills make a charming and feminine decoration for clothes—smocked frills are even prettier. What was once a decoration solely for children's clothes has now become a fashion note for adults, lifting dresses and blouses to a new elegance. Add smocking at necklines, cuffs or in panels down the front of classically styled garments, working and insetting the panels before finally making up the garment.

Decorative smocking stitches

Surface honeycomb stitch
This is worked in the same way as honeycomb stitch (see Embroidery Chapter 22) except that the thread lies on the right side of the work all the time instead of being taken through to the back. It is worked from left to right as shown.

Double feather stitch
This is a fairly tight stitch which is worked like ordinary feather stitch, picking up two tubes of the fabric for each stitch and working from right to left. This stitch needs a little practice to achieve the even effect required for smocking.

Vandyke stitch
This is a small, tight stitch worked from right to left. Bring the needle through from the back of the work at the second tube from the right. Then work a back stitch over the first two tubes. Go down to the second row, take the needle through the second and third tubes and work a back stitch over them. Go back up to the first row and work as before with the third and fourth tubes. Continue in this way across the width of the work.
The next row is worked similarly, starting on the third row and working up to the second row. Simply thread the needle behind the previously worked back stitches of the second row, as shown. Continue working in the same manner.

▼ *Surface honeycomb stitch*

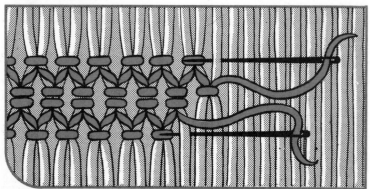

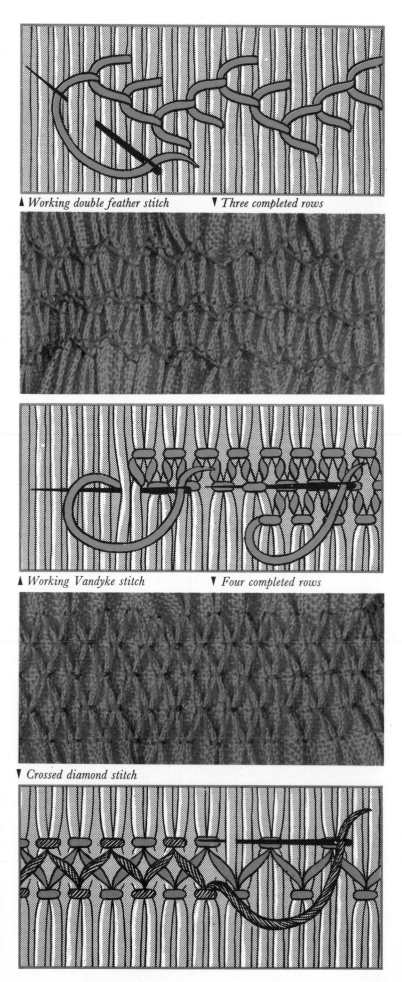

▲ *Working double feather stitch*   ▼ *Three completed rows*

▲ *Working Vandyke stitch*   ▼ *Four completed rows*

▼ *Crossed diamond stitch*

▲ Detail of inset sleeve panel

▲ Inset smocked panels on the sleeves and a smocked neckline make a simple dress pretty

Putting smocking to work

Smocking stitches are never really complicated and once you have mastered the basic ones it is simply a matter of combining several stitches as in this spotted dress. It may look like an ambitious project but you will be amazed at how easy it is once you break down the pattern to individual stitches.

This simple dress has been given a touch of glamour by inserting a panel of smocking into the sleeves and adding a smocked collar. You can decorate a handmade dress by inserting a smocked panel, remembering to cut the fabric three times the actual width of the finished panel, plus seam allowances. Once the smocking is completed, stitch the panel in place.

The stitches used on the sleeve from the top downwards are:

Crossed diamond stitch, rows 1, 8, 12, 29, 33, 50, 54, 61.
Cable stitch, rows 2, 5, 10, 15, 18, 23, 26, 31, 36, 39, 44, 47, 52, 56, 59, 62.
Diamond stitch, rows 3, 4, 6, 7, 9, 11, 13, 14, 16, 17, 19, 20, 21, 22, 24, 25, 27, 28, 30, 32, 34, 35, 37, 38, 40, 41, 42, 43, 45, 46, 48, 49, 51, 53, 55, 57, 58, 60.

Crossed diamond stitch is worked with two rows of diamond stitch immediately over each other, interlocking one row with the other by working in contrasting colours on alternate sets of tubes, (see diagram).

The stitches used on the collar are:
Cable stitch rows 1, 4, 7.
Crossed diamond stitch rows 2, 9.
Diamond stitch rows 3, 5, 6, 8.

Chapter 24

Dress pattern to smock for 6-10 year olds

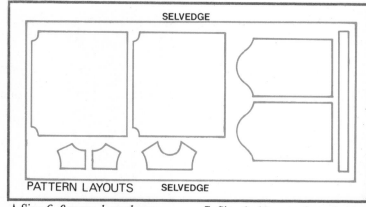

▲ Size 6–8 years, long sleeves

It should only take a few evenings to complete this charming child's dress with its pretty smocked collar and cuffs. It is made up in a crisp, fresh gingham so that the small checks can be used as a guide for working the smocking panels. The same pattern will also make a lovely little nightdress.

Measurements

To fit a size 6–8 (9–10) year old

Materials you will need

Short sleeved version

☐ 170 (190) cm small check 90 cm gingham (2cm across each square)

Long sleeved version

☐ 220 (240) cm gingham

Both versions

☐ Anchor Pearl Cotton No.8: 1 ball orange

☐ Anchor Pearl Cotton No. 8: 1 ball white

☐ Press studs or small buttons for back neck fastening

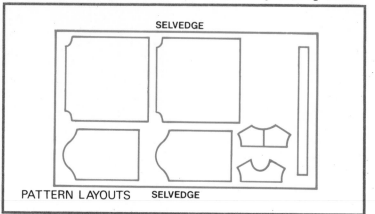

▼ Size 9–10 years, long sleeves

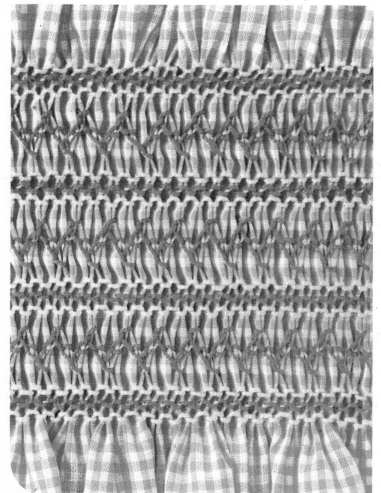

▼ Detail shows effect of working three patterns for a deeper panel

▼ Blue: size 6–8 years; red: size 9–10 years, short sleeve version

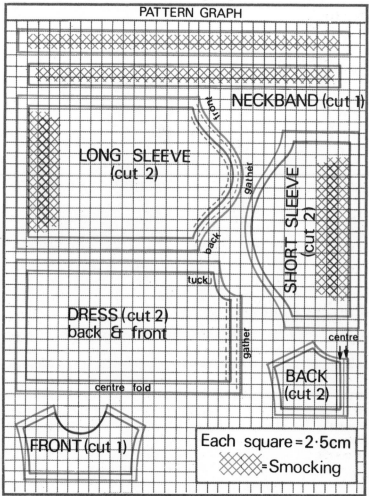

To make the pattern

Mark up a large sheet of brown paper in 2·5cm squares and copy the pattern graph on to it, square by square. Cut out the pattern pieces.

To cut out

When cutting out the dress, allow 1·5cm seam allowances and 10cm for the hem. Lay the material flat and pin the pattern pieces to it as shown in the pattern layout.

To make up

Make a small hem at the top of the neck band, and at each end of it, either by hand or machine. Gather up the smocking bands on the collar and sleeves by picking up the white squares on the wrong side of the work. Pull up the threads quite tightly so that the right side of the work is firm and evenly pleated. Smock three rows of cable stitch, one of feather stitch, three of cable stitch, one of feather stitch and three of cable stitch (see detail) on neck and sleeves.

Join the shoulder seams of Front and Back yokes. Cut a 10cm opening down the Centre Back of skirt top. Gather the top of the skirt to measure the same as across yokes. Join the side seams, then mark one inch out to either side of the seam and bring these two points together over the seam to make a pleat. Turn the pleat to the Front of the dress (see diagram).

Slip stitch the neckband by hand to the neck of the yoke, picking up each tube separately, leaving seam allowance plus 2cm at the back of the yoke to be hemmed for opening. Machine stitch round edge of yoke to secure the neckband turning. Hem neck opening as in diagram and finish with poppers or tiny buttons, making buttonhole loops to fasten. Stitch the sleeve seam, then gather round the top of the sleeve to fit the armhole and set the sleeves into armholes. Make a narrow hem on sleeve cuffs. Oversew all raw edges or neaten with machine zigzagging. Turn up hem.

▲ *No worries about washing her dress, made of small check gingham and decorated with pretty panels of smocking*

▼ *Making a pleat in the side-seam*   ▼ *Tacking the neckband to the yoke*   ▼ *A detail of the back opening*

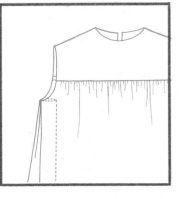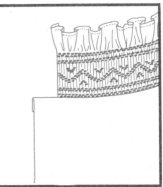

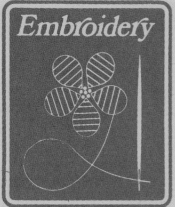

Chapter 25

Embroidery

Lattice smocking

Lattice smocking is worked without a foundation of gathering and produces an effective form of pleating on the right side of the fabric.

Fabrics

Fabrics with a pile, such as velvet and corduroy, are the best to use, but any heavy quality fabric which does not crease easily, such as satin, will do. Allow approximately double the quantity of fabric to the required finished measurement.

Yarns

Use strong sewing yarns such as buttonhole twist, button cotton or nylon sewing thread in the needle.

Method

Commercial transfers are made for stamping the dots used in the smocking, (see Embroidery Chapter 21) but it is possible to mark your own if you prefer. The dots are spaced in rows 3cm apart. All the smocking is worked on the wrong side of the fabric. The stitches will not show on the right side after the smocking pleats are formed. After the dots are marked on the wrong side of the fabric, start the smocking at the upper left hand corner. Knot the end of the yarn.

Pick up the dots by inserting the needle into the fabric to right of dot and out through the left side of the same dot. The thread is carried from dot to dot on the working side of the fabric. Pick up dot 1 with the needle and make a second holding stitch as shown in diagram 1. Then pick up dot 2, go back to dot 1 and pick up again as shown in diagram 2. Pull dots 1 and 2 together and knot securely as shown in diagram 3. Pick up dot 3 then, with the thread above the needle, slip the needle under the thread between dots 1 and 2 as shown in diagram 4, pulling the thread tightly at dot 3 to form a knot. Be sure to keep the fabric flat between dots 1 and 3. Pick up dot 4, then go back and pick up dot 3 again as shown in diagram 5. Pull the dots together and knot them securely. Pick up dot 5 as shown in diagram 6, slip the needle under the thread between dots 3 and 5 and knot as in diagram 4. Continue to work down the row of dots in the same manner, starting with diagram 2 and picking up dot 6 next. Secure all ends firmly.

Far right: lattice smocking worked in velvet for the sleeves of this delightful dress ▶

▼ *Trace-off guide to repeat as necessary*　　　　*Step-by-step working instructions ▶*

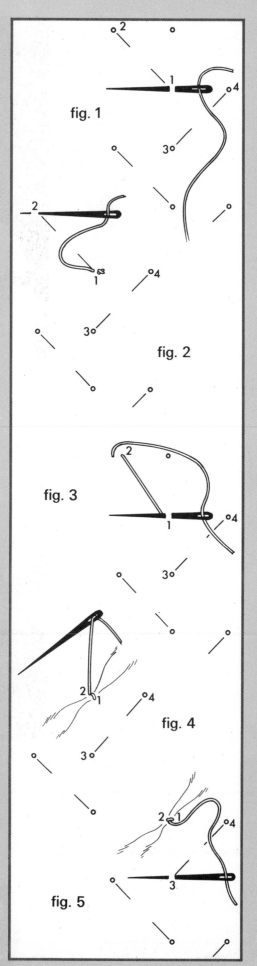

fig. 1

fig. 2

fig. 3

fig. 4

fig. 5

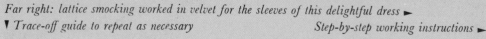
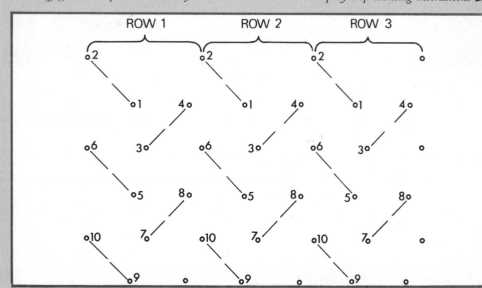

ROW 1	ROW 2	ROW 3

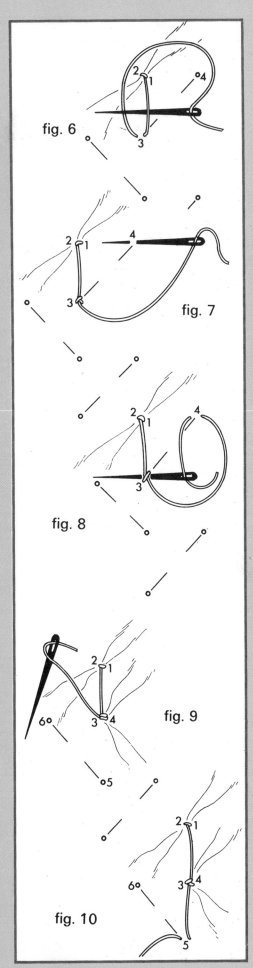

fig. 6

fig. 7

fig. 8

fig. 9

fig. 10

Chapter 26

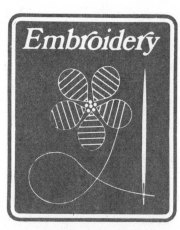

Introduction to drawn thread work

Drawn thread work is a form of counted thread embroidery in which the threads are cut and pulled out from open-weave fabric and the remaining, exposed threads are stitched together in patterns. It originated as a decorative embroidery in ancient Egypt more than two thousand, five hundred years ago. One of the simplest and best known ways of using this fascinating technique is for making decorative hems on handkerchiefs and household linen, particularly sheets, pillowcases, tablecloths, napkins and traycloths.

Making a drawn thread traycloth

Although ready-hemmed traycloths can be purchased, it is better, for drawn thread work, to make the cloth from a length of fabric because bought cloths rarely follow the true grain of the fabric.

For a traycloth measuring 51cm by 36cm with a 2·5cm hem all round, you will need:
- ☐ 60cm 90cm wide even weave material (such as linen or crash)
- ☐ Anchor Stranded Cotton in a matching or contrasting colour.

To make the traycloth
Working on a flat surface, find the centre of the material by folding it in half horizontally and then tacking along the crease, following the grain (see Embroidery Chapter 3). Fold the material in half vertically and tack along the crease, following the grain. The material is now divided into four sections and the centre marked. Leave the tacking stitches in position until the work is completed because they are essential to the placing of embroidery.

Working with a long side horizontal, measure 25·5cm to the left and 25·5cm to the right, from the centre point, to find the length of the traycloth. Measure 18cm up and down from the centre point to find the depth of the cloth. Mark the area all round with a line of tacking stitches, following the grain of the fabric.

From the line of tacking, measure inwards the depth of the hem on all four sides (2·5cm). With a needle, lift one horizontal thread and snip it carefully with scissors. Still using the needle, carefully unpick this thread working away from the centre towards the corners and similarly, draw a thread on all four sides until the drawn threads meet and form a square hole at the corners. Don't unpick any further than the corners but leave the ends long enough to darn back into the fabric to avoid fraying. One to three threads withdrawn is sufficient; if more are pulled out the fabric may be weakened. Measure the hem depth (2·5cm) outwards from the tacking line all round and mark with another line of tacking stitches.

Trim off the excess fabric 1·5cm outside the second line of the tacking. The cloth should now measure 59cm wide by 44cm deep. Fold the crease on the first line of tacking and then on the second to form a 2·5cm hem. Tack the hem to within one thread of exposed threads. Before hem stitching, mitre the corners.

Mitred corners
Working on the wrong side, fold each corner point down so that the point lies where the drawn threads meet. Press each point down, open out and trim the point off diagonally, 6mm above the crease. Fold the 6mm turning back on the crease and bring points A and B together (see diagram). Slip stitch along the creases.

Handkerchief hemstitch
Embroidery threads used for drawn thread work are usually matched to the fabric but coloured thread can be used for a pretty contrast. Stranded cotton, coton à broder, cotton and metallic yarns can be used effectively.

Choose a thread in relation to the thickness of the fabric. For coarse fabrics such as linen, three or four strands of stranded cotton or similar weight of thread is suitable. For lighter fabrics, such as organdie or lawn, one or two strands of stranded thread would be sufficient.

Working on the wrong side and from left to right, with the end of the thread inside the hem, place the needle in from the right, picking up four of the exposed threads. Pull the needle through and pick up two threads of the turned hem. Make sure that the same two horizontal threads are picked up all along the hem.

The instructions for making the traycloth can be applied to making napkins, place mats or table cloths.

Inset borders
Hemstitching can also be used for appliquéd inset borders with drawn thread work. Working from the right side, three or four of the exposed threads are picked up and then two threads of the inset border fabric.

For larger cloths, cut the contrast fabric into long, separate strips, and join with a mitre at the corners before hemstitching.

▼ *Darning back drawn threads* ▼ *Mitreing a corner*

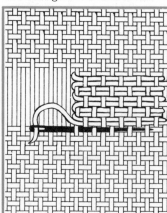
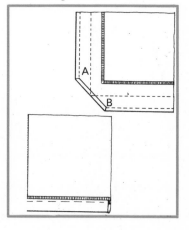

Yarn used for making traycloth
Anchor Stranded Cotton

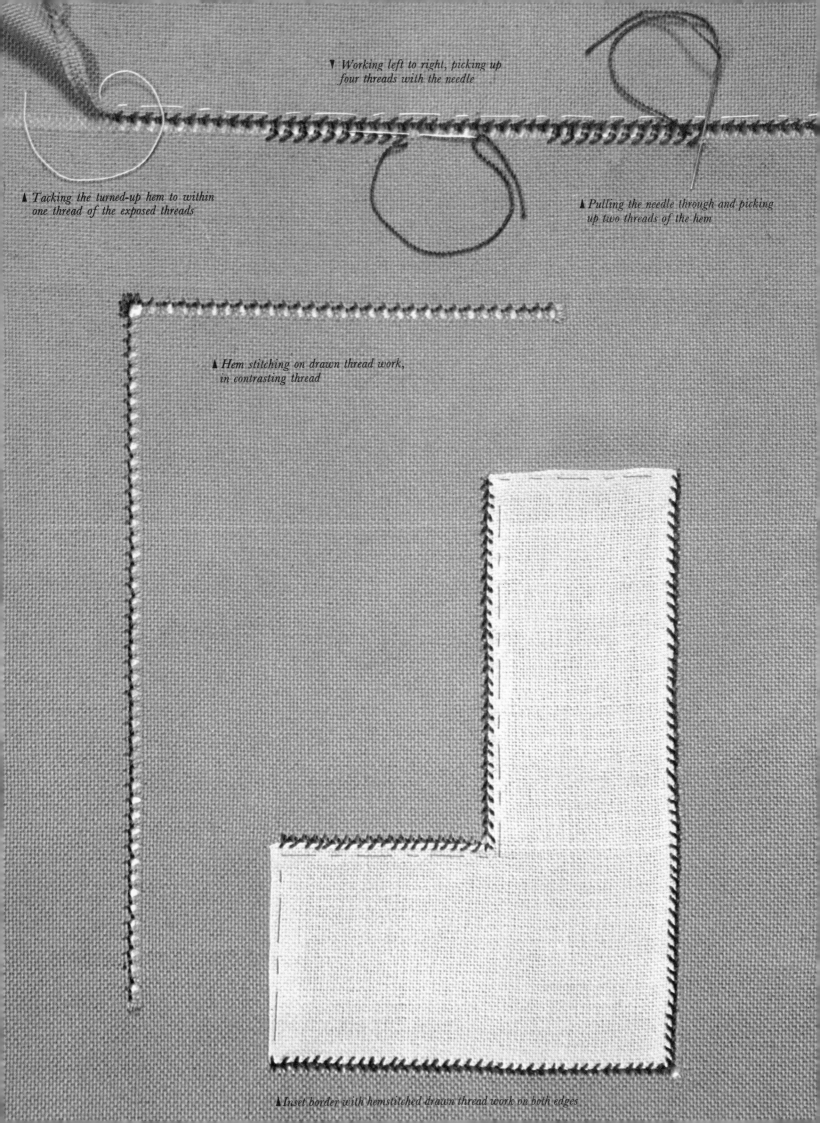

▼ *Working left to right, picking up four threads with the needle*

▲ *Tacking the turned-up hem to within one thread of the exposed threads*

▲ *Pulling the needle through and picking up two threads of the hem*

▲ *Hem stitching on drawn thread work, in contrasting thread*

▲ *Inset border with hemstitched drawn thread work on both edges*

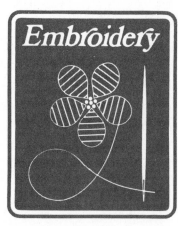

Chapter 27

Variations in drawn thread work

Decorative, reinforced corners are an important stage in drawn thread work and the three pretty corner finishes described here will help you to achieve a professional-looking finish on your handmade linen.

Several attractive variations can be worked on the basic hemstitch described in the previous chapter—ladder hemstitch, zigzag hemstitch and one of the effects obtained by knotting groups of threads, are described here. By grouping and twisting the threads in other ways and using different yarns, you will be able to work out other variations yourself.

Decorative, reinforced corners

When two or more rows of threads have been drawn out, as for instance on the traycloth (see Embroidery Chapter 26), a square empty space is formed at the corners, where the drawn threads meet. After the ends of the threads have been darned in, the edges of the square are worked very closely with satin stitch or buttonhole stitch, to prevent the hole fraying. With fine fabrics the hole is very small and may be left with just the edges finished off. With coarse fabrics the hole is larger, and is filled with a worked web to decorate and strengthen the corner. Both dove's eye filling and loop stitch filling are simple to do and form the basis for more complicated and decorative fillings.

Each of these fillings is based on a simple, reinforced corner—a corded or buttonhole stitched edge is worked very closely along the edges of the square (see illustration).

Dove's eye filling

To work dove's eye filling, fasten the embroidery thread to one corner of the square and take it across diagonally to the opposite corner of the square. Return to centre and work in the same way across the other two corners. Where the threads cross, work the dove's eye by stitching round and round until the eye is large enough. Take the thread across to one of the corners and fasten off.

Loop stitch filling

Loop stitch filling, which has a pretty, lacy look, is used when the corner hole is not very large. Follow the diagram (right) for the method of working this simple decorative filling.

Variations on hemstitch

Ladder hemstitch

This simple hemstitch variation is worked where four to six threads have been drawn. Work hemstitch on both sides of exposed thread area, making a series of vertical groupings. Two, three or four threads are taken up by the needle to form the groups.

Zigzag hemstitch

Begin this stitch by working a single row of hemstitch, taking up an even number of threads (two, four or six). On the opposite side of the drawn threads, take up half of the same group of threads with half of the adjacent group, making a zigzag effect.

Knotting groups of threads

The knotting of groups of threads produces more attractive variations on ladder hemstitch. The knot which holds the groups of threads firmly fixed, twisted chain stitch—(see illustration), is obtained by placing the needle as for chain stitch and passing the needle under the group of threads. The embroidery thread is left visible and forms part of the pattern. You can remove more threads, working more rows of chain stitch to form zigzag patterns.

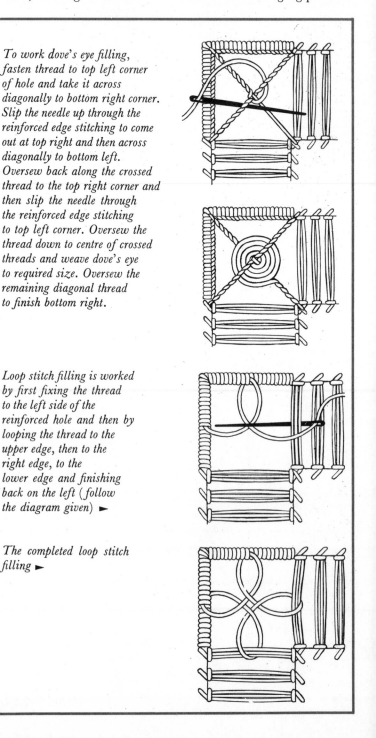

To work dove's eye filling, fasten thread to top left corner of hole and take it across diagonally to bottom right corner. Slip the needle up through the reinforced edge stitching to come out at top right and then across diagonally to bottom left. Oversew back along the crossed thread to the top right corner and then slip the needle through the reinforced edge stitching to top left corner. Oversew the thread down to centre of crossed threads and weave dove's eye to required size. Oversew the remaining diagonal thread to finish bottom right.

Loop stitch filling is worked by first fixing the thread to the left side of the reinforced hole and then by looping the thread to the upper edge, then to the right edge, to the lower edge and finishing back on the left (follow the diagram given) ►

The completed loop stitch filling ►

1 *Simple reinforced corner using buttonhole stitch in contrasting colour*
2 *Zigzag hemstitch worked over groups of four drawn threads*
3 *Three groups of threads knotted together with twisted chain stitch*
4 *Dove's eye filling worked on satin stitch reinforcing, in contrast colour*
5 *Loop stitch filling on satin stitch reinforcing in matching thread*
6 *Ladder hemstitch worked on both sides of the drawn threads*

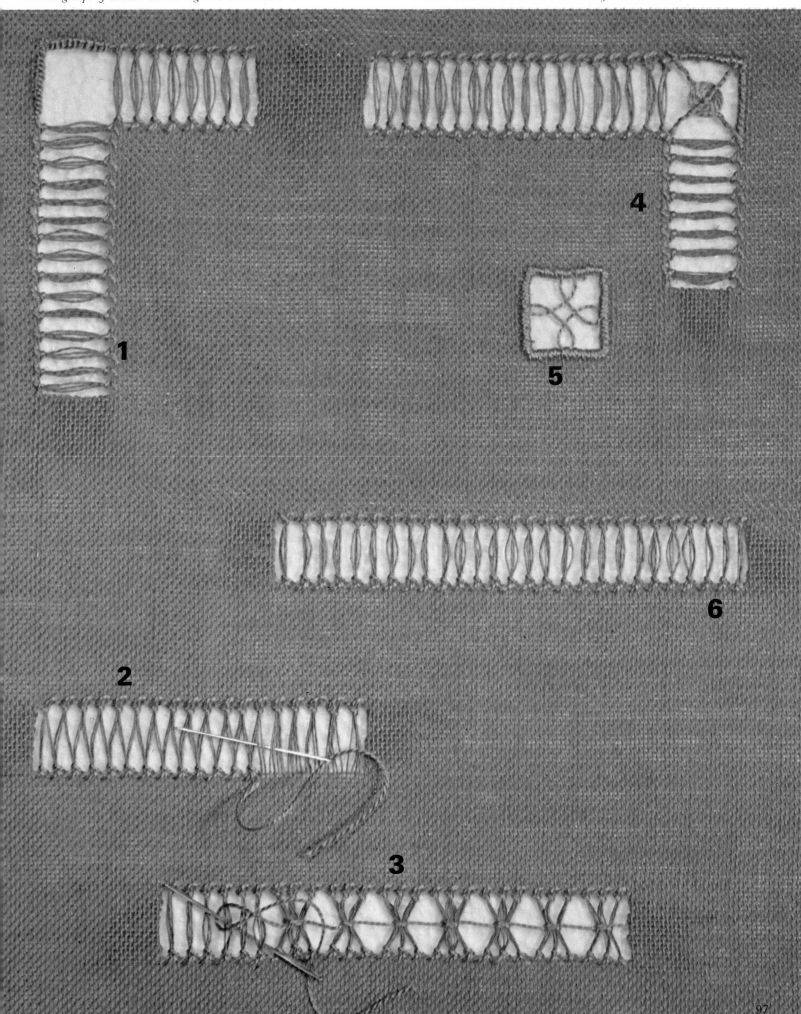

Chapter 28

Design in drawn thread work

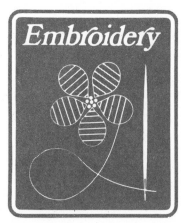

The stitches shown in this chapter can be adapted to form beautiful modern designs such as the waistcoat, cushions and wall panels illustrated on the following pages.

Drawn thread work is an interesting form of embroidery based on the removal of either the warp (lengthwise) or the weft (crosswise) threads from a precise even-weave fabric. The remaining threads are grouped together into patterns by knotting or interlacing, based on a foundation of ladder hemstitch (see Embroidery Chapter 27).

Each group should contain the same number of threads, usually an even number, so that the threads can be divided evenly when knotting or interlacing, to form a pattern.

For an interlaced pattern a large number of threads have to be withdrawn from the fabric to allow sufficient play to form a pattern. The actual number of threads drawn depends greatly on the fabric and thickness of the weave, so it is a good idea to practice on a spare piece of the material before starting the actual work. Avoid withdrawing so many threads that the fabric is weakened.

Fabrics
The best fabrics to use for this technique are even-weave linen or furnishing fabrics of man-made fibres with precise even-weave, such as Draylon. If the fabric weft threads are of a different thickness to the warp threads, the patterns will be distorted and, depending on the thickness of the threads, this will show up in a design to different degrees.

However, if the design is of a free or abstract nature, this unevenness of weave can be turned to advantage. The more experienced embroiderer can experiment with unusual and interesting fabrics to create different effects.

For wall hangings, great effect can be achieved with even-weave woollen fabrics, hessian, sacking and the various types of canvas normally used in canvas work. With canvas an interesting contrast of textures can be achieved by combining drawn thread work and canvas work stitches.

Yarns
Traditionally, linen yarns were used for drawn thread work, but these are no longer easily obtainable. Some extremely interesting results can be achieved with modern threads however, by using a combination of unusual fabrics and yarns such as gold, silver or copper lurex, weaving yarns or plastic raffia, as well as the more usual yarns such as pearl cotton, coton a broder, soft embroidery cotton and stranded cotton. Cords, braids or fine ribbon make interesting interlacings.

Stitches
There are several ways of using the basic foundation of ladder hemstitch with knotting or interlacing to create different pattern effects.

Four of them are shown here. Zigzag hemstitch (see Embroidery Chapter 27) can also be used as a foundation stitch, but for some special effects a foundation stitch is not necessary. The results are looser and more open but also less hard-wearing.

Complementary stitches
In modern embroidery almost any combination of stitches is acceptable provided the finished result is attractive and does not look jumbled. Drawn thread work and canvas work stitches combine well because they are both worked over counted threads. Many other filling and line stitches go with drawn thread work too. For example, rows of drawn threads separated by rows of blocked satin stitch, richly worked spiders' webs or detached eyelets all build up into instant designs. The Stitch Library gives two such complementary stitches.

Colour
In drawn thread work the decoration relies more on texture contrast than colour combinations, and the best results come from a restricted use of colour. Whichever colour you choose for the embroidery yarn, be it a lighter or darker tone of the fabric colour, an exact match or a complete contrast, use the same colour tone range throughout. A combination of several yarn contrast colours simply detracts attention from the design.

Where to use drawn thread work
Drawn thread work gives an individual and expensive look to household items or clothes—cushions, curtains, wall panels, dresses, waistcoats, blouses and children's wear. Contrast ribbon or fabric can be placed behind the embroidery to dramatise the effect.

Stitch Library

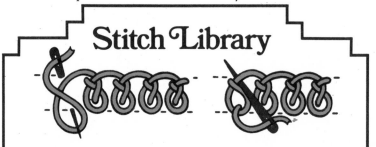

Rosette chain stitch
This stitch gives a braid effect if worked closely, a petal shape when openly spaced. It can be used in straight or curved lines and is worked from right to left or top to bottom.

Sorbello stitch
This is a knotted stitch which looks best worked in a thick yarn. In a thinner yarn it has a completely different effect. Use it close together as a filling, in single or groups of rows as a border or as a powdering.

Needleweaving

Because the withdrawn threads are replaced by closely woven blocks of stitches, this is a hard wearing form of the drawn thread technique.

Woven hemstitch

For the simplest form, withdraw five or six threads. Weave over the first group of threads (three, four or five, depending on the texture of the fabric—if the fabric is coarse, work over fewer), and under the second group. Work back and forth over these two groups, continuing along the upper half of the threads. The next block is then worked over the lower half of the second group and the new third group. Pull the weaving firmly so that spaces are left between the blocks. Work with a tapestry needle.

Pyramid border

The needleweaving border is worked over ten groups of threads tapering off to two groups. The number of threads withdrawn and the number in each group depend upon the texture of the fabric.

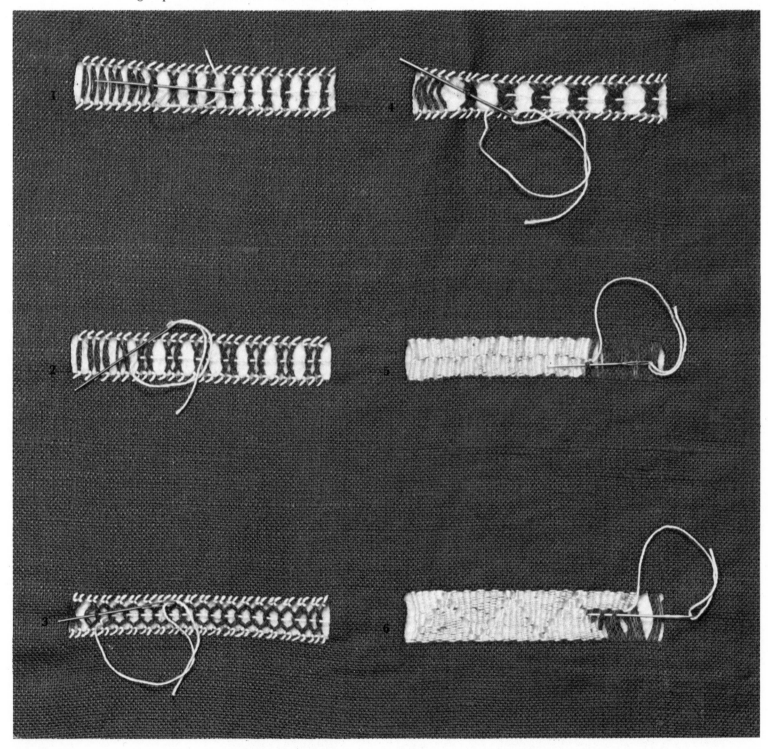

1 *The simplest form of interlacing worked over groups of four threads*
2 *Interlacing worked over groups of two and four threads*
3 *A pattern worked over groups of three threads*
4 *Interlacing worked over four groups each of four threads*
5 *Woven hemstitch*
6 *Needleweaving a pyramid border*

The articles shown on these pages are examples of modern drawn thread work showing a variety of textures, and uses to which drawn thread work can be put.

Abstract panel

This is in the nature of a sampler worked on textured stripes of open weave vision net curtaining. Some threads have been pulled out giving two very open areas. The rest of the design is a combination of a variety of pulled fabric stitches further decorated with surface stitches such as twisted chain, rosette chain, raised chain band, French knots and couching. Some braids and lampshade trimmings have been stitched onto the surface to give a more solid effect. Further texture has been added by using curtain rings, wooden button moulds and wooden beads. The sampler is mounted on a contrast fabric over a wooden frame and measures about 38cm by 51cm.

Dragonfly

As the nature of drawn thread work is to follow the grain of the fabric, the rounded shapes of the insect have been reduced to basic geometric shapes. The design uses a combination of Hardanger embroidery and drawn thread techniques. The design is worked on even weave linen with threads pulled out for the body stripes which are worked in simple drawn thread stitches. Surface stitches such as raised chain band, woven spider's web and couching for the body outlines give strength and texture to the design. Needle weaving has also been incorporated using a self colour yarn on the body, feelers and tail.

Blue-green cushion

The fabric used is a loosely woven Draylon furnishing tweed which lends itself well to drawn thread work. The decoration is formed by using small blocks of satin stitch interspersed with large eyelets. The band of withdrawn threads is threaded with narrow, navy blue satin ribbon. The raised

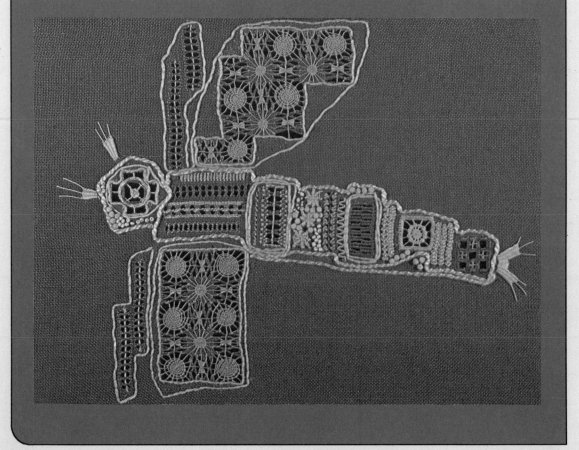

▲ *Abstract panel in the nature of a sampler worked on vision net curtaining fabric*
▼ *A dragonfly worked in a combination of Hardanger embroidery and drawn thread stitches*

decoration and border at each end of the cushion is formed with a row of shell crochet worked in 4 ply crepe knitting yarn.

Cream cushion

Courtelle curtain fabric with a narrow woven stripe has been used for this cushion. Working from the centre outwards, the decoration has been formed as follows. The centre band of withdrawn threads has been interlaced with two thicknesses of Perlita which has been knotted at regular intervals. Next, a row of square stitch in a broken line is worked using cream pearl cotton.

A row of sorbello stitch follows worked in apricot coloured pearl cotton. Close to this a row of coral stitch is worked in cream coloured soft embroidery cotton.

A row of shaggy weaving cotton follows, couched down, and the next row is knotted stitch in dark cream pearl cotton. The final row of embroidery is pulled satin stitch in broken blocks using dark brown pearl cotton. The border edge is worked in sorbello stitch and pulled satin stitch blocks. The raised bands are rows of shell crochet, which also decorate each end of the cushion.

Waistcoat

The waistcoat is made in cream rayon curtain fabric consisting of stripes of solid and open weave upon which the embroidery design is based. The panels on either side of the waistcoat are identical. The stitches used, working from the centre of each panel outwards, are as follows. The centre row of stitching is coral knot stitch using thick cream wool worked over the open threads. The next row is raised chain band worked in alternate lengths of crunchy nylon weaving yarn and six strands of stranded cotton. The next row is formed with lengths of square stitch and French knots using pearl cotton, Nos. 5 and 8. The outer row is raised chain band worked in thick wool over the open threads of fabric.

▲ *A fashionable waistcoat richly decorated in a variety of simple stitches*
▼ *Detail of stitches on the cream cushion*   ▼ *Detail of stitches on the green cushion*

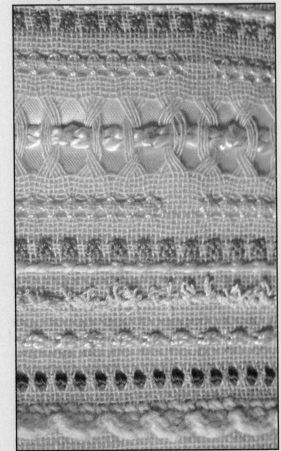

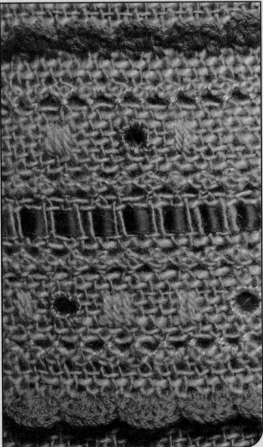

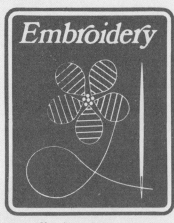
Embroidery

Norwegian Hardanger embroidery

Hardanger embroidery comes from a district of that name in West Norway. Traditionally the embroidery was worked in white yarn on white fabric but modern designs have introduced colour. It is basically a drawn thread technique and is used to decorate either household linens or items of dress.

Hardanger is worked on hardanger fabric or fine linen with a precise even weave. Pearl cotton is the most suitable embroidery yarn but it is possible to substitute coton a broder or stranded cotton. Two different thicknesses of pearl cotton are used, No.5 for the thick satin stitch blocks and the finer No.8 for the woven bars and fillings. The satin stitch surrounds to the spaces are always worked first and this is best done in an embroidery frame. Working the spaces and drawing out the threads which is done without a frame is the second stage of working. Care must always be taken to count the fabric threads and the stitches worked with great accuracy.

The stitches used

The filled-in areas are worked in satin stitch while needleweaving and cording is used for the bars and buttonhole stitch for edges. Four sided stitch is used for both straight and diagonal lines and as a filling stitch.

After the edges of the design have been completed the threads are then cut with very sharp scissors and drawn out, first in one direction and then in the other. The work can then be further decorated with bars with picots, or eyelets.

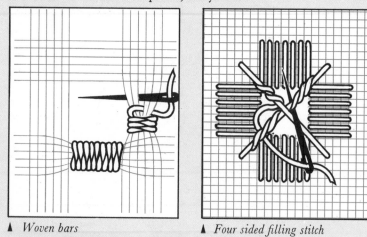

▲ Woven bars   ▲ Four sided filling stitch

Hems and edges

There are a variety of ways to finish hems and edges depending on what the embroidery is to be used for. A hemstitched hem or a plain hem make strong edges for household linen while a buttonhole stitch (see Embroidery Chapter 9) worked round the edge and the fabric cut away makes a more delicate edge for clothing.

Trolley cloth

You will need
☐ Anchor Pearl Cotton No. 5: 2 balls white
☐ Anchor Pearl Cotton No. 8: 2 balls white
☐ 69cm 56cm wide even-weave linen
☐ Tapestry needles sizes 20 and 24

Needles and yarn
Use pearl cotton No.5 for all satin stitch with tapestry needle size 20. For the rest of the embroidery use pearl cotton No. 8 with tapestry needle size 24.

Working the design
Mark the centre of the fabric both ways with lines of tacking stitches. Begin the embroidery from the point where the tacking stitches cross and work the quarter of the design as given, following the chart overleaf.
The chart gives a little more than one quarter of the design and the arrows indicate the centre to be marked with tacking threads. The chart also shows the arrangement of the stitches on the fabric threads which are represented by the background lines.
Work all the satin stitch blocks before cutting the threads. Six threads are cut and withdrawn each way from the sections shown blank. Woven bars are then worked over the loose threads on the large areas and the fillings worked last.
Work the three other quarters of the design to correspond. Press the embroidery when completed on the wrong side. Trim the fabric to 44cm by 65cm, turn back 1·5cm hem, mitre the corners and stitch.

Woven bars
These are worked over the loose threads of the fabric remaining after the other threads have been withdrawn. Weave the needle over and under three threads until the loose threads are completely covered. When passing from one bar to another take care that the passing yarn is hidden behind the fabric.

Four sided filling stitch
Two twisted bars are worked by carrying the yarn diagonally across the space, entering the fabric and twisting the yarn over the first threads back to the starting point. The twisting of the second bar is taken only to the centre. Then pass the yarn over and under the bars twice in a circular motion, then under and over twice. Finally complete the other half of the second bar.

▼ Detail of trolley cloth embroidery

▲ *A charming Hardanger cloth to grace a trolley or a tray*

Stitch Library

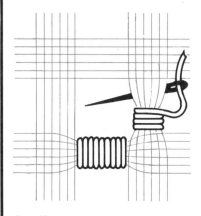

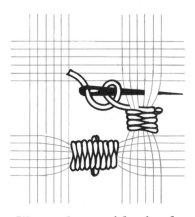

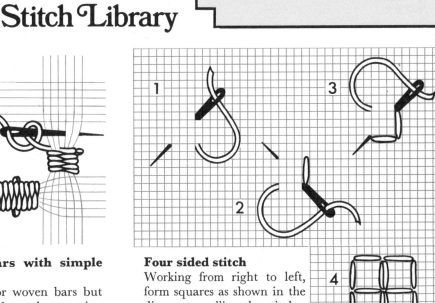

Cording
Withdraw the number of threads required from the fabric and separate the loose threads into bars by overcasting firmly over these threads as many times as required to cover the groups of threads completely.

Woven bars with simple picot
Work as for woven bars but half way along the weaving work a picot with each half of the next stitch. This is done by twisting the thread once round the needle before inserting the needle between the loose threads in the usual way. Complete the bar.

Four sided stitch
Working from right to left, form squares as shown in the diagrams, pulling the stitches firmly. For a filling stitch turn the fabric at the end of the row so that you are still working from right to left.

Chart giving just over a quarter of the design
Each line of the grid represents one thread of fabric

⬆ Centre

Chapter 30

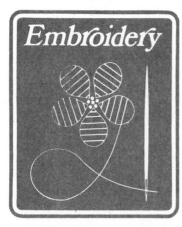

Introduction to cut work

Cut work is more correctly called Richelieu embroidery, named after the famous Cardinal who was Minister to King Louis XIII of France. Cardinal Richelieu, eager to develop industry in France, arranged for skilled Venetian lace-workers to set up schools and workshops encouraging the application of new techniques, thus helping to establish a new skilled industry in France. Cut work remained in vogue throughout the seventeenth century.

There are various forms of embroidery that come under the heading of cut work—Richelieu cut work, Renaissance cut work and reticella cut work. Richelieu is the most solid and reticella the most open. Renaissance cut work is more elaborate in design and is joined by plain buttonhole bars without the use of picots.

The nature of cut work

Cut work is a form of embroidery where the motifs such as figures, flowers and other shapes are surrounded with closely worked buttonhole stitch linked with bars, the rest of the fabric being cut away.

Stitches used in cut work

Outlines. All the outlines of the motifs in a cut work design are worked in buttonhole stitch.

Bars. Bars are buttonhole stitched or worked in cording and can be decorated with picots (for method of working bars see Embroidery Chapter 29).

Details. These can be worked in several ways: stem stitch, which can be whipped to give greater relief; back stitch, seeding, satin stitch, French knots or other simple filling stitches.

Yarns and fabrics

Coton à broder is used for this form of embroidery or, alternatively, stranded cotton, using two or three strands depending on the thickness of the fabric being stitched.

It is essential to choose fine, stiff, firmly woven fabrics for cut work. Linen is the best but good quality cotton can be used as a substitute.

Preparing the work

Apply the design using a commercial transfer or dressmakers carbon paper. Tack the fabric onto stiff, strong paper so that it is well stretched with the grain of the fabric straight. With two or three strands of cotton in the needle work small running stitches round the lines of design on the fabric only, until you come to a bar. Fasten the running thread with a tiny back stitch on the right side of the fabric without cutting off the thread. pass over the bar and pick up two or three threads of fabric, pass back to the far side and continue the running stitches (see diagram).

Bars are worked at about 1cm to 1·3cm intervals, following the curves of the design. Where a large area of fabric is to be cut away, branched bars are worked to fill in the space.

Working cut work design

When running stitches and foundations for the bars are completed cover them with closely worked buttonhole stitch, keeping the stitches very neat and even. To give more strength and a raised edge, the buttonhole stitch is worked over a laid thread of one strand of coton à broder or two or three strands of stranded cotton, in the same way as for cording (see Embroidery Chapter 16). The buttonhole stitch (see Embroidery Chapter 9) is also worked with either two or three strands of cotton depending on the thickness of fabric being embroidered. When a bar is reached, pass another thread across the two existing ones and cover all three threads with cording or buttonhole stitch, working over the passing threads only and not picking up the fabric underneath. The buttonhole stitch bars can be decorated with picots. When making the bars great care should be taken to ensure that the tension of the stitches is even— not too loose or too tight—as any unevenness will spoil the work. Fasten off the work by taking a few running stitches along the line of the design where they will be covered by buttonhole stitch. To join onto buttonhole stitch, make a few running stitches and bring the needle up through the back of the work and up through the last buttonhole loop made. Do not fasten off work when making a bar because it looks unsightly.

Branching bars

Work two tacking threads between A and B. Work buttonhole stitch from B to C and from there work another two tacking threads to E. Work buttonhole stitch from E to D and from there work another two tacking threads across to F. Cover the length from F to D, D to C and C to A with buttonhole stitch (see diagram).

Cutting away fabric

When all the embroidery is complete unpick the tacking stitches

▼ *Cut work in progress and a bar being worked*

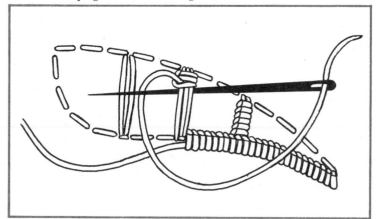

▼ *The motif completed with picots worked on each bar*

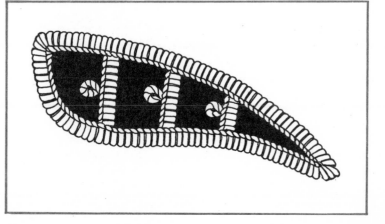

and remove the paper from the back of the work. Press the embroidery carefully on the wrong side of the work over a soft pad, using a damp cloth. Using a small pair of very sharp and pointed scissors, trim the fabric away up to the buttonhole stitched edges of the design, cutting as close as possible to the stitching so that no rough or raw edges show. When cutting be extremely careful not to damage bars or buttonhole stitches. Work of this kind can be ruined by using blunt scissors or by careless cutting, resulting in a limp piece of work with ragged edges. After cutting is complete, press the embroidery again on the wrong side over a damp cloth.

Uses of cut work

Cut work is mainly used on table linen, but it makes an elegant decoration for sheets and pillow cases. It can also look attractive on clothes—on the collar of a dress, for instance, or on a blouse in the form of panels down sleeves and as an edging for sleeves and hems.

For an individual fashion detail, embroider a deep border of cut work on the hem of a wedding dress.

Designs

Designs can be either simple or intricate. The simpler designs generally have sections cut out of the actual motifs, but more complicated designs leave the motif or shapes solid, linked to the background with bars. Most of the designs available in transfers are traditional, very few of them show a modern feeling. Look for inspiration for designs of your own in church windows where the leading of stained glass windows suggest the bars of cut work. The intricate crispness of cut work is accentuated by using white embroidery on white, or neutral on neutral fabric. The simplicity and beauty of the work is lost by introducing a variety of colours. Texture can be added by using various line and filling stitches for details.

▼ *Method of working branching bars*

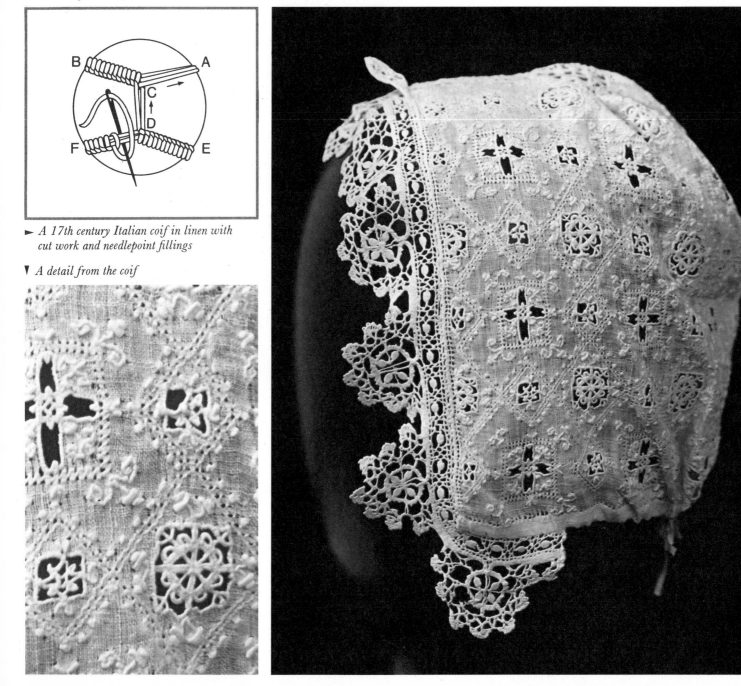

► *A 17th century Italian coif in linen with cut work and needlepoint fillings*

▼ *A detail from the coif*

Chapter 31

A modern interpretation of cut work

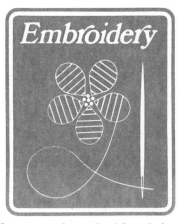

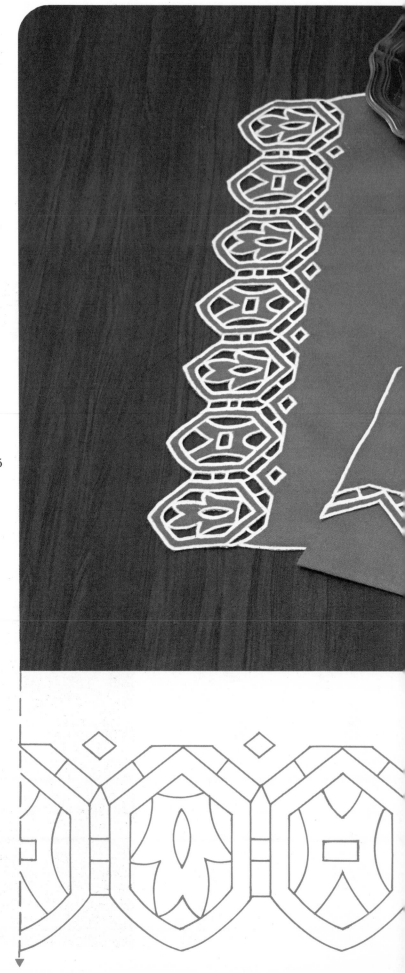

This modern interpretation of cut work embroidered in brilliant white on dark blue linen makes a striking decoration for a place mat and napkin holder. The embroidery would look equally attractive worked on any strong contrasting coloured linen, or for a more traditional look work the embroidery in the same colour as the fabric. The quantities for fabric and yarn are given for making one set only. For a set of six place mats and holders you will require 2·52m of linen and 48 skeins of yarn. Make or purchase a plain napkin to tuck into each holder. If you make the napkins, use one of the borders to decorate the edges.

To make a place mat measuring 30cm by 45cm and a table napkin holder measuring 13cm by 27cm.
You will need:
- [ ] 40cm by 92cm fine blue linen
- [ ] 8 skeins snow white DMC Brilliant Embroidery Cotton No. 25
- [ ] Blue sewing thread to match fabric
- [ ] Crewel needle No. 8

Preparing the fabric
Cutting on the straight of the material, cut one rectangle measuring 36cm by 51cm for the place mat and another rectangle measuring 32cm by 39cm for the table napkin holder.

Transferring the design
Trace the outlines of the place mat and the napkin holder design from these pages. Transfer these designs onto the fabric using white or yellow carbon paper, placing the borders one inch in from the cut edges.
Trace a single line to mark the top and bottom borders of the place mat. Trace a single line on the lateral edges of the napkin holder flap; the flap should measure 10cm deep from the pointed edge of the border.

Working the design
The cut work embroidery is worked entirely with snow white Brilliant Embroidery Cotton No. 25. Embroidery Chapter 30 gives the instructions for preparing and working the buttonhole edging and buttonhole bars.
Work the pointed edge over 2 threads of the linen material taken as cord foundation.
Once the work is complete, press with damp cloth, placing the right side of the material downwards on a thick, soft pad.
Cut away the edges of the openwork. Press a second time on the wrong side of the work over a pad.
Finish the plain edges of the table mat and napkin folder by making a hand sewn hem about 1cm wide.
Fold the napkin holder and close the side seams with small slip stitches.

▲ *Crisp white cut work on dark linen makes a modern looking place mat and napkin holder to complement modern tableware*

◀ *Actual size trace off design for half of the place mat border. The arrow head indicates the centre of the border*

Actual size trace off design for half of the napkin holder flap. The arrow indicates the centre ▶

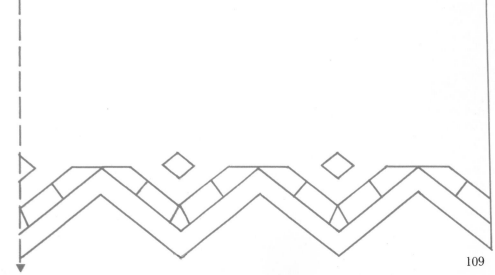

Chapter 32

Decorating with insertions

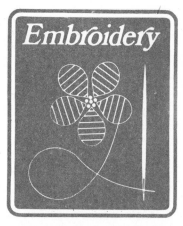

Insertion trimmings are enjoying a new popularity. It is a delightful form of decoration involving solid areas of fabric which are joined together with lace-like stitches. This chapter deals with yarns, fabrics and the methods of working.

Insertion is a method of joining two edges of fabric with decorative stitches. It looks charming on table linens and linen guest towels but it can be used with particular advantage on some kinds of clothing.

Rouleau or ribbon, alternated with insertion stitches, make a more interesting decoration for inset panels or edgings. Use either narrow or deep bands of rouleau on clothing such as on yokes or midriffs. Sleeves take on a distinctive look decorated with inset bands at intervals down their length.

Insertions are also an ideal method of adding length or letting out a garment. A deep band of rouleau set in a skirt can be worked in self fabric or fabric of a similar weight.

Fabrics
Work an insertion on a firm fabric such as fine linen cotton, fine wool or silk. Plain colours make better backgrounds than prints or patterns.

Yarns
Any medium weight embroidery yarn, with the exception of stranded cotton which is not strong enough, is suitable. All the insertions shown in this chapter are worked with pearl cotton No.5. If the piece of embroidery fabric is made of yarn-dyed linen or wool, threads drawn out from the fabric can be used for the insertion stitching.

Preparing the work
Make neat narrow hems on the edges to be joined or make lengths of rouleau by cutting 2·5cm wide bias strips of the fabric. Fold in half lengthwise, right sides together, and make two rows of machine stitching either 3mm or 6mm from the folded edge, depending on how deep a rouleau is required. The extra fabric gives a padded, rounded effect to the rouleau. Thread the ends of the sewing cotton left from the machining into the eye of a bodkin and secure these ends with several back stitches. Slot the bodkin through the rouleau, pulling it through to the right side.

Tack the pieces of fabric, or rouleau, to heavy wrapping paper with the hemmed or rouleau edges 3mm to 13mm apart, depending on the finished effect desired. The further apart the hems are placed, the weaker the join will be. The two edges are then joined together with any of the following insertion stitches.

Bullion bar insertion
This is worked from right to left. Bring needle out on top edge. Cross over open space and insert needle directly below. Wrap

thread around the bar just formed one or more times depending on the width of the open space. Insert the needle in the top exactly where the thread first emerged and slide the needle through the hem to position for next bar.

Knotted insertion
Work from left to right. Bring the thread out on the near edge and insert the needle from the front into the opposite edge. Make a loop as in buttonhole stitch then thread the needle through as shown. Pull tight. Repeat the knot stitch on the opposite edge. Continue working a knot stitch on each edge alternately. When worked closely, this makes a firm, strong stitch.

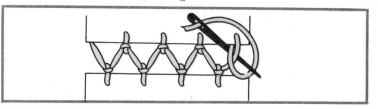

Laced insertion
Before tacking the fabric to the paper work along each edge separately a row of plain knotted insertion stitch. Tack the pieces of fabric to the paper and then lace with yarn in a self or contrast colour. Work the lacing in open Cretan stitch (see Embroidery Chapter 11) or merely whip the edges together.

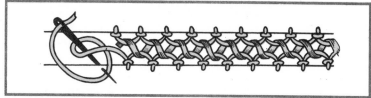

Buttonhole insertion
Working from left to right, make one or more buttonhole stitch on the top edge then make the same number on the lower edge. The size and number of stitches can vary but should be consistent throughout the one piece of work.

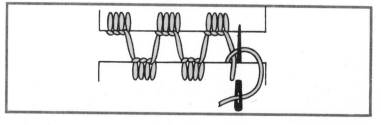

Open Cretan insertion or faggotting
This is worked in the same way as Cretan stitch (Embroidery Chapter 11), picking up a small amount of fabric from alternate edges.

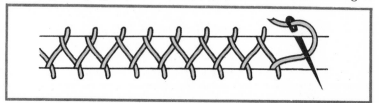

▲ Blue linen place mat decorated with open Cretan insertion worked in white

Half Cretan insertion
Work the stitches of this insertion very small and close together. A twist is formed only on one side compared with open Cretan insertion in which both sides are twisted.

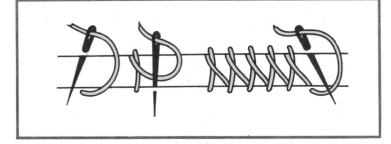

Italian buttonhole insertion
Although this stitch looks complicated it is relatively simple and rich in effect. Begin with a loop base and buttonhole in the sequence shown. The stitches are in fact worked close together, the diagram is spaced openly for clarity.

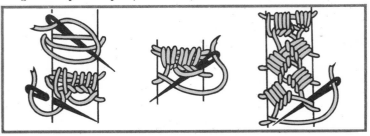

Twisted insertion
This stitch is also known as faggotting and is worked in a similar way to open Cretan insertion, but as each stitch is worked the needle takes a twist over the thread of the last stitch made.

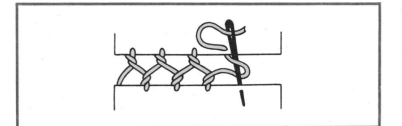

Faggot bundles insertion
The bundles are worked as shown and should be fairly close together with a firm thread otherwise the stitch is not rigid and will wear badly.

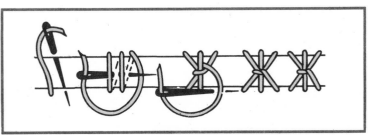

111

Chapter 33

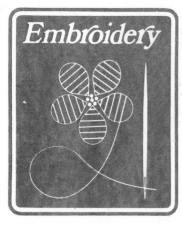

How to use a decorative alphabet

Embroidered initials, whether simply or elaborately worked, add a distinctive and individual touch to personal items or household linen. Letters can also be used as a basis for designs and pattern formations. The shape and style of the letter can suggest the stitches to use. For example, angular letters translate well into counted thread work.

Letters, usually thought of in terms of initials and monograms for personalising household linen and accessories, can also represent a rich source of inspiration to the embroiderer. Modern trends in embroidery design and techniques can make a letter an exciting and interesting shape on which to work.

Letters come in hundreds of different shapes, styles and sizes—Roman faces, Egyptian, seriffed, italics and scripts—and all of them can be interpreted into embroidery. Look for unfamiliar and attractive letters in newspaper and magazine titles, in advertisements and in old books. Keep a scrapbook of those that appeal to you and don't overlook the fascinating symbols and characters of other languages, such as Chinese, Japanese, Arabic and Persian.

Using letters for decoration

Letters can be depicted in almost every embroidery stitch and technique. They can be simple, applied in brightly coloured fabrics, felts and leathers or intricate, worked in hand and machine embroidery. Work single letters or monograms on pockets and fashion accessories, using the basic shape as a framework for decorative flowers or other small motifs. Build up a design of letters in bold appliqué for casual skirts and trousers or work a single, small letter for an unusual and attractive brooch or pendant. Letters can also be used as an integral part of wall panel designs. For instance, an educational yet attractive panel for a child's room could comprise of large letters with motifs worked within the shape or groups of letters and motifs telling a simple pictorial story. Letters are also used to tell a message in church embroideries, banners and flags.

Three basic methods of working letters

Satin stitch and cording

This is a very simple and basic embroidery method for working letters. Transfer the letters onto the fabric and pad the solid areas with rows of running stitch, back stitch or chain stitch. The fine lines are padded with back stitch or stem stitch. The solid areas are then worked over in satin stitch and the fine lines in cording. The example shown in this chapter is very simple and suitable for items which receive hard wear such as towels. For a pretty effect on guest linen, the initials can be decorated with a scattering of eyelet holes or small flowers and worked on sheets and pillow cases or dainty guest towels.

Decorative letters

Classic letters take on a decorative illumination style if superimposed over simple flower motifs. One of the 'N's opposite is sewn in double back stitch. The outline of each leaf is worked in stem stitch, the inside in couching and French knots have been added to give texture to the design. The third 'N' is worked in Pekinese stitch. This is easy to do. Simply work a row of back stitch (see Embroidery Chapter 4) and interlace with a different coloured thread, looping the stitch in and out. Pull the loops slightly so that the work becomes regular. See diagram of Pekinese stitch in Embroidery Chapter 36.

Machine embroidered letters

These can be worked on a zigzag machine, in satin stitch or running stitch using the free machine embroidery method and decorated by hand afterwards. Some machine manufacturers supply a set of semi-automatic templates to be fitted to the sewing machine, and instructions for using these are supplied by the manufacturer. The scarf illustrated here was worked using the template method.

◄ *A fashionable scarf with machine embroidered initials*

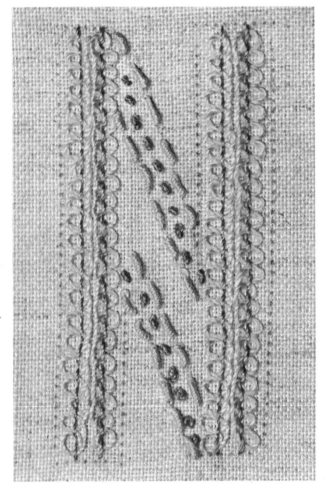

▲ *The letter 'N' worked in Pekinese stitch*
▼ *The letter 'N' worked in satin stitch*

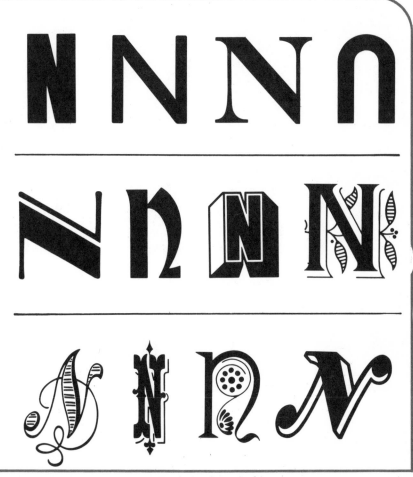

▲ *Twelve types of the letter 'N', all suitable for embroidery*
▼ *The letter 'N' worked in double back stitch*

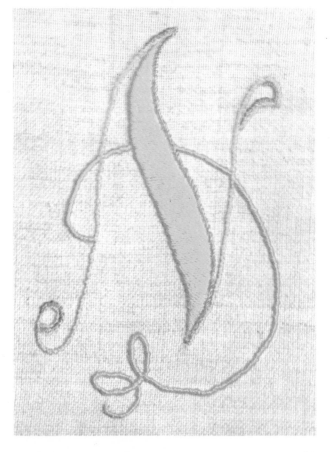

A B C D E F G
H I J K L M
N O P Q R S T
U V W X Y Z

*Trace and enlarge any of the letters from these alphabets
and embroider them in different colours and stitches*

A B C D E F G
H I J K L M
N O P Q R S T
U V W X Y Z

Collector's Piece

The sampler below was worked in the early 18th century. It is a clear piece of work embroidered in flowers and animals. The borders are typical of this period. Later samplers became much more extravagant and cluttered. The piece of work on the left shows the beginnings of this trend.

The alphabet and figures feature on the sampler opposite. Hannah Taylor has also worked her name and age on the bottom which is more typical of the late 18th century.

Towards the middle of the 19th century samplers were worked in wool, and design played a more important part than the educational factor.

Learning from samplers

Originally the sampler was worked as an exercise in different stitches. They also served to teach young girls their alphabet and figures.

Embroiderers' Guild, London.

ABCDEFGHIKLMNNOPQ
RSTVVWWXYZ&1234567

Then Teach us to the underticke fum
of our hore Days to Tell
that is thy Wildom will confidert
may Ever be inclind Pfalm XC

ABCDEFGHIKL
MNOPQRSTV
WXYZ& TAYLOR

Hannah Taylor 1774

Virtue alone Can Never die but Lives to imortality
from haughty looks Ill turn Afide & mortifie my Pride

Hannah Taylor
born December 17
1763 and made
this August 18 1774
at NewPort
RhodIsland
1774

Chapter 34

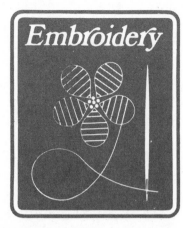

Introduction to cross stitch

Cross stitch is one of the oldest and most international embroidery stitches, frequently found in the national costumes of Europe and the Orient where it is often worked in gay, bright colours. It lends itself to fillings and building up traditional geometric patterns, as in Assisi designs, and is also used for interpreting realistic and precisely detailed pictures in the modern Danish manner.

Ideally, cross stitch should be worked on an even-weave fabric because this makes it easier to count threads and the whole effect of the stitch depends on its regularity. Each cross stitch should make a perfect square, being worked down and across over an equal number of threads of an even-weave fabric.

The main point to remember is that in whichever direction you work the stitch, the upper stitches must always lie in the same direction (usually from bottom left to top right). If they do not they will reflect the light differently from the other stitches and will stand out clearly as mistakes.

Methods of working

The most even finish for filling in large areas of colour is obtained by working a row of diagonal stitches (half cross stitches) in one direction and then completing the stitches by working another row in the opposite direction. If you are working a complete design in cross stitch, keep the texture even by working the whole design in half cross stitch and then complete in the other direction. This also helps you to build up the design at a very encouraging rate! If there is only a small area to cover, it is permissible to use the alternative method where one stitch is completed at a time but this will look less even. To embroider very fine or uneven fabrics, use the canvas method to keep the stitches even. Place a piece of soft

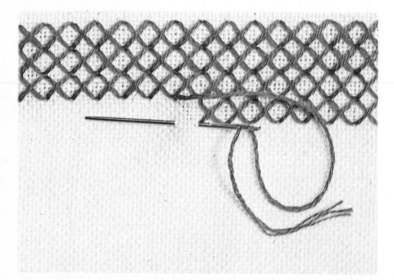

When filling small areas complete one stitch at a time. Take care to count the threads, using the weave of the fabric as a guide so that the stitches line up evenly. Work from either left to right or right to left

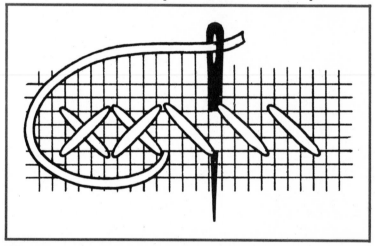

▲ *For large areas it is best to work the cross stitch in two journeys*
▼ *Double cross stitch steps should be worked in the same order throughout*

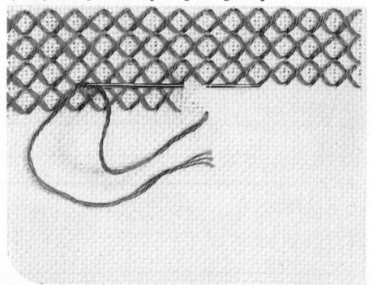

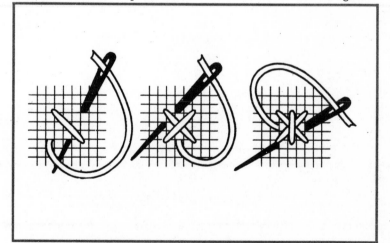

cotton canvas on top of the fabric, matching the warp and weft of the canvas to that of the fabric. Tack it in place. Work the stitches over the threads of the canvas and through the material underneath, taking care not to catch the canvas or pull the stitches too tight. When the embroidery is completely finished, gently pull out from under it the canvas threads one by one.

Home is where the heart is

This gay picture brings a fresh modern approach to the old sampler idea. It was designed to be a very special birthday greeting for the designer's husband, but it could equally well be mounted on a teapot stand and covered with heatproof glass.

Working charts and full instructions are given on the following two pages, together with colour suggestions.

These charts are planned in such a way that you can either use the motifs individually or group them to add up to the complete composition. Each motif has its own colour coding with numbered reference to Anchor Stranded Cotton colours. One of the best features of charted designs is that they provide a permanent reference which you can use again and again.

All colour numbers given are for Anchor Stranded Cotton.

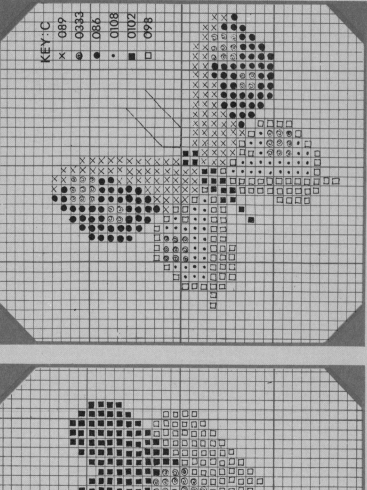

KEY·C

×	089
⊚	0333
●	086
·	0108
■	0102
□	098

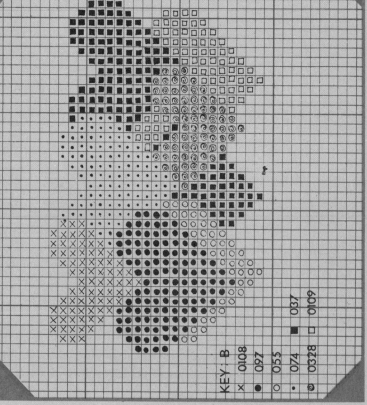

KEY·B

×	0108
●	097
○	055
·	074
■	0328
□	037
	0109

KEY·A

×	034
□	055
·	0333

Materials

To make the panel shown (finished size 23cm by 21·5cm) you will require:

☐ 35cm even-weave linen (12 threads to the centimetre, 56cm wide)

☐ 1 skein each of Stranded Cotton colours given in key to the charts, except for the leaf green which needs 2 skeins

☐ Crewel needle size 8 or 9

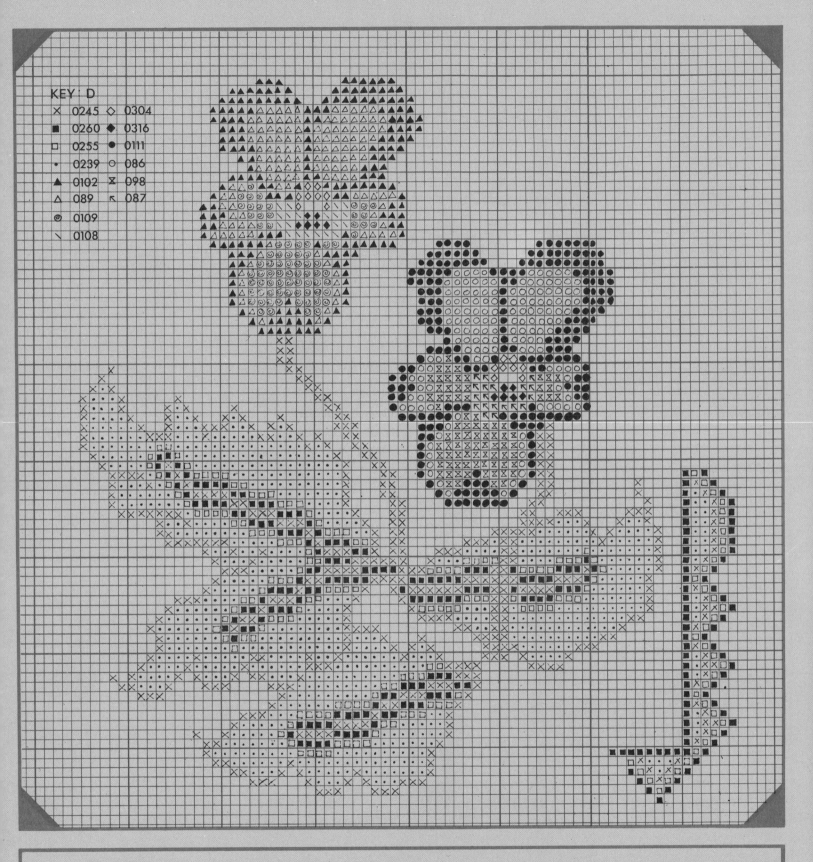

KEY D

✕	0245	◇	0304
■	0260	◆	0316
☐	0255	●	0111
·	0239	○	086
▲	0102	⊠	098
△	089	⺌	087
◉	0109		
╲	0108		

How to work the sampler

Mark a centre line on the fabric with tacking stitches. This applies whether you are going to use a single motif or the complete composition. Always start at the centre of the design working outwards because this makes the counting easier.

Each square of the chart represents 2 threads of fabric so work the stitches accordingly using 3 strands of stranded cotton throughout.

When completed, press the embroidery lightly on the wrong side. If you are going to use the embroidery for a teapot stand, trim the excess fabric and make 1·3cm hem on all sides, mitreing the corners for a neat finish. Press the hemmed edges on the wrong side. If you are making a picture, take the embroidery to an expert for mounting and framing unless you feel able to do it yourself (see Embroidery Chapter 16).

Collector's Piece

The Hastings Embroidery

This embroidery was commissioned by the Borough of Hastings from the Royal School of Needlework to celebrate the 900th anniversary of the Battle of Hastings. A team of 18 embroiderers took just over a year to complete the embroidery which consists of 27 panels, each measuring nine feet by three feet, 243 feet in all. They depict important events in British history, from the arrival of William the Conqueror to the present day. Shown here are panels nos. 7, 14, 16 and 17.

14th-15th century
At the Battle of Bannockburn in 1314, Robert the Bruce of Scotland defeats Edward II of England.
Relations between England and France become hostile, and the year 1337 witnesses the start of the Hundred Years' War.
The French are defeated in 1346 at the Battle of Crecy by the English army under the leadership of Edward III and the Black Prince.

16th-17th century
Queen Elizabeth I commissions Sir Walter Raleigh to found the first colony in America, Virginia. Mary Queen of Scots, accused of originating a plot to assassinate Queen Elizabeth, is found guilty and condemned to death in 1586. The Spanish Armada sails into battle with the English fleet in an attempt to overthrow Elizabeth I's campaign of Protestantism.

17th-18th century
Early in the 17th century, the *Mayflower*, with Pilgrims aboard, sets sail for America, or the New World. Civil war rages in England, the monarchy against Parliament. The crowd rejoices at the restoration of the monarch in 1660.

17th-19th century
The Great Plague of 1665 ravages London, killing people in their thousands. A year later, London is hit by the Great Fire which started in a baker's shop and burned for three days. Many of London's buildings and churches were destroyed, including St. Paul's Cathedral which was rebuilt by Christopher Wren.

Chapter 35

Introduction to blackwork

Embroidery

Stitch Library

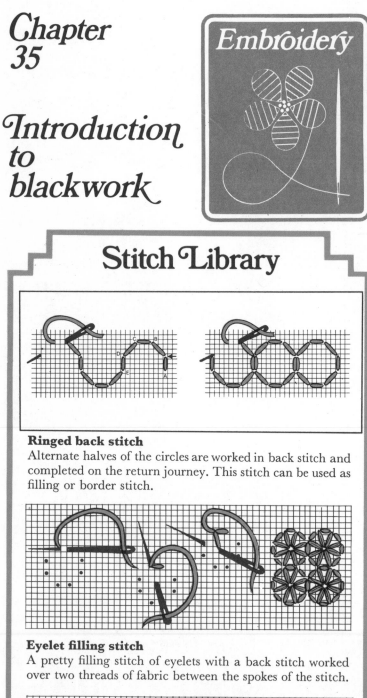

Ringed back stitch
Alternate halves of the circles are worked in back stitch and completed on the return journey. This stitch can be used as filling or border stitch.

Eyelet filling stitch
A pretty filling stitch of eyelets with a back stitch worked over two threads of fabric between the spokes of the stitch.

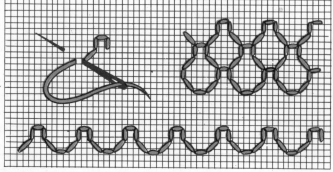

Festoon
This filling stitch is worked in back stitch. It can also be used in horizontal lines.

Blackwork embroidery was probably of African origin and introduced to Spain by the Moors. Although blackwork was not entirely unknown in England, Henry VIII's Spanish wife Katharine of Aragon increased its popularity, and throughout Tudor and Elizabethan times the embroidery was used extensively on clothes and was gradually extended to use on household linens such as bed hangings.

The delightful panel of fishes in this chapter has been specially designed for us as a modern interpretation of blackwork, and though it may at first sight appear complicated the design can be easily copied from the trace outline on page 126, where instructions for making the panel can also be found.

In simple terms, blackwork is a monochrome method of embroidery. It relies for effect on the relationships of tone values and consists of a variety of light fillings in well planned shapes with neatly defined outlines. Traditionally worked in black on white with additional touches of gold and silver threads, it is the dramatic tone contrast which has always been its main attraction.

In modern embroidery design, however, colour has been introduced. The choice of colour or colours needs considerable care and the stronger the contrast the more dramatic the effect. Experiment with colour contrasts and combinations of colours such as white embroidery on black, red on pink, brown on cream or beige, until you achieve the desired effect and your own individual style.

Blackwork can be used to great effect on all types of clothing such as blouses, dresses and skirts, or on household linens such as runners, tablecloths, place mats, curtains, cushions and wall panels. Stitches in blackwork are worked over counted threads of even weave fabric and as a result designs tend to be angular. However, areas of filling can be tapered off to produce more rounded or pointed shapes which need not necessarily be enclosed in an outline stitch. Alternatively, flowing lines of stitching can be incorporated as an integral part of a design to give a freer feeling. Certain pattern lines and shapes can be strengthened by using a thicker yarn or by working over fewer threads of fabric, whereas lighter areas are created by working with finer yarn or by working over more threads of fabric.

Fabrics
Suitable fabrics include embroidery linen, or synthetic dress or furnishing fabrics with a precise even-weave of between thirteen to thirty-nine threads to the inch, provided the threads are clear enough to count.

Yarns
Generally speaking, the thickness of the yarns should correspond to the threads of the fabric but this can vary, depending on the final effect required.

Stranded cotton, pearl cotton, sewing cotton (Sylko), machine embroidery cotton, soft embroidery cotton and various kinds of metal threads (see Embroidery Chapters 37 and 38) can all be used in blackwork. To keep the effect precise it is best to use single thread in the needle, but for a softer effect use two or three strands of stranded cotton.

Stitches
Blackwork outlines can be worked in a variety of stitches such as stem stitch, back stitch, whipped back stitch, coral stitch and couching.

Filling stitches, which are used to form the patterns, are based on straight stitches — running stitch, back stitch and double running or Holbein stitch. Cross stitch and its variations are also used as filling stitches and darning, which is one of the simplest forms of embroidery, makes an interesting filling.

Double running stitch (Holbein stitch). This stitch is worked in two stages by working running stitch over the counted threads and then a second row filling the spaces left by the first.

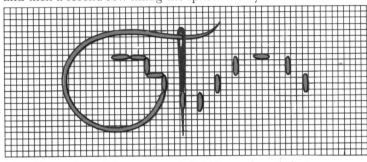

▲ *Double running stitch stage two*   ▲ *Double running stitch stage one*

Eye stitch. Worked with eight stitches of equal length radiating from a central point.

Coral stitch. Working from right to left, bring thread up through the fabric and hold with the thumb of the left hand. Take a small stitch at right angles to the thread, going under and over it. Pull up to form a small knot.

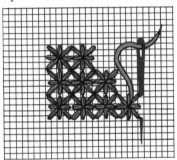 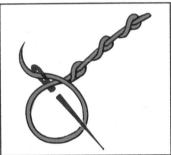

▲ *Method of working eye stitch*   ▲ *Method of working coral stitch*

Transferring designs
Use the trace and tack method for transferring designs, described in Embroidery Chapter 3.

Using a frame
It is advisable to use a frame for this type of embroidery. A tambour frame is suitable for small pieces of work and a square or slate frame for larger pieces.

A blackwork panel of fishes for you to copy shown life size ►
▼ *One of the fishes in the panel enlarged to show stitch detail*

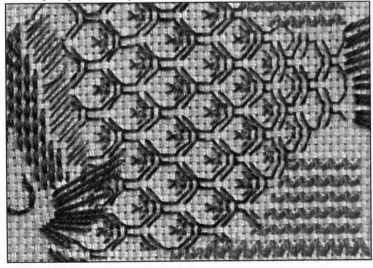

Blackwork fish panel

Add sophistication and style to your home. Make this fish panel in blackwork and try out different stitch patterns to create your own exciting effects. The diagrams on the opposite page give you an idea of the basic pattern and stitch forms you can incorporate into your work.

Materials you will need
☐ Hardanger cotton 22 pairs of thread to the inch
☐ Tapestry needle No. 24
☐ Crewel needle No. 7 or 8
☐ Yarns

Fish A
tail	Coton à Broder
fins	Coton à Broder
face	Pearl Cotton No. 8: one skein
body	Stranded Cotton: one skein

Fish B
face	Coton à Broder
tail	Coton à Broder
fins	Coton à Broder
(below face)	
body	Stranded Cotton: one skein
main fins	Pearl Cotton No. 8: one skein

Fish C
outline	Coton à Broder
eye	Coton à Broder
lower shape	Coton à Broder
tail	Coton à Broder
fins	Coton à Broder
body	Stranded Cotton: one skein

How to transfer the pattern and design
Trace the outline drawing onto tissue paper and tack to background fabric (see Embroidery Chapter 3) making sure the sides are parallel with the grain. Tear away tissue paper carefully and stretch the background material in a frame, or pin it to a rectangular one, keeping the fabric perfectly square. Start with a line of the stitching down the centre of an area and work outwards, stopping wherever it touches the tacked outline.

How to enlarge the design
A heavier fabric can be used to enlarge the design. However, if the stitches are copied direct from the photograph on page 125 they will automatically be more open, but by using a thicker thread a closer texture will be achieved. Alternatively, see what additional pattern you can add to a stitch in the way of diagonal, horizontal or cross stitches.

> *The yarns used here are Anchor Coton à Broder, Anchor Stranded Cotton and Anchor Pearl Cotton*

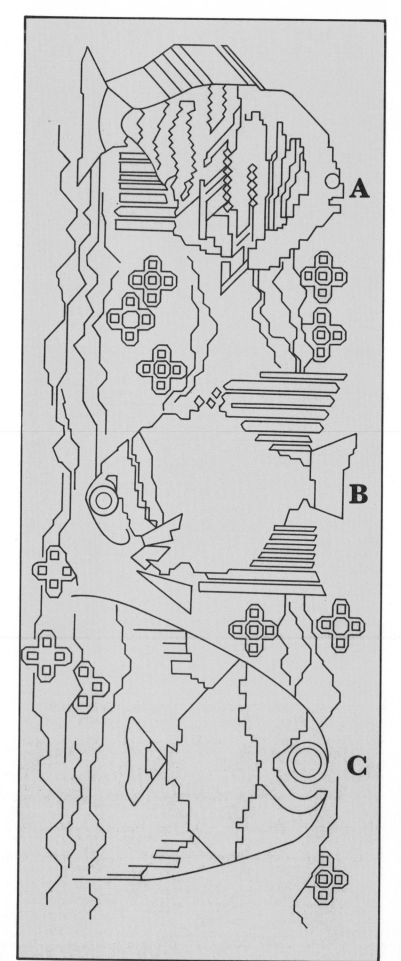

Try out different stitch patterns

Have plenty of material so that stitches can be tried out on the side. This is important in order that you can see what thickness of thread gives the weight and achieves the effect you want in the design. The same stitch worked using a thick thread and then a thin thread gives a very good idea of the total values you can achieve. Look, for instance, at the zigzag stitches on the fins of Fish A and then at those on its back.

Remember, stitches normally go over one thread or square at a time, so if you want a long line or longer stitch it must be divided and worked as a back stitch. This can be illustrated by the working on the head and body of Fish A. The exception to this can be seen in the tails and some of the fins. You can always break a rule providing the effect achieved is correct.

Designing your own stitches

Start with a simple, basic stitch and add to it in different ways, so building them up to make your own designs. Remember to leave the original stitch open in order to make room for additions.

The pattern on the back of Fish C is achieved by filling in the basic pattern with crosses of different weights so that an even texture is formed. Basic patterns for you to start working from are shown below.

Basic patterns to start working from

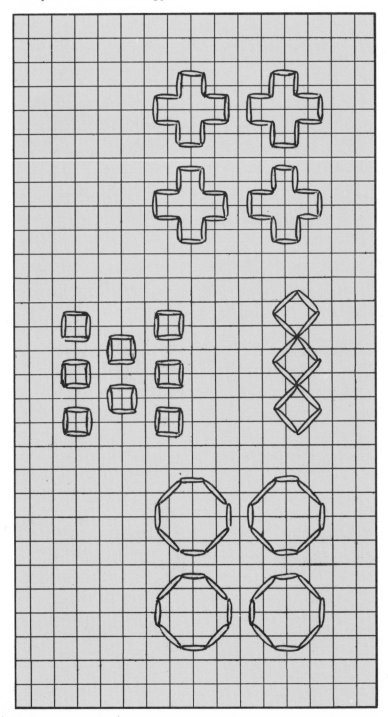

Cross stitch forms the basis of each stitch pattern

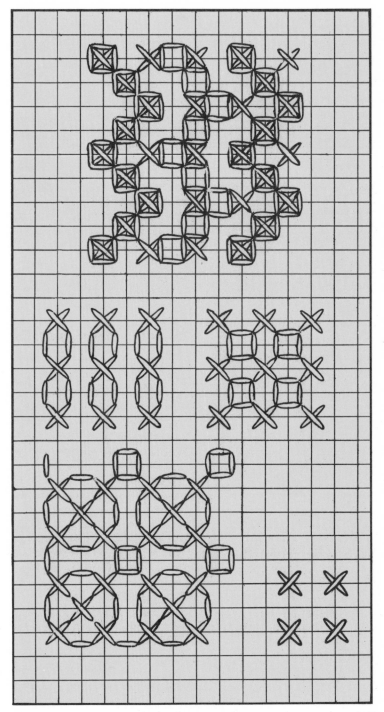

Chapter 36

Eastern fantasy panel in blackwork

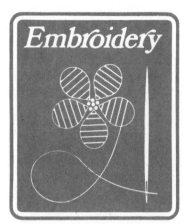

This intriguing Eastern fantasy panel shows a modern interpretation of the ancient form of embroidery known as blackwork. The completed effect is merely a build-up of straight and simple stitches. Each building is a complete design in itself and can be used on its own. On the following pages is an almost life size reproduction of the panel with a thread count at the bottom, and this can be used as a working chart.

Materials you will need

☐ 50cm 150cm wide even-weave linen with 9 threads to the centimetre (finished size of panel 60cm by 35 cm)
☐ Anchor Stranded Cotton: 6 skeins black
☐ 1 spool Penelope metallic cord gold
☐ 3 cards Penelope gold lurex
☐ 1 card Penelope silver lurex
☐ Tapestry needle size 22 (for working gold and silver threads)
☐ Tapestry needle size 26 (for working stranded cotton)
☐ Hardboard 60cm by 35cm
☐ Slate frame

Working from the picture overleaf

This is a counted thread design and the stitches are worked over the counted threads of the fabric. The almost life size picture of the panel on the following pages can therefore be used as a working chart. The diagrams show how some of the more complicated filling patterns are built up, and these are numbered to identify them with the areas to be worked in the patterns on the outline diagram. Each grid line of the filling pattern diagrams represents one thread of the fabric.

Using the yarns

Stranded cotton. Use two strands for the filling patterns and outlines, one strand for the paving, and four strands on the towers of the left hand building.
Gold and silver lurex. Use single for stitching, double for couching.
Metallic gold cord. Use double throughout.

Stitches in the design

Outlines

In blackwork, the outline is worked before the filling patterns. The main outline stitch in this design is whipped back stitch worked in stranded cotton. Other outline effects are as follows:
Couched gold. Two lengths of couched lurex gold thread caught down with one thread of stranded cotton on the large towers of the left hand building and on the outline of the centre front roof of the right hand building.
Whipped back stitch. This is worked entirely in lurex gold on the base of the large towers of the left hand building, round the diamond shape on the centre roof of the same building, on the side turrets and the top centre dome of the centre

building, and round the large dome of the right hand building.
A row of back stitch is worked over as shown in the diagram, using either a self colour or a contrast.
Double whipped back stitch. Black back stitch with lurex gold whipping on the side domes of the right hand building.
This is worked in the same way as whipped back stitch, and a second row of whip stitches is worked back along the line of back stitches in the opposite direction.
Back stitch. Worked on the edge of the section immediately below the domes on the right hand building.
Pekinese stitch. This is worked with black back stitch and lurex gold interlacing on the centre section of the large dome on the centre building. A foundation line of small back stitches has a second thread looped through with larger loops on the top and smaller loops below the line of stitching (see Embroidery Chapter 33).
Filling stitches
Pattern fillings are worked after the outline has been completed and consist of straight stitches worked over counted threads. The two smaller rounded towers and the doors of the large building are worked in double cross stitch. The filling pattern on the large central dome consists of satin stitch blocks worked and interlaced with gold metallic cord.
Threaded satin stitch. The blocks of satin stitch are threaded through in zigzag fashion using self or contrasting colour thread.

Mounting the panel

When the embroidery is completed, remove it from the frame and press lightly on the back of the work, using a dry cloth to protect the metal threads from heat. Mount the panel on a piece of hardboard, as described in Embroidery Chapter 16.

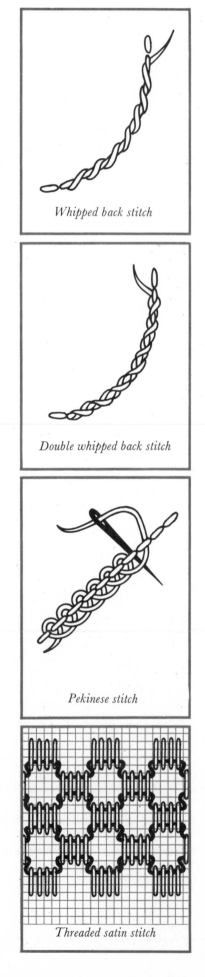

Whipped back stitch

Double whipped back stitch

Pekinese stitch

Threaded satin stitch

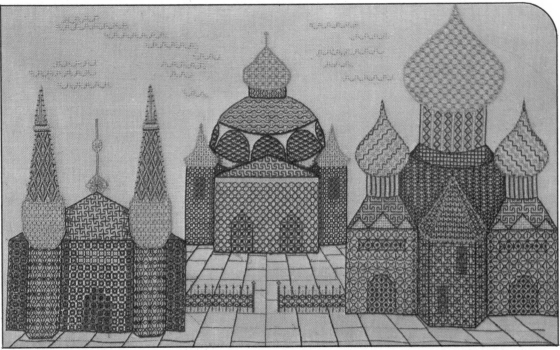

▲ *An Eastern fantasy wall panel* ▼ *The numbered areas in the diagram refer to the filling patterns on this page*

10   20   30   40   50   60   70   80   90   100   110   120   130   140   150   160   170   180   190   200   210   220   230   24

Each mark on the scale indicates every tenth thread on the fabric

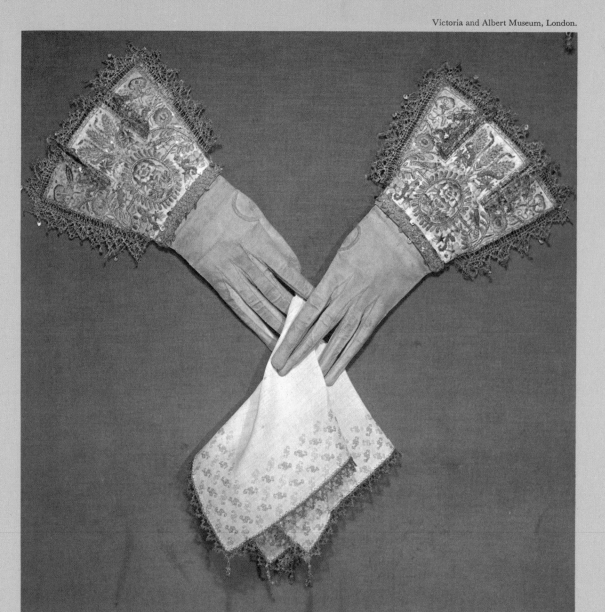

collector's piece

Gloves fit for a Queen

At the court of Queen Elizabeth 1, the practice of giving presents at New Year was an important part of court life, and embroidery was considered a valuable gift, worthy of being presented to the Queen. Elizabeth received presents from all her high-ranking officials—embroidered gowns, petticoats, doublets and other articles of clothing—and embroidered gloves featured high on the list. The Queen was presented with costly embroidered gloves on other occasions also; she received a pair from both Oxford and Cambridge Universities when she visited them. The embroidered gloves of this period were so ornate and heavy that they were no longer regarded as useful articles but purely as ornamentation. They were rarely worn, and subsequently examples of the beautiful work have survived, the colours only slightly faded. The gloves illustrated are made of pale coloured doeskin with gauntlets of silk cut into six scallops or tabs. The crimson velvet 'mittens' have their gauntlets cut into eight tabs. The designs worked on both gloves are typically Elizabethan, consisting of flowers, fruits, insects and entwined stems, with each of the tabs containing a different flower or plant motif. Coloured silks, gold threads and small jewels were used for the embroidery, and the doeskin gloves are trimmed with gold lace.

Chapter 37

Introduction to metal thread embroidery

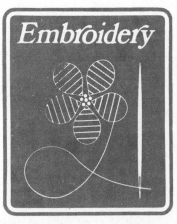

The character of metal thread embroidery is completely different from that of other kinds of embroidery. Gold or silver threads are couched on to the surface of the fabric, while beads, pieces of kid, gold purl and coloured yarns add contrast, richness, and texture to the design.

Everyone who becomes interested in gold work experiences a thrill in working with the precious metal threads. The shimmer and glitter of the embroidery evokes images of rich tapestries and fabulous jewels, and even the simplest designs have a satisfying splendour about them.

The success of gold work lies in a thorough understanding of the materials used, careful planning, and skilful manipulation of the metal threads.

This chapter deals with the basic materials and equipment needed for this fascinating craft.

Tools and equipment

The various pieces of equipment needed for metal thread embroidery, or gold work, as it is generally known, may seem at first to be somewhat numerous. However, there are different techniques in gold work and all the items listed here are important to the success of the work.

Slate frame or gold work frame
It is essential that a frame is used for metal thread embroidery. The fabric must be held taut in order to support the threads in smooth lines and to avoid puckering. A slate frame is recommended for large pieces of work while a gold work frame is suitable for pieces measuring up to 20cm by 30·5cm.

Needles
Three sizes of crewel needle are required: No.5 for framing up; No.8 for general use and No.10 for couching and applying purl gold. A chenille needle size No.20 is used for finishing off ends of metal threads and a heavy embroidery needle is used for string.

String in gold work
A strong string or twine is used for framing up and you will also need two balls of good quality string, of different thicknesses, for padding purposes.

Felt sausage
Pure gold threads are kept wound on a roll of felt to prevent kinking. Make a 'sausage' by rolling a 9in by 9in piece of felt and slip stitch along the edge to hold the roll in shape.

Purl cutting board
Prepare a cutting board by glueing a rectangle of felt or velvet

measuring 3 inches by 4 inches to a piece of card. Purl gold pieces are cut above the board so that the pieces fall on to the fabric. The pile prevents the springy coils from jumping away.

Gold thread storage
Gold threads are fairly costly, particularly the pure gold qualities, and care should be taken to see that the unused threads do not become damaged. Keep threads wound on rolls of felt and stored in an air-tight container. A tin with a press-on lid would do or an opaque plastic pot with a fitting top.

Acid-free tissue paper
This is essential for covering gold work while it is in progress, for protection and to help prevent tarnishing.

Varieties of metal threads

There are several qualities of metal embroidery thread (see Yarn Chart pages 10 and 11 ranging from pure gold and silver to the synthetic types. Some of the threads are inclined to tarnish but they are, nevertheless, worth including in a design for the contrast which slightly discoloured threads can lend to gold work.

Japanese gold
Japanese gold is pure gold thread and because it does not tarnish it is often used for the main lines of a design. Japanese gold consists of a core of fine silk floss thread over which finely beaten and cut gold is coiled. The silk core varies in colour and if the coiled gold unwinds, the core shows through spoiling the look of the work. It is sometimes necessary to twist the metal thread between thumb and forefinger before and after each couching stitch is made. Jap gold should be kept wound in double threads round a felt roll.

Passing gold
Passing gold thread contains a high proportion of gold and has a soft, smooth appearance. This thread is easier for beginners to use because the gold is coiled more tightly than Japanese gold and the core doesn't show through when corners are turned.

Admiralty quality
These threads contain a high proportion of gold but are less expensive than the pure gold quality. Admiralty quality is inclined to tarnish but so slowly that it is often unnoticeable.

Synthetic gold thread
Synthetic metal thread will not tarnish but the surface is even and the shine almost hard compared with pure gold which has a much warmer appearance. Contrast is, however, an essential part of embroidery design and, combined with real gold threads, synthetic gold supports and enriches the overall effect of gold work.

Silver thread
Silver threads are available in the same range of qualities and types as gold threads.

Braids, string and cords
There are a number of braids, novelty gift wrapping strings and cords which can be used in metal thread embroidery. These are mostly synthetic. Braids and strings can either be used as they are or unravelled. Used in their wrinkled state, unravelled threads can give a three dimensional quality to a design.

Types of gold purl
Purl looks like a fine metal spring coil and is usually made from

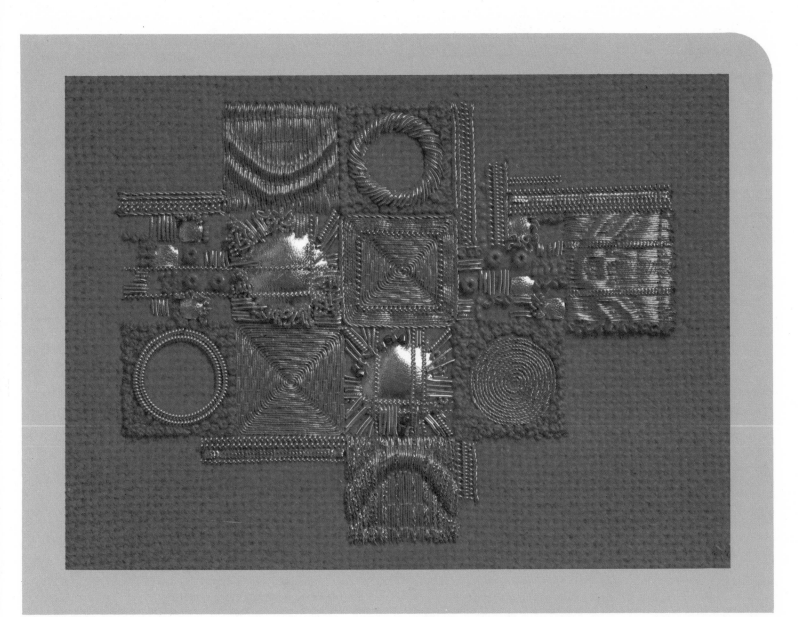

▲ *This modern design in metal thread embroidery shows examples of many of the threads mentioned here. Working techniques are given in the next chapter*

Admiralty quality metal. Purl is purchased in lengths and various surfaces and thicknesses are available.

Pearl purl This is a coarse and slightly inflexible purl and is usually couched in lengths rather than cut into small pieces.

Check purl A fine metal thread which has been bent into angles before being coiled, check purl has a sparkling, chequered appearance.

Smooth purl Smooth purl is a flexible plain coil with a highly polished surface.

Rough purl Rather misnamed, rough purl has not got a rough surface but it does have a softer effect than smooth purl.

Threads and yarns

In gold work designs, coloured embroidery threads can be used for contrast and for breaking down the glare from flat, highly reflective areas.

Maltese silk

This is recommended for couching. Several shades of yellow are available for working on gold thread and grey is used when working on silver thread.

Materials for padding

Pieces of non-woven material, such as kid, leather, PVC and felt are used in gold work designs, either applied flat to the surface or padded out.

Fabrics and backings

Almost any material can be used for metal thread work providing it isn't too loosely woven. Dress-weight fabrics made from man-made fibres should be avoided because they are likely to split when the metal threads are pulled through.

In metal thread embroidery, as with other forms of embroidery, contrast of texture is an important part of design. Tweed, soft wool, and furnishing linen, as well as pure silk and velvet, can be used very effectively.

It is advisable to back background fabrics before starting gold work, choosing a material of approximately the same weight. Linen, calico, holland or cotton can be used, but backing material should be pre-shrunk before being used.

The next gold work chapter deals with design and methods of working the materials used in gold work.

Chapter 38

How to work metal thread embroidery

Beautiful metal thread work depends to a large extent on the manipulation of the precious metal threads. The techniques are simple, but the results are exotic.

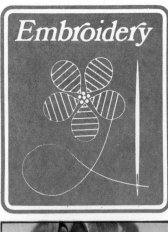

Preparing to work. Once you have collected the various pieces of equipment (Embroidery Chapter 37) choose a suitable background fabric and back it for extra strength. Trace the design on to the right side of the fabric (Embroidery Chapter 3) using the tacking method and a thread matched to the background fabric.

Mount the backed fabric into a slate frame (see Embroidery Chapter 13) or gold work frame.

Couching with metal threads. Work with two lengths of fine gold thread for both single lines and solid areas. Drag a length of Maltese silk once through a block of beeswax to strengthen it against the friction of the metal threads. Using a No.1 crewel needle, first make a knot at the end of the silk and then work one small back stitch on the design line. Hold the two gold threads together in position, leaving about one inch from the beginning free, to be worked through the fabric later. Work two couching stitches over the gold thread, stitching through the same hole in the fabric, and continue along the length of the metal thread, working single couching stitches about 6mm apart. Pull the gold threads slightly taut as you work.

Stop about 6mm from the end of the design line being worked and make two couching stitches, as you did at the beginning, and

finish with two back stitches. Cut off excess gold thread, leaving about one inch to be worked through later.

Finishing off ends. Ends of gold thread should be left on the right side of the fabric until work is completed. If the ends are taken through while work is in progress, they are likely to tangle or unravel.

Using a No.18 chenille needle, insert the point into the fabric where the metal thread is to go through. Thread the inch of metal through the eye of the needle (diagram 2). Supporting the work with the left hand underneath, quickly and firmly pull the needle and thread through the fabric. Some threads may be too thick to go through all at once. These should be divided and each strand taken through separately. Once the metal threads are at the back of the work, cut to 1·3cm and oversew them to the backing fabric with two or three stitches.

Couching over string. An interesting effect is achieved by couching several lengths of gold thread close together over a 'ladder' of string (see sample). The string must be stitched firmly to the background before the metal threads are couched down.

Cut off lengths of string. Hold one piece of string in position, leaving an inch free, and at the beginning of the line make two stitches, working through the same hole to secure the string to the background fabric. The stitches should go through the core of the string and not over the surface. Work stitches each side of the string (diagram 3) and finish off with double stitches at the end. Cut off excess string, as close to the double end stitches as possible. When all the pieces of string required for the padded area have been couched down, work the gold threads over the string 'ladder' (see sample). The gold threads should be worked lying close together so that the string is completely covered.

Turning corners and angles. Sometimes a design demands that the metal threads turn at angles on the surface of the fabric (see sample). To work corners and angles, make normal couching stitches along the two metal threads to within $\frac{1}{4}$ inch of the corner or angle. Each single thread is taken round separately, the outer one first. Make a sharply defined angle in the metal thread, using a pair of tweezers, and then make two diagonal couching stitches into the corner, one on each thread, first stitching the outside thread and then the inner one.

Solid areas of couching. When a large area of gold thread couching is worked, instead of cutting both ends of the threads on each row, one of the two threads is brought back on the second row with a new single thread (see sample). A double stitch is required on the turn and a hidden double stitch is worked to hold the new thread in place.

For circular or irregular shapes made up entirely of metal threads, start at the outer edge to establish the shape and work towards the centre. Pure gold thread is usually used for outlining a design because this thread does not tarnish and the outline stays clearly defined. Make sure that the metal threads lie close together in

solid areas. If the needle is angled towards the metal thread · when the couching stitches are being made, this will help to achieve the effect (diagram 1).

Using purl. The sample shows several different ways of using pieces of purl. They can be built up into geometric patterns, formed into loops on the surface and used for powdering or seeding on the background. Purl gold cut into short pieces, up to 1cm long, can be stitched like beads on to the background.

Purl can be used over padded areas to give a raised, purl area or stitched around the edges of applied gold kid. It can also be couched in rows over string, either at right angles or diagonally across it. Purl can either be used in short pieces or couched in lengths.

To make purl loops, bring the needle through to the right side and thread on a small length of purl. Put the needle back into the work a shorter distance than the length of the piece of purl, and pull the thread tight until the loops stand up.

Bring thread through to the right side and repeat.

Always cut purl over a cutting board (see Embroidery Chapter 37).

Padded areas

Any material which does not fray can be used in metal thread work—kid, suede, leather, PVC or felt.

To pad fabrics, draw the shape to be padded on to felt and then cut out the shape fractionally smaller all round. For more raised padding, consecutively smaller layers of felt are cut out. The smallest piece of padding is stitched to the background fabric first and then each larger layer in turn, the stitches going right through to the background fabric (see diagram). The surface fabric of the shape is then pinned over the padding and secured with three or four stitches around the edge, or in the corners. Complete the stitching all round, using stab stitch and working the stitches at right **angles to the cut edge.**

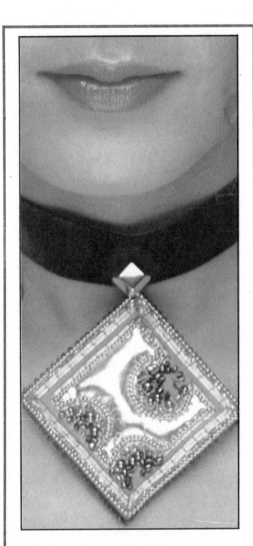

To make a pendant

Materials
- ☐ Piece of silk 18cm square
- ☐ Piece of firm card 5·5cm square
- ☐ Small scrap of gold kid
- ☐ Metal threads of various types
- ☐ Metal link: gold and green beads
- ☐ 50cm velvet ribbon
- ☐ Hooks and eyes

Trace, enlarge and transfer the design from this page on to the background fabric using the tacking method described in Embroidery Chapter 3. Work the design using the metal threads as shown, stitching beads and purl loops into position. Mount the piece of work over the card and secure firmly by lacing as if mounting a panel (Embroidery Chapter 16). Cover the back of the pendant with a piece of the fabric or a small piece of fine Jap silk to match the background colour and stitch neatly in place. Sew the metal link securely to one of the corners of the pendant and then on to the ribbon. Hem raw edges of ribbon and sew on two sets of hooks and eyes.

This sample illustrates the methods of working and some of the effects that can be achieved in metal thread embroidery. Read from the top.

1. *Top row, left to right:*
Simple couching effects. The method of couching down metal threads, the needle angled to ensure that the stitches lie closely together; double stitches worked at the beginning and end of a row and bricked couching; couching stitches evenly distributed; two ways of couching down flat braids using large couching stitches or small diagonal back stitches; flat plaited braid couched down with tiny back stitches down the centre of the braid; a method for couching down twisted metal thread, the stitches, made at an angle to the twist and into the middle of the thread; a method of couching pearl purl, small angled stitches being made between the twists of purl.

2. *The method used for pulling metal threads through to the wrong side of the work.*

3. *Couching over string. Stitched down string, the ends cut close to the double stitches; three effects of couching over string, left to right, passing gold thread with two double couched stitches between; flat lurex braid with one double couching stitch between the pieces of string and uneven bricking; using several different types of gold thread.*

4. *Couched threads turned at an angle on the background fabric.*

5. *Four different effects when working couched threads over a large area, reading downwards. For a round or irregular shape, start on the outside of the shape and work inwards towards the centre; turning alternate threads back and introducing new threads, the couching worked in a bricking effect; simple even couching stitches alternate threads turned back and new threads introduced; small pieces of card stitched to the background fabric first and metal threads couched down over the card.*

6. *Progressive stages of making a raised padded area. The smallest piece of felt is stitched down first and each larger layer is stitched over the smaller layer in turn. Four stab stitches are made at equidistant intervals round the edge of each piece of felt to ensure even spread of fullness, then the rest of the stitches filled in. The piece of gold kid is stitched down over the felt padding, using the same method.*

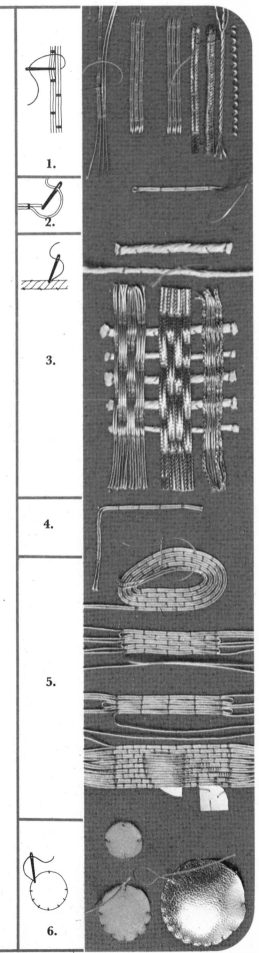

1.

2.

3.

4.

5.

6.

Chapter 39

Experiments in metal thread embroidery

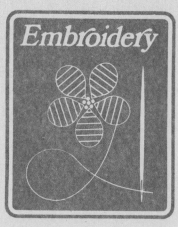

This chapter on metal thread embroidery illustrates some of the different effects which can be achieved by varying the threads and the techniques of applying them.

Although gold threads are rich and exciting to work with, silver and silver lurex threads produce embroidery with a cool and exquisite look.

Uses

Metal thread embroidery is traditionally associated with ecclesiastical work as a decoration for copes, mitres, altar frontals, pulpit falls and prayer book covers, but in modern embroidery it is used for wall panels, and as a decoration for lids of fabric jewellery boxes.

On fashion garments metal thread embroidery adds luxurious richness, and need not cause cleaning problems as a variety of washable lurex yarns are available.

Fir cone

The background fabric is a cotton/Terylene mixture in dark brown. The applied fabrics are Jap silk in a bronze colour, gold kid in a variety of tones, and gloving leathers in shades of brown. The metal threads used are Jap gold, pearl purl, lurex in antique gold and gold fingering knitting yarn. The Jap silk was applied first, couched down with Jap gold and lurex. Shapes cut from leather and gold kid form the cone seeds detail. Couched gold threads and gold fingering knitting are used for the finer design lines.

Tree bark

The background fabric used here is natural coloured hessian, and the applied fabric is gold orion cloth which resembles kid. The raised, padded sections were worked first. Several layers of felt in varying sizes were stitched in place beginning with the smallest and finishing with the largest, giving a smooth, rounded padding. The orion cloth was then stitched down over the padding. The textured stitchery is a combination of gold and lurex threads couched down in vertical flowing lines to form rhythm in the design.

Silver on blue

This interesting sampler is worked on a slub textured furnishing fabric, using a variety of materials in tones of silver. Narrow silver ribbon was bunched in a random fashion and tiny matt silver beads were stitched into the folds. Silver checkered purl, cut in lengths, is applied in small loops. Finer silver and lurex threads and pure silk lightly scatter the background in the form of small star stitches and random crossed threads to contrast with the heavier textures. The circles of silver kid make interesting focal highlights.

▼ *The design entitled 'fir cone' worked in gold kid and leather*

'Tree bark' which uses padded areas ▼   *Silver on blue, cool and lovely* ►

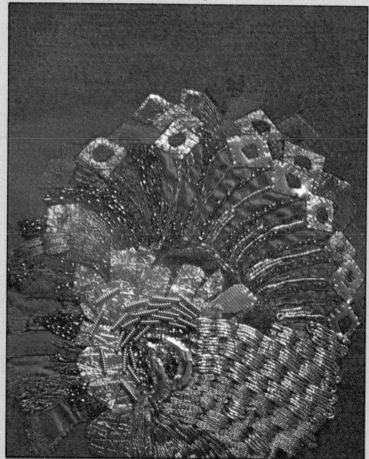

Chapter 40

Introduction to beading

Methods and materials used for modern bead embroidery.

Materials and equipment

Thread
Cotton or silk thread is used for bead embroidery, and should be of the finest and strongest quality available. Before use, the thread is drawn once across beeswax and is used double thickness. Generally, in beadwork, the thread should not show on the right side of the work and a colour suited to both the background fabric and the beads should be chosen.

Needles
Beading needles are long and fine and are available in sizes 10 to 13.

Frame
A frame is generally advisable for working beading and is essential for tambour beading, both hands being left free for working—one hand using the hook and the other setting the beads.

Beads and sequins
There are many different types of beads and sequins available, each in a wide range of colours and sizes. Sequin material, which can be cut into pieces and various shapes, is obtainable in sheets of 3·70m lengths, about 60cm wide. Sequin waste, the material left over after sequins have been cut out, is useful; it is about 7·5 cm wide and is available in lengths.

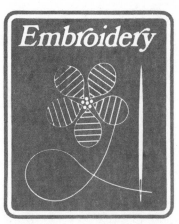

Applying beadwork designs

Designs are marked out on the background fabric in the same way as for embroidery. Mark designs on the right side for hand stitched beading and on the wrong side for tambour beading. Beading should always be worked on the pieces of a garment before it is made up. For perfectly worked seams, work the beading up to the seam line. Stitch the garment seam by hand, and if there are any gaps showing in the beading, fill the odd beads in.

Methods of beading

Six methods of attaching beads and sequins to the background fabric are given. The illustrations and diagrams show beads and sequins applied in straight lines, but design lines can of course curve, and can be broken or added to. The tension of the stitches used for beading should be firm but not too tight or the effect is spoiled. Make sure that the thread is fastened off securely at both ends of a row of beads.

Method 1
Bring the needle through to the front of the work and pick up one bead. Slide it along the needle and just onto the thread. Pick up one thread of the background fabric, the length of the bead along the design line. Draw the needle through the fabric to place the bead on the fabric and pick up the second bead.

Method 2
This method requires two needles and thread in use at the same time. Needle No.1, the beading needle, picks up two or more beads and stitches them to the fabric (following the technique in method 1). Needle No.2 then works the second stage, making a small slanting stitch between each bead, catching down the linking thread.

Method 3
Bring the needle up through the hole of the sequin, set the sequin on the fabric and take a tiny stitch to the side of it on the line of design. Bring the needle up through the next sequin and continue to the end of the line. This results in a scale-like effect.

Method 4
Bring the needle up through the hole in the first sequin. Set the next sequin on the fabric and insert the needle. Set the third sequin on the fabric and bring the needle up through the hole and then, making a back stitch, into the hole of the previous sequin. Continue applying further sequins using a back stitch each time.

Method 5
Each sequin is sewn to the fabric with a single back stitch, and again a contrasting thread can be used.

Method 6
Each sequin is held in place by a small bead which must be larger than the hole in the sequin. Bring the needle up through the hole, pick up a bead on the needle and insert the needle back through the hole in the sequin. Bring the needle up through the hole of the next sequin and continue.

Tambour beading

This is a method of attaching beads and sequins by means of a small, sharp hook in a holder. Set the fabric in the frame with the wrong side uppermost.

Thread the beads onto a spool of cotton—they can be threaded in a pattern sequence if required. Hold the hook in the right hand above the frame, the left hand holding the thread, and flick up a bead beyond the hook as each stitch is made. For a 'speckled' effect, flick up a bead for every second stitch only. Tambour beading is an especially good method for attaching small beads, bugles and sequins if the pattern is linear. Combine tambour beading with hand stitched beading for even more unusual effects.

Beaded cuffs

To bead two cuffs you will need:
- [ ] Sheet of sequin material measuring 76cm by 61cm
- [ ] 2½mm gold pearls
- [ ] 5mm cup sequins in coral shade
- [ ] Yellow chalk beads
- [ ] 5mm flat sequins in blue-green shade
- [ ] White chalk beads
- [ ] Gold beads
- [ ] Small size pale blue chalk beads
- [ ] Sewing thread (cotton or silk)
- [ ] Beading needle

Working the cuffs
Prepare the thread by dragging it through a block of beeswax. Thread the needle with double thread. Mark the oblong shapes on the sequin material, using a fine ball point pen and a ruler. The size of the shapes can be adjusted to fit the depth of the cuff and the measurement round the wrist. Cut the shapes out with a sharp pair of scissors and pierce the holes with a pin, holding the sequin shape over a soft felt pad. All the beads, sequins and sequin shapes are sewn on by passing the thread through a small bead on top (method 6). Complete all the beadwork before making up the cuff and attaching it to the sleeve.

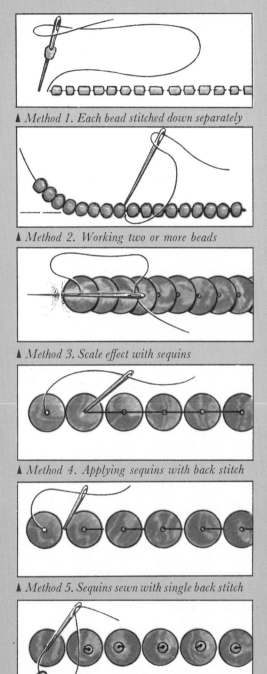

▲ Method 1. Each bead stitched down separately

▲ Method 2. Working two or more beads

▲ Method 3. Scale effect with sequins

▲ Method 4. Applying sequins with back stitch

▲ Method 5. Sequins sewn with single back stitch

▲ Method 6. Sequin held with a small bead

◀ Shimmering effect of toned beads and sequins   ▼ Diagram for working the beaded cuff

Gold oblong shape cut from large sheet
attached by 2½mm gold pearls.

Coral 5mm cup sequin – yellow chalk bead.
Blue/green 5mm flat sequin – white chalk
bead.

Gold beads attached with small pale blue
chalk bead – sewn on fold line.

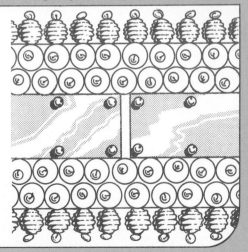

Chapter 41

Beading in fashion

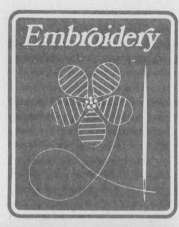

This second chapter on beading deals with uses of beading for fashion garments and accessories, how to work out beading designs, and gives methods for applying designs and working out the quantities of beads and sequins required.

Beading in fashion

Beading should be planned as an integral part of the garment design, enhancing the line, and giving the garment an added richness and an exclusive quality.

Beading for fashion must be bold enough to read well at a distance and yet have sufficient detail for close-up interest. The arrangement of the embroidery on a garment is particularly important. Use perhaps two or three patterns on one garment. For example, a rich small scale pattern on the yoke; a small spaced spot motif over the main part of the garment, and a narrow border for edges. Dress accessories of all types can be beaded to form luxurious and exclusive fashion highlights to simple garments. One plain, well cut dress, for example, can ring the changes with a set of different beaded belts, collars or cuffs. A set of beaded buttons can completely transform an otherwise ordinary garment, though beaded buttons are rather impractical and should only be used for decoration. Beaded buckles for belts or shoes are fun to embroider, quick to make, and are ideal items for the beginner to experiment upon. Hats, headdresses, evening bags and gloves are also ideal for bead embroidery, but particular care must be taken when attaching beads to ready-made items to ensure that the tension of the stitching is firm and even.

Designs for beading

Generally it is the least complicated designs which are the most effective for bead embroidery. Select designs with bold shapes and avoid those formed of small shapes and thin lines as these give little scope for creating the rich, clustered textures which are possible with beading. As with all forms of embroidery, texture plays an important part and beads should be chosen in various sizes and shapes, complementing both each other and the background fabric. Many of the embroidery designs already given in this book can be adapted to bead embroidery or can be enhanced by the addition of beads. For solid effect all-over designs, such as those used on evening bags and belts, charted geometric designs can be used. These are worked on fine double mesh canvas, each bead being stitched separately using a tent stitch over one set of double threads each time. For added texture, larger beads can be applied over the grounding design.

Designing directly onto fabrics

Beads lend themselves to free designing without the use of a pattern or a chart. Select beads in a colour scheme to complement the fabric and mount the fabric in an embroidery frame.

Scatter the beads onto the mounted fabric and arrange them in patterns, anchoring the beads in position by pushing a pin through the hole, as the pattern develops.

Combining beading with embroidery

Beading can be combined with other forms of embroidery to great effect. Machine or hand embroidery can be used as the basis of the design, which is then highlighted and enriched with beading. For a rich and interesting effect on velvet, for example, using machine embroidery, use a thick thread, such as chenille, in the bobbin. This gives a lively texture on which to base beading. Metallic threads can also be used in the same way, or couched on by hand or zigzag machine stitch. For further texture interest, apply

◄ *Machine embroidery and rich beading on hand printed fabric combine to lift a simply cut evening dress into the haute couture class*

shapes of silver or gold kid. Beads can also be combined with smocking designs which look marvellous for evening or bridal dresses. For a peasant look, combine hand embroidery with wood and china or chalk beads. Padded appliqué and quilting also take on a new richness when combined with beading.

Printed fabric and beading
Printed fabrics can provide inspiration for the basis of a beaded embroidery design. On the elegant evening dress shown in this chapter, for instance, the beading is worked over a hand printed design combined with free machine embroidery. When working on printed fabrics, choose bold prints and select focal areas of the pattern to highlight. Small, complicated prints should be avoided as the beading will only complicate the design. Avoid over-beading a pattern or the result will be a confused mess. If you are not sure whether you have done enough, hang the beaded section somewhere where it can be viewed easily and leave it for a day or so. When you return to it, you will find it easier to be critical and be able to decide whether to add more beads or to leave it as it is.

Transferring designs
Method 1. Pricking and pouncing. Draw the design onto tracing paper and lay the paper face downwards over a soft pad, such as a folded blanket or a sheet of felt. Perforate the lines of the design with a pin (or a sewing machine needle may be easier to handle), keeping the holes closely spaced. Tack the pricked design rough side uppermost (the right way round) to the fabric and, using a small round pad made from a 5cm deep strip of tightly rolled up felt, dab powdered chalk through the holes. Use powdered chalk on dark colours and powdered charcoal mixed with a little chalk on light colours. This method is especially suitable for complex designs and designs which need to be repeated two or more times. Fix the pounced design by painting over the dotted lines with water colour paint, using a very fine brush. Because the design is thus permanently marked onto the fabric, the lines of the design must be strictly followed during beading.
Method 2. Tracing. For beading on semi-transparent fabrics, place the design under the fabric and very carefully trace through using a hard lead pencil with a very fine point. Alternatively, trace the design onto tracing paper using a felt tipped pen. Pin the design securely in position underneath the fabric, and with small running stitches follow the line of the design without working through the paper.
Method 3. Tacking. Place the traced design onto the right side of the fabric and tack the outlines, using small stitches, through to the fabric. To remove the paper without damaging the fabric perforate it with a needle between and under each stitch, then tear the paper away carefully.

Calculating quantities
If the area to be beaded is large or includes a number of repeats, it is essential to work a sample of any design first to calculate how many beads are required.
Measure the length and depth of the worked sample and then work out how many repeats of the sample are required to cover the area to be beaded. Count the number of beads used on the sample and multiply this by the number of repeats required to find the total number of beads of each kind required.

Stretching beadwork
When planning a design, bear in mind the weight of the beads and their 'pull' on the fabric. If the beading is likely to be heavy, use the fabric double, particularly when working with sheer fabrics, or for added strength mount each piece of the garment on unbleached calico before beading.

Sometimes, a completed piece of beading may show signs of puckering, and if this happens the work will require stretching. Place two or three sheets of damp blotting paper over a wooden surface larger than the area of the finished work, such as a drawing board. Place the beading right side uppermost over the paper and, making sure that at least one edge of the work is straight, pin it out with gold headed drawing pins (which do not rust so easily) at about 5cm intervals. Work round the embroidery, easing it into shape as you pin. Continue pinning until the pins are touching each other. Leave the work to dry for at least 24 hours.
If sequins have been used in the embroidery, extra care is needed. Sequins are made on a basis of gelatine and will curl up and melt when they come in contact with water. To prevent this, damp the first sheet of paper only, and place a layer of dry paper over it before pinning out the work.

Ways with beads
Piling beads. Beads and sequins can be sewn piled on top of each other, and it is great fun to experiment with combinations of different shapes and surface qualities. For example, pile six sequins decreasing in size, some cup shaped, some flat and of different colours, topped with a small chalk bead to secure. The examples given in this chapter show eight permutations on the 'round shape'. Several beads sewn on at a time can give a lovely raised, loopy effect, two bugles sewn on at a time result in a spiky texture.

▲ *Top row: swing motifs for exotic fringes. Centre and bottom row: eight variations of piling beads and sequins for encrusted designs*

Swing motifs. Sewing swing motifs can be fun, too, and these can be extended to fringes which can be as light and fragile or as heavy and chunky as desired. Some examples are shown in this chapter but the permutations are unlimited. Any of the swing motifs shown can be continued along the edge of fabric to make a fringe. For picot edgings, sew beads along the edge of the fabric, each bead held in place with a tiny chalk bead. Different effects can be achieved depending on the shapes of the beads used.

Chapter 42

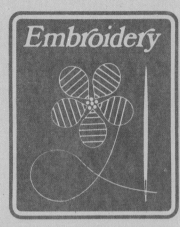

Panel in crewel work

Crewel embroidery, named after the yarn used, is a very early form of English embroidery. It reached its height of popularity during the 17th century in the reign of James I, and is also known as Jacobean work.

The house and garden panel featured in this chapter, especially designed for us, is a modern interpretation of this type of embroidery. The basically simple stitches and encrusted areas of beads create lively texture.

Yarns

Crewel embroidery is worked in crewel wool, a thin two-ply worsted yarn. Other yarns can be introduced as desired to add highlights and texture to a design. Stranded cotton, pearl cotton, soft embroidery cotton and metal threads are all suitable.

Fabrics

The embroidery is generally worked on a background fabric of linen, but any fabric similar in weave can be used. Dress and furnishing fabrics in man-made fibres are suitable, and those with a slight texture make an interesting background to complement the embroidery.

Stitches

Long and short stitches and couching in its various forms (see Embroidery Chapters 4 and 16) are the stitches most commonly associated with crewel embroidery, but any embroidery stitch or combination of stitches can be used in a design.

House and garden panel

Use the ideas shown in this picture of a charming house and garden to design a panel depicting your own house and garden. To make this panel you will need:
- ☐ Fine even-weave fabric measuring 62cm by 46cm
- ☐ Large wooden beads in assorted colours
- ☐ Small wooden beads in assorted colours
- ☐ Glass beads in assorted colours
- ☐ Tapestry needle size 22 for double strands of yarn
- ☐ Tapestry needle size 18 for several strands of yarn
- ☐ Crewel needle size 7 for single strands of yarn
- ☐ Appletons Crewel Wool in the following colours:
   1 skein each of burgundy 148; terra cotta 223; dark grass green 256; sea green 405; scarlet 501; bright yellow 554; pale fuschia 801; fuschia 803; dark fuschia 805; dark rose pink 948; iron grey 967; light elephant grey 971; elephant grey 972; medium elephant grey 976
   Two skeins each of bright grass green 253; grass green 254 and medium grass green 255
- ☐ Embroidery frame

Stitches and colours

Use two strands of crewel wool in the needle unless otherwise stated.

Landscape in foreground. Chain stitch in 253, 254 and 256.

Path. Top rectangle—cross couching, two strands of 971 couched down with one strand of 972. Lower path—two strands of 971 couched down with one strand of 971.

Steps in path. Double knot stitch using four strands of 971.

Roof. Fly stitches in 976. Horizontal lines of couching, two strands of 976 couched down with one strand of the same colour.

Balcony. Cable chain stitch, worked as small as possible, using one strand of 148. Horizontal lines of couching edging to balcony worked in two strands and couched down with one strand of 976.

Front door. Roumanian stitch worked to the full width of the door shaping into the curve at top, 803.

Door frame. Raised chain band in 971.

Grass. Top patches—worked in rows of back stitch positioned alternately, each stitch taken over two threads of the fabric and in rows spaced three threads apart, using one strand of 254. The rows of back stitches are then threaded diagonally with one strand of 253. Lower patches—simple couching with the stitches matching in vertical lines. Use two strands of 253, couched down with one strand of 254.

Outlines. Stem stitch, using two strands of 967 round paths and wrought iron gate. Use one strand of same shade round house and upper curve of paths.

Wall. Couching and Roumanian stitch; Roumanian stitch is worked in 223. The couching is worked in continuous bands in the gaps between the pillars, the couching stitches forming vertical lines. Use two strands of 223 couched down with one strand of 948.

Weeping willow trees. Cretan stitch worked with 253, 254, 255 and 256.

Flowers. French knots and bullion knots in 148, 801, 803, 805, 501 and 554 together with wooden and glass beads sewn on with one strand. Stitch the larger beads on with six stitches in the form of a star.

Windows and plant plots. Roumanian stitch in 976 for windows and 223 for plant pots.

Shrubs in pots. Bullion knots in 405. Work a line of bullion knots with three twists round the needle on the outline of each shrub. With four twists round the needle, fill in the centres leaving some gaps.

Round windows and outside of house. Twisted chain in 223.

▼ *Detail of the bead flowers*　　*Crewel embroidery in rich texture* ►

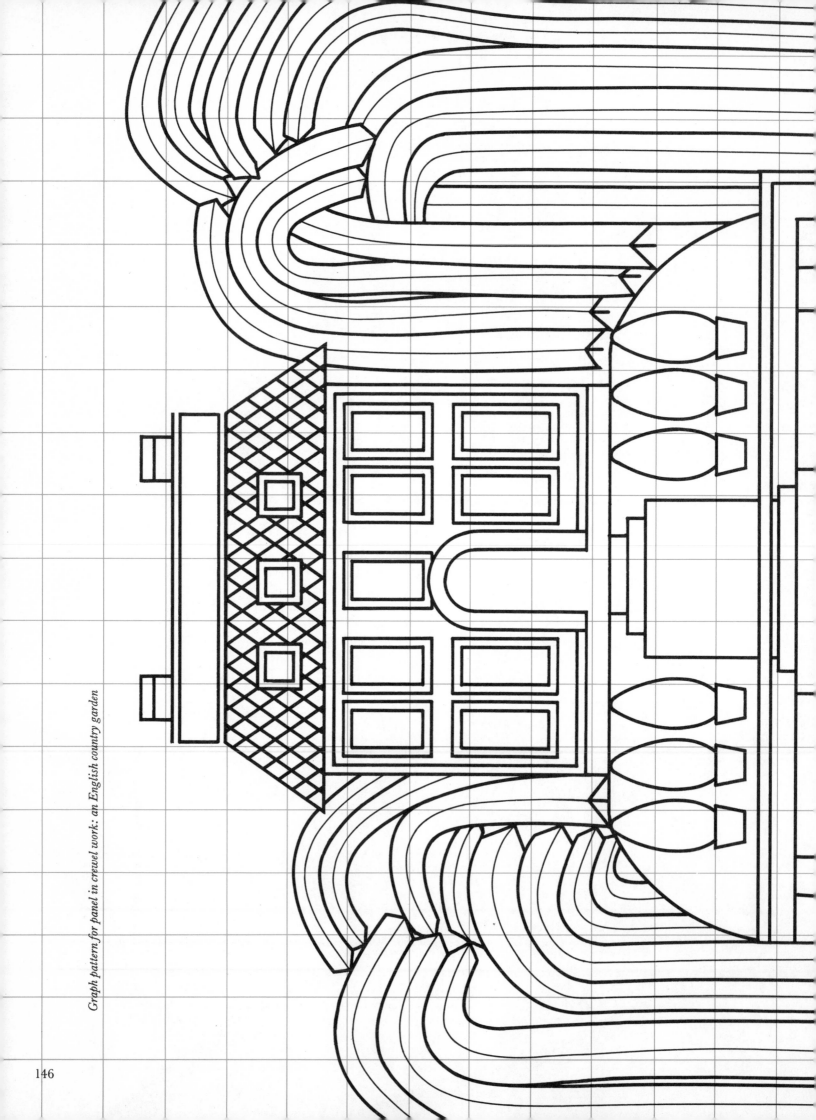

Graph pattern for panel in crewel work: an English country garden

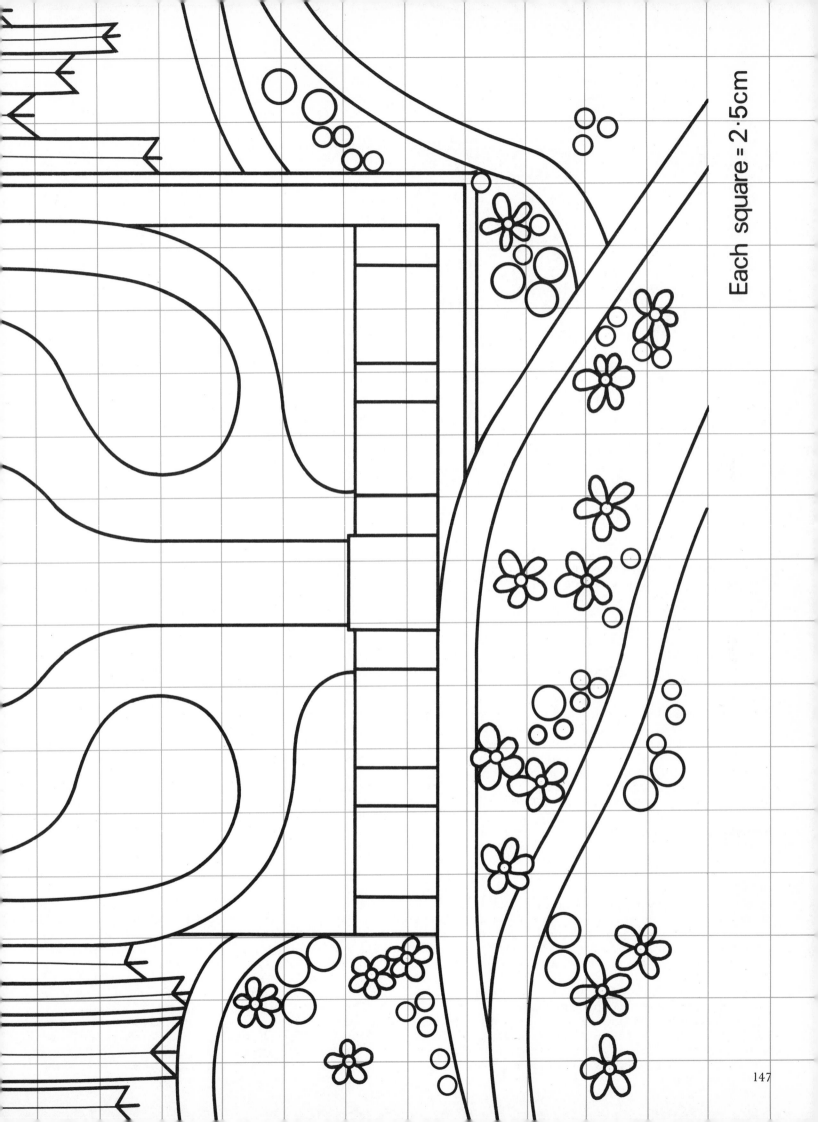

Each square = 2·5cm

147

Chapter 43

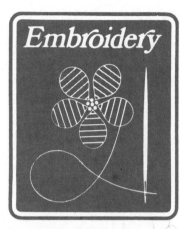

Introduction to quilting

This chapter deals with the basic quilting techniques and how to make an evening bag. Fine examples of modern and traditional quilting can be seen over the page.

Materials

The materials for quilting consist of backing, a layer of wadding and a top fabric. The backing can either be of the same fabric as the top layer or a contrast in both colour and texture. A dull surfaced fabric is better for backing if for a bed or cot cover, because it prevents the quilt from slipping. Light to medium weight fabrics such as cotton, linen, satin or silk can be used for quilting. Originally, quilts were padded with carded sheeps wool, and later with cotton wool. Today, muslin-backed nylon wadding, available by the yard, is ideal; it is easy to handle, washes well and retains its 'spring'. Domett, a wool and cotton mixture fabric, is ideal for padding quilted garments where lightness and warmth are required. Surgical cotton wool or cotton wool wadding should never be used. It is treated to make it absorbent and tends to take in dampness from the atmosphere.

Setting up work in a frame

It is possible to quilt very small pieces in the hand, but it is generally advisable to quilt with the work stretched on a slate frame. Apply the design onto the right side of the top fabric to be quilted. The bottom layer is then set up first in the frame as instructed in Embroidery Chapter 13. Stretch the bottom layer taut ready for working and place the wadding smoothly over it. The top fabric is then placed in position and all three layers are tacked together firmly ready for the design to be stitched. All the work is carried out from one side of the frame, and the work should not be turned as this can cause cockling in the quilting.

Stitches and working method

The traditional wadded quilt is sewn with an evenly spaced running stitch. One hand is held under the work to receive the needle as it is stabbed through the layers of fabric, and the same hand passes it back to the right side of the work on the line of the design. Several needles are used at once, each one following a line of the design, and each needle worked a little way forward at a time to maintain tension and smoothness of work. The stitches and the spaces between them must look the same on both sides of the quilt, for reversability is a characteristic feature of wadded quilting.

Transfer and tracing method

There are several methods of marking designs onto fabric to be quilted. A commercial transfer, or the dressmakers carbon paper method, can be used, but as the design is usually applied to the right side of the fabric and worked in running stitch the design lines are not completely covered, and will remain visible until the quilting is washed.

Needle marking method

Marking designs for quilting with a needle gives a more clearly defined line on which to work. Tailors chalk can be used but tends to smudge unless it is kept very sharp during use. With the needle marking method, the design can be applied to the fabric before it is set up in the frame, or bit by bit as the work is in progress. It depends on the workers preference as to which method is chosen.

For the needle marking method, the pattern shapes of the design are cut as templates of stiff paper or cardboard. Or, alternatively, simple patterns can be marked directly onto the fabric using a ruler, coins, drinking glasses or saucepan lids as templates. The main outlines of the shapes are drawn round the template using the point of a large, thick needle such as a tapestry needle. If the design is to be marked out before framing, lay the top fabric over a piece of thick fabric, such as felt, on the kitchen table and mark the outlines by drawing firmly round the templates, holding the needle at a slant so that it does not catch or tear the fabric. It is better, however, to mark the design in sections whilst working.

Quilted evening handbag

Materials you will need:
- [ ] 50cm heavy quality satin and 50cm lining to match
- [ ] 2 pieces of Terylene wadding 23cm square
- [ ] 2 pieces of muslin 23cm square
- [ ] 2 spools of button hole twist thread to match satin
- [ ] 1 sewing needle Crewel No. 7
- [ ] Small quantity of tiny gilt beads
- [ ] 1 spool of invisible sewing thread and 1 beading needle
- [ ] 1 spool of sewing silk to match satin
- [ ] 1·85m fine piping cord
- [ ] 1 gilt bag frame, 15cm between mounting isles

Preparing for quilting

Cut two pieces of satin 23cm square. Cut two crossway strips from the satin 69cm long and 2·5cm wide for piping and cut another 5cm wide by 51cm long for the gusset. Trace the design from the diagram and transfer it onto the right side of the satin for each side of the bag, including outline and dotted line.

Prepare the muslin backing and the wadding in the frame for quilting, and then place one of the satin pieces on top.

The quilting is worked in back stitch using buttonhole twist in the needle, and the stitching should be worked so that the stitches are as even as possible. Tighten the work in the frame if it becomes slack while quilting.

When all the stitchery has been completed, sew the beads in position at the intersection of the lines.

Repeat for the second side.

To make up bag

Trim the wadding and muslin. Outline the shape of the bag on both back and front, following the dotted line on the diagram, in small running stitches using a contrasting cotton. This is the piping line. Trim quilting along the outer line on the diagram. Cut the piping cord in half so that you have two pieces each measuring 36 inches long. Tack the piping cord into the crossway strips. Tack the covered cord into position on the dotted outline on both the back and front of the bag. Back stitch firmly in position.

Position the completed bag on the bag frame, and hold it in position with tie tacks through the holes on both sides of the frame, at the corners. Sew in position using sewing silk and hiding the stitches in the seam of the piping. Back stitches will make a strong and firm fitting. Cut and make a lining to fit the finished bag.

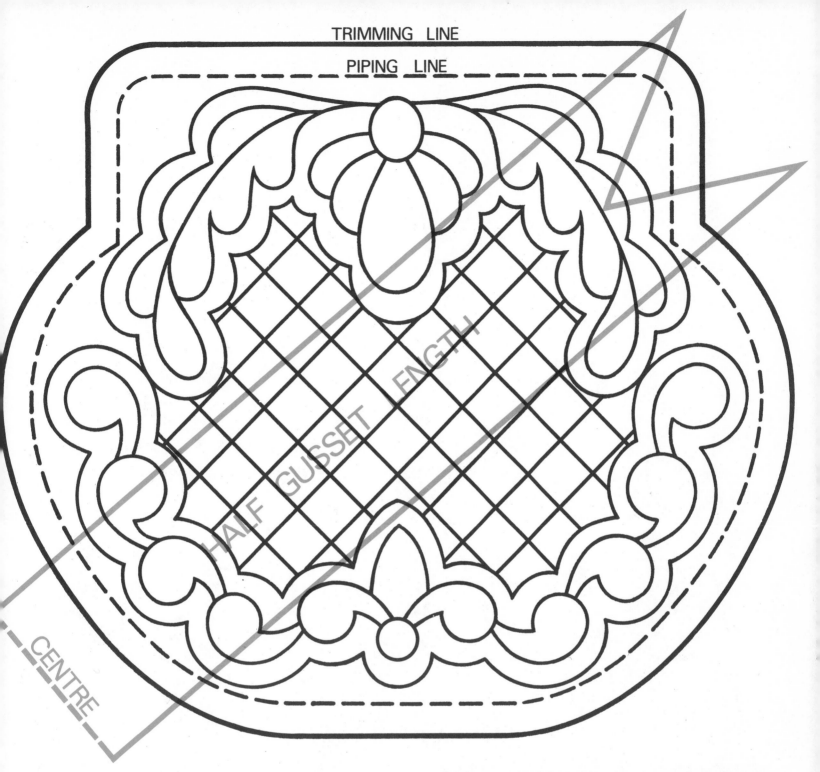

TRIMMING LINE

PIPING LINE

HALF GUSSET LENGTH

CENTRE

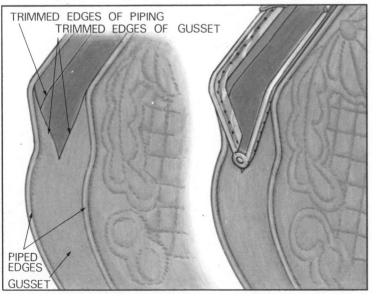

▼ *Inserted gusset with edges trimmed* ▼ *Bag stitched to frame*

TRIMMED EDGES OF PIPING
TRIMMED EDGES OF GUSSET

PIPED
EDGES

GUSSET

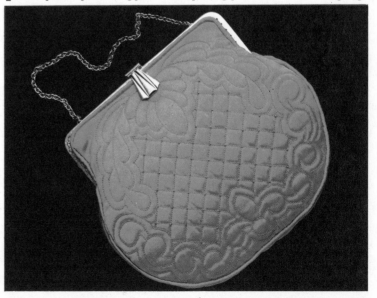

▲ *Trace pattern for cutting fabric and quilting pattern* ▼ *The evening bag*

Traditional quilting

Quilting is a centuries old technique. It has served many other purposes over the years besides that of providing warmth. In the 16th century it was in high fashion as it padded out the clothing to the desired shape, and combined with surface stitching and drawn fabric made up into a very beautiful garment. The quilting at this time, was composed of three layers of fabric in contrast to the flat quilting of the 18th century, which consisted of only two layers.

18th century coverlet
The coverlet illustrated opposite has two layers, which is typical of this century. They are sewn together with fine back stitching in yellow silk and worked in a trellis pattern which covers the whole of the background.

Trellis and other simple geometric patterns were popular as a background to silk embroidery. These and a vermicular pattern of continuous curving lines were an easy way out for the less skilled embroiderer, as it is much easier to work in a curving line than evenly in a straight one. The embroidery on the coverlet is sewn in many coloured silks. The work conjures up the 18th century image of Chinese design, which was fashionable at this time.

The centre motif is that of a bird with wings outspread, all curves and movement. The birds are repeated at the corners and face in towards the centre of the quilt, surrounded by the trailing leaf circle which again forms the same pattern in the centre. The embroidery is worked in long and short stitch, split stitch and satin stitch.

The coverlet can be seen in the Victoria and Albert Museum, London, together with many other beautiful quilts in different colours and designs. Quilting was also worked on pillow cases, headresses and bags and served as a padding for wartime armour in the 16th century.

Modern quilting

Quilting is as popular today as it was in the 16th and 18th century. Dresses, coats, bags and many other fashion accessories are made up of quilting and modern embroiderers work them in panels for decoration in the home, and for exhibition purposes.

The work itself is freer than it was originally, the lines curving and falling in irregular patterns, which is well illustrated by the piece shown below.

Quilted exhibition piece
The exciting quilted panel below updates traditional methods to complement the flowing, clear-cut lines of modern furnishings. The design is reminiscent of wood grain with its rough texture and uneven, rugged pattern, while the use of white on white in both stitch and fabric provides sophistication and subtlety. The light of the larger padded areas is emphasised by the slight sheen of the fabric and the corded areas contrast in narrow bands of light and shade. Trapunto quilting is used for the large padded areas and the corded quilting for the flowing lines. We give instructions for both these methods of machine quilting in Embroidery Chapter 45. This particular piece of quilting can be seen at the Embroiderers' Guild, London, where it is available for viewing and study purposes.

Chapter 44

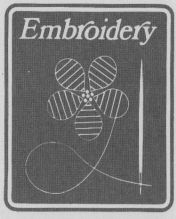

Quilted waistcoat for a man

Quilting, like many other craft forms, lends itself beautifully to being interpreted in contemporary designs and colour schemes. The luxurious man's waistcoat shown in this chapter, designed especially for this book, shows an interesting use of quilting for a fashion garment.

To make a man's quilted reversible waistcoat to fit size 38 chest you will need:
- [ ] 70cm cotton velvet (curtain velvet)
- [ ] 140cm Viyella fabric
- [ ] 70cm domett
- [ ] 1 spool sewing silk in colour matching the velvet
- [ ] 12 2cm button moulds for covered buttons
- [ ] 1 spool embroidery silk matching Viyella
- [ ] Tissue paper

Instructions

Set up the fabrics in a slate frame for quilting as described in Embroidery Chapter 43. Frame up the Viyella first then reverse the frame and place the domett smoothly onto the wrong side of the Viyella. Place the velvet in position on the domett.

Tack the three layers of fabric together, working through the fabric from one side to the other.

Turn the frame to the right side, Viyella uppermost.

Trace the design onto tissue paper. Make another tracing and reverse it for the second front.

Place the two tracings onto the Viyella side of the framed fabrics, making sure that the straight grain lines match the grain of the fabric. Leave sufficient space round the two fronts for seam allowance. The velvet pile should run down the body. Tack the pattern onto the Viyella around the outside edge. Follow the instructions in Embroidery Chapter 43 for working the design in running stitch, working through the tissue paper. When the evenly spaced running stitches have been completed, gently tear away the tissue paper and remove the work from the frame.

Making up the waistcoat

Cut and join cross way strips of Viyella, 2·5cm wide. Fold the strips in half and place the raw edges together around the armholes, down the fronts and along the lower edges. Stitch 6mm away from the raw edge. Fold binding over the edge and hem invisibly on the wrong side, along the line of machine stitching.

Cut out two backs for the waistcoat in the Viyella. Stitch one back to the front joining at shoulder and underarm seams. Turn up lower raw edge to wrong side. Take the second back and fold and tack all turnings to the wrong side. Placing wrong sides together, tack and slip stitch the second back over the first back. Press back and seams but not the quilting.

Cover button moulds with Viyella and sew 6 buttons on the inside of the left front and 6 buttons, exactly in line, on the outside of

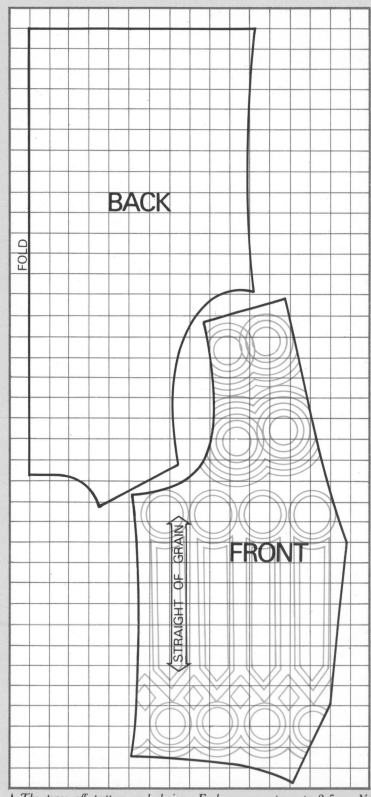

▲ *The trace off pattern and design. Each square represents 2·5cm. No seam allowances are given*

Quilting makes a rich decoration for a reversible waistcoat ▶

the right front. The buttons should be 4cm apart and 1·3cm in from the bound edge. Make sure that no stitching shows through to the right side.

To make buttonhole loops, crochet a length in chain stitch with embroidery silk or linen sufficient to make button loops for both sides. Stitch the length of crochet chain stitch along both edges of the waistcoat, making a buttonhole loop opposite each button.

Chapter 45

Quilting by machine

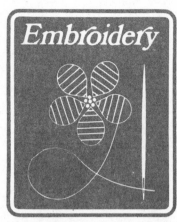

The beauty of machine quilting is that it is extremely quick to do, and is ideal for large pieces of work and fashion garments when fast results are desired. This chapter gives three types of machine quilting and an alternative hand method to Italian quilting.

The main types of quilting can be worked using the machine in the normal way with the presser foot on the machine. Straight-stitch and zigzag stitch are used, with the machine threaded with machine embroidery cotton No. 30, or a mercerised sewing cotton such as

▼ *Detail of machine quilting design on a skirt*

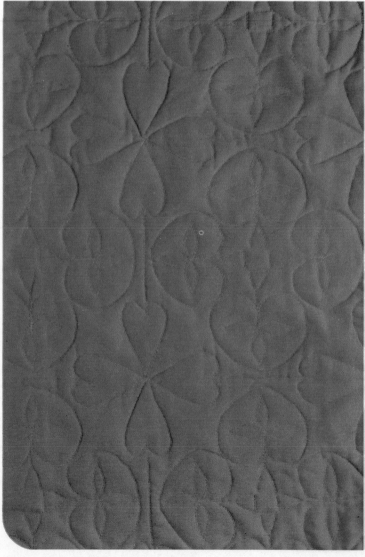

Sylko. It is often desirable to add portions of applied fabric to a design as these quickly make a solid shape which otherwise would have taken ages to cover completely with machine stitches.

Straight lines or simple curves, which can easily be followed with the presser foot on the machine, must be used for the designs. The work should be mounted on greaseproof paper before beginning machining to prevent puckering and stretching.

Quilting

There are three kinds of quilting that can be easily worked on a sewing machine. They can be used separately or combined to create more complex designs.

English quilting. Also called wadded quilting, this is the most commonly known and simplest form of quilting where the complete surface is padded. Terylene wadding is placed between the top fabric and the backing fabric and all three layers are stitched together. The stitching is usually worked with a running stitch and the conventional motif is a diamond shape, but other geometric forms or gently curving forms can be used. The work can be stitched on the wrong side if the design needs to be marked on paper, as for a quilt for example, but work is usually carried out on the right side, in the normal way.

Trapunto quilting. The two fabrics (the top fabric and backing) are stitched together with a running stitch, the backing is slit and the shape is filled with animal wool (obtainable from chemists), or kapok, and the slit sewn together again by hand. The shapes must be enclosed with stitching and should be of a shape easily stitched with the foot on the machine. Use animal wool for small shapes, and kapok for large shapes. Use a strong, firmly woven fabric, such as cotton sateen, on the back of the work to support the padding, and to keep the padded effect on the front of the work. Use these small padded areas in conjunction with appliqué and embroidery for evening bags, cushions, quilts and wall panels.

Italian quilting. The padding is formed by threading wool, such as 8 ply wool, rug wool or quilting wool, through the backing fabric between channels of stitching from about 3mm to 6mm wide. Two layers of fabric are used and the channels are most easily made using a double needle on a zigzag sewing machine. They can also be worked with a straight stitch machine making the second line of stitching parallel to the first. Thread a tapestry needle with thick wool and insert it between the lines of stitching. The backing fabric must be open weave, such as muslin, so that the needle carrying the padding thread can come out through it and be inserted again following the curve of the design. Leave a small loop each time the needle is inserted into the fabric. This makes a practical and pretty decoration on dresses, cushions, bed and cot quilts. If the top fabric is semi-sheer, an interesting effect can be achieved by using a contrasting colour wool. Some zigzag stitch and automatic sewing machines will automatically sew in cord or wool as you work. All three methods mentioned above are quick and simple to do and can easily be worked by beginners.

Italian quilting by hand

The main difference between Italian quilting and other forms of quilting is that no warmth is added by the quilting, and instead of being padded all over the outlines of the design only are padded to give a raised or corded effect. The transfer or design used must be one especially designed for this type of quilting, or bold appliqué designs can be used by drawing double outline 6mm or less inside the original design line. The design can be applied to either the top fabric or the lining, but generally to the top fabric. Stitch the lines of the design by hand using either small back stitches or a running stitch, using sewing cotton or pure silk. Pad the double lines of stitching in the same way as described for the machine method.

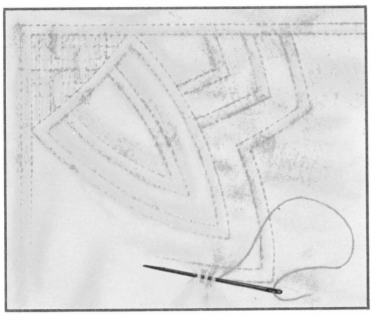

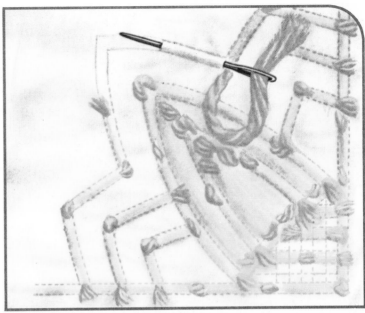

▲ *Method of working Italian quilting by hand*
▲ *Method of padding Italian quilting by hand*
▼ *A cot quilt worked in Italian quilting by hand*

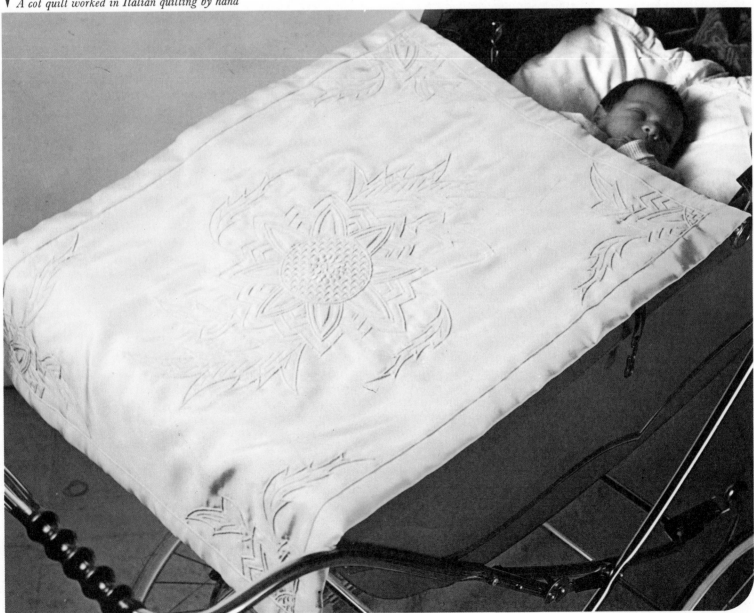

Chapter 46

Introduction to machine embroidery

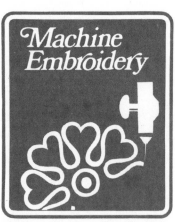

In recent years, embroidery designers have become more fully aware of the tremendous design potential of machine embroidery—not only for clothes and household linen but also for pictures and wall hangings.

Whether you have an up-to-date fully automatic machine or are still using your mother's old treadle, you can produce beautiful effects and patterns yourself. In the next four chapters we describe the different types of machine and explain their various stitch and technique capabilities. The sampler opposite illustrates the many stitch formations that can be achieved by working with a machine.

The main advantage of machine embroidery over hand embroidery is obviously one of speed. How much you can achieve is naturally related to how sophisticated your machine is and although it is possible to do some machine embroidery even if you only have a treadle or hand-operated machine, there must be limits.

There are three types of machine embroidery; straight stitching with the foot on the machine, using varying threads for decorative effects; free embroidery with the foot off the machine; automatic pattern embroidery. (Interesting effects can be achieved using the straight stitch method, by winding thicker thread on to the spool).

Free machine embroidery

For free machine embroidery, the foot of the machine is removed and the teeth which feed the material under the needle, lowered. Once this has been done, the fabric itself can be moved in every direction while the machine is running.

Uses of machine embroidery

The adaptability of machine embroidery is, of course, similar to that of hand embroidery. It helps to make clothes look more individual, adds interest to household items like towels and table-cloths, or becomes an art form making appliqué pictures.

Once you have followed the machine embroidery chapters and mastered the basic technique, you will then be able to experiment and work out new and original ideas.

What your machine can do

The old treadle machine was foot operated, strong and could be relied upon to do a running line of stitching on almost any fabric, however thick. It was used for dressmaking and household sewing. With the machine foot still in place it is possible to do several simple, thicker stitches with thicker than normal threads in the spool. With the foot off, you will be able to experiment with a basic running stitch of varying thicknesses and with different tensions.

The hand-operated models came next and these were smaller, portable and more convenient except that they were only straight stitch machines and slow to work with as they leave only one hand free to guide the fabric.

Once again, with the foot on the machine it is possible to experiment with thicknesses of yarn. But free embroidery with the foot off the machine is not possible because you need both hands free to guide the fabric.

The simple electric model enabled the operator to use both hands to guide the fabric and to sew faster in a straight stitch.

Again, with the foot on, this machine will work simple stitches in thicker yarns. Once you have taken off the foot you will be able to experiment with yarns, stitch sizes and tension variations.

The electric zigzag machine which was introduced after the second world war was more versatile and this machine made zigzag as well as straight stitches available to the public. It also added the facility to sew a stitch with a width as well as length.

With the foot still on this model you will be able to experiment with thicker stitches, zigzag and satin stitches. On some models there is a shuttle design for twin needles to work tucking, appliqué, eyelet holes and hemstitching. In free embroidery you will have a choice of basic running stitch plus zigzag stitch and variations.

Fully automatic machines with built-in patterns set in motion with the flick of a lever were the next advance.

There are obvious advantages in having this kind of machine to do embroidery. With the foot still on the machine you can try thicker stitches plus zigzag and satin stitch patterns, using the twin needles for double patterns and tucking, appliqué, eyelet holes and hem-stitching. In free embroidery the basic running stitch plus the zigzag stitch can be used.

Free arm machines are not very suitable for machine embroidery unless they adapt to an ordinary flat-bed style.

Preparing to work

Needles for machine embroidery

With machine embroidery, needles should be carefully selected because the eye will have to accommodate a thread which might not normally be teamed with the particular fabric.

As with straight-forward sewing, care should be taken with the choice of needle used in the machine. A thin fabric requires a thin needle, for example, No.11 English or 70 Continental, and fine cotton. A medium fabric requires a No. 12 to 14 English needle, 80 Continental and medium thread. A thick fabric should be worked with a No.16 English needle or 90 Continental and a slightly thicker thread.

Threads for machine embroidery

As well as the normal sewing cottons in varying thicknesses, embroidery and decorative stitches can be worked in machine embroidery cotton No.50 or No.30. Thicker embroidery threads can be wound on to the spool.

Stitch length and tension

Experiment with altering tensions and length of stitch. In most cases tensions must be adjusted for the top thread and are marked in numbers on a disc or indicated by a plus or minus sign. Spool cases have either one or two screws. When there are two, the one on the left is a set screw which holds the tension bar in place and the one on the right is the tension screw. When the spool case has only one screw, then that is the tension screw.

Turn the tension screw clockwise with a small screwdriver to tighten the thread and anti-clockwise to loosen it. Embroidery generally requires a tension slightly looser than normal.

The stitch length, if adjustable, is usually indicated by a numbered dial or lever.

Machine embroidery, raised areas ▲
Hand-winding a spool ▼

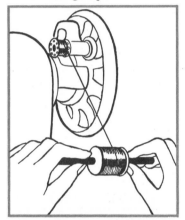

Machine embroidery on velvet ▲
Machine with the foot off ▼

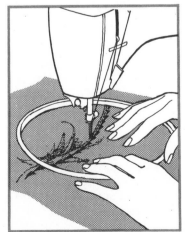

Treadle and simple electric

1. Stitching with loose tension, thick yarn in spool
2. Vermicelli effect in a free pattern using a small stitch
3–6. Straight stitch with a thick yarn in the spool
7. Free pattern in straight stitch, hand applied beads
8–13. Different yarns on the spool
14. Applied ribbons using a straight stitch down each edge
15–20. As for rows 8–13

Zigzag machine

21. Satin stitch
22. Pattern built up using varying widths of satin stitch which are linked with lines of straight stitching using a thicker thread in the spool
23. Satin stitch
24–28. Satin stitch and zigzag worked in varying widths, spacings and tensions
29. Satin stitch worked in varying widths by moving the stitch width lever by hand
30. Decoration worked in free embroidery using zigzag stitch. Hand stitched beads
31. A simple geometric pattern worked around felt diamonds and decorated with square wooden beads. The second row out from the diamonds is a length of wool couched to the fabric with a small zigzag stitch
32. Narrow tuck stitched with two rows of straight machining, one row simple the other using a thicker yarn in the spool and a loose spool tension
33. A deeper tuck stitched with a wide satin stitch and a thick yarn on the spool

Automatic machine

34 & 35. Automatic patterns
36 & 37. Satin stitch holding narrow velvet ribbon in place
38 & 39. Automatic patterns
40. As for 33
41. As for 32
42–48. Variations of tucking. Rows 42 and 48 are decorated with glass beads sewn on by hand

(The numbers identify the row)

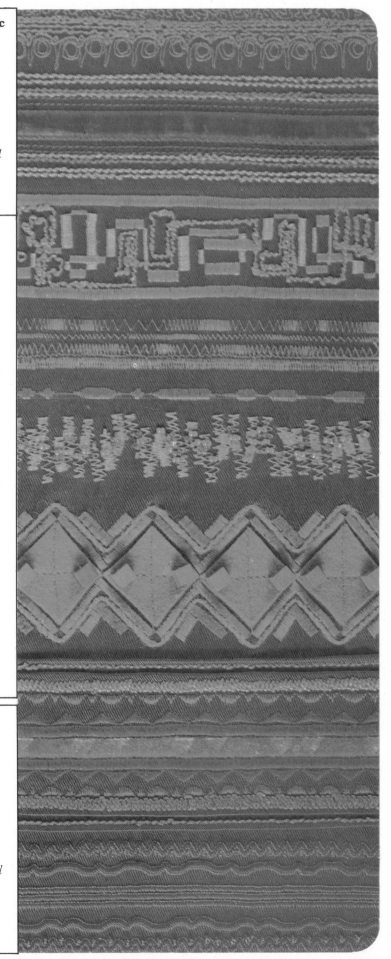

Chapter 47

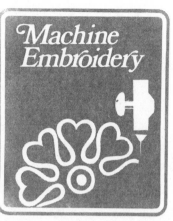

Straight stitch and automatic patterns

This chapter deals with decoration and embroidery worked with the foot on the machine and the use of automatic patterns. The effects are different from free embroidery which is worked with machine foot removed and feed teeth lowered.

The machine is used in the normal way as for dressmaking but sometimes threads, tensions and needles differ according to the required result.

Decoration of this kind can be applied to clothes and accessories, to useful items such as cushion covers, curtains and pictures or wall hangings. Stitches worked with the foot on the machine are neat and practical and lie flat on the surface of the fabric and are easily washed and cleaned.

Both the pretty dresses illustrated are decorated using techniques described in this chapter.

Designing

Long straight lines or simple curves are better than short lines because if the lines of the design are not continuous, the ends of the thread will have to be darned through to the back of the work.

Applying design to fabric

Guide lines of the design, which will have to be followed by the machine needle, can be marked on the fabric with soft white crayon (never use a pencil on the right side unless it has a very soft lead and then use it lightly, otherwise the lead will mark both the fabric and the thread).

Sometimes it is possible to trace the design on to thin paper such as tracing or typing copy paper. Tack this on to the back of the work and stitch the main guide lines from the back. Turn the work to the right side to work the embroidery.

Hard, unpliable, closely-woven fabrics with a shiny finish are difficult to use as they pucker badly.

Method of embroidery

For all work stitched with the foot on the machine (except for eyelet holes and tucking) the fabric is placed on thin paper. This paper prevents puckering especially when the zigzag or satin stitch is used. The paper does not have to be tacked to the fabric and is pulled away after all the embroidery is completed.

Thicker threads

Cotton No.30 or sewing cotton is used on top of the machine and the work stitched on the wrong side. Paper is still used on the back and the design guide lines can be drawn on it.

Thicker threads such as pearl cotton No.5 and No.8, stranded

cotton and thin wool are wound on to the spool by hand. The tension screw in the spool case is loosened or completely removed so that the thread runs very loosely. The top tension should be reasonably tight. This technique can be used on a straight stitch machine, a zigzag machine or for automatic patterns. The length of stitch should be adjusted and also the width of stitch on a zigazg machine to get varied results.

Metallic threads

When using metallic threads it is not possible to wind the thread on to the spool on the machine in the usual way. This kind of thread is so brittle that running it through all the thread guides would only damage or snap it. Instead, slot a pencil through the reel and feed it directly from this on to the spool winder. Keep the thread untwisted if it is a flat sided lurex thread (see Chapter 46). The spool tension must be loose and the top tension fairly tight so that only the metallic thread shows on the right side of the work. This technique is worked face downward and can be used on a straight stitch machine, a zigzag machine or for the patterns on an automatic. Fine metallic threads are available now which can be worked from the top with a slightly looser top tension.

Stitches, patterns and techniques

Zigzag, satin stitch and automatic patterns

Machine embroidery cotton No.30 and sewing cottons are used for these stitches. The spool and top of the machine are threaded with the same kind of cotton.

Experiment by altering the length and width of the zigzag stitch—when the zigzag stitch is closed up it becomes satin stitch. The zigzag stitch and satin stitch should look smooth, the stitches locked together at the back of the work, which means a slightly looser top tension than bottom tension. If tension is too tight the embroidery will not lie smoothly and the fabric will pucker.

The automatic patterns can look very effective when worked with double needles and different coloured threads. This kind of work is always embroidered right side up.

Hemstitching, tucking and eyelet holes

Hemstitching can be worked with single or double hemstitching needles. Embroidery cotton is used and this form of decoration is usually done on organdie or organza.

Tucking is worked with twin needles and a matching pin tucking foot. These come in different widths. Some machines insert a cord automatically as you sew, making the tucks broader and more durable. Backing paper is not used for this decoration as the top threads have to be pulled together by the bottom thread to make a raised tuck. Although this technique is based on the simple straight stitch, it can only be achieved on a zigzag or fully automatic machine with twin needles.

Eyelet holes

These require a special eyelet embroidery plate and foot. Pierce a hole in the fabric with an embroidery stiletto and then place the fabric in an embroidery frame. The feed is lowered so that the frame can be swung freely round in a circle to make the satin stitch around the hole.

All these fascinating techniques are quick to do which is the main advantage of machine embroidery. They are easily learned but as some machines differ from others, any extra information can be found in the instruction booklet of your particular machine. If you bought it second-hand without a manual, the manufacturers are usually able to supply one.

▲ *Stitch detail of light green dress*
Automatic patterns—instant charm ►
▼ *Stitch detail of pink/grey dress*

Collector's Piece

Machine embroidery at its most exquisite

This machine embroidered mat was worked by Rebecca Crompton in 1938. It is made of a fine, off-white fabric with a translucent quality, which adds a delicacy to the figures. The stitches include crazy stitch, cording with lace fillings, eyelet holes and zigzag stitch and has been worked on a swing-needle machine. The zigzag stitching has been worked freely with the teeth dropped and the needle straight to allow the embroiderer to draw out the patterns. It has been used for the filled in areas on the mat, such as the ladies' bodices. Silver thread is embroidered onto the design which serves as a contrast to the all-white effect and adds textural interest to the work.

Embroiderers' Guild, London.

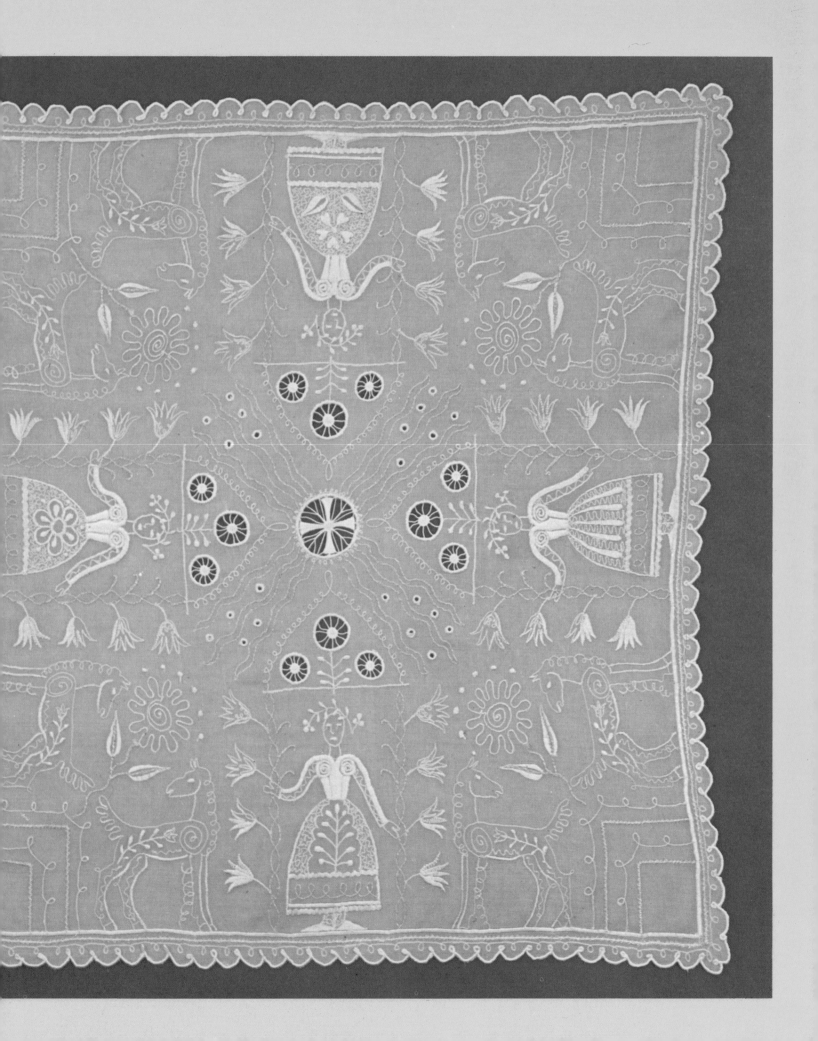

Chapter 48

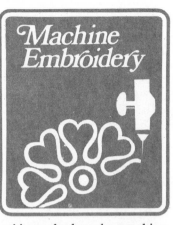

Free machine embroidery

These two charming dresses are worked using the free machine embroidery

The term 'free machine embroidery' is used when the machine is released from the control of the presser foot and feed teeth so that you can stitch in any direction quite freely. Although designs are usually worked to a pattern, machine embroidery has a degree of spontaneity about it and you will develop a style that is all your own.

Free machine embroidery

This is an exciting technique because the designs which can be achieved are infinitely more interesting than those obtained with the foot on the machine or with programmed patterns.

A limited amount of free embroidery is possible on a treadle machine or an ordinary domestic electric machine but the greatest variety of effects is achieved on swing-needle models.

Embroidery frames

In free machine embroidery, the work itself is guided under the needle, the fabric held taut in a frame. Special machine embroidery frames which have a screw fitment are available and these frames are made of either wood or metal. Choose a size suitable for the work—a 10cm, 15cm or a 20cm diameter are used with domestic machines. Hand embroidery frames can be used for machine embroidery but because they are rather deeper than the special frames they make the control more difficult.

It is advisable to bind the embroidery frame with bias strips of material or bandaging, if you are working with very fine or light coloured fabric, to prevent your work becoming snagged or soiled.

Materials

Machine embroidery cotton is available in two thicknesses—No.30 and No.50. Many embroiderers prefer No.30 because it is thicker and less likely to break. A fine sewing cotton can also be used—No.60 works very well and is available in a much wider variety of colours than the machine embroidery threads.

A No.11 English or No.70 or No.80 Continental size needle is recommended for machine embroidery but make sure that the needle used is sharp. Damaged or bent needles will cause stitches to be missed and snags in the material.

Refer to the previous chapter before choosing your fabric.

Setting up the machine

First, remove the presser foot and then lower the feed teeth which lie immediately below the presser foot. Some modern machines have a lever for lowering the feed but if your machine has not got this lever, the feed teeth will have to be covered with a special plate for working free machine embroidery. The manufacturer of your machine or the local service centre will help you to obtain the plate.

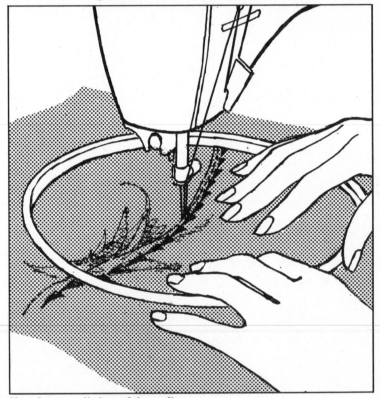

Keep fingers well clear of the needle

Thread the machine in the normal way, using machine embroidery thread. While you are practising stitches and effects, use a different colour thread in the spool from that used on the top of the machine so that tension mistakes can be spotted easily. Tension is difficult to check when both threads are of the same colour.

Both top and bottom stitch tensions should be equal and not too tight—a tight stitch will pucker the fabric. The thread from the spool affects the look of the stitch on the top of the work, so learn to adjust the tension screw in the spool case. For instance, if the spool thread is too loose, a beady, rough stitch results on the surface of your embroidery.

To work machine embroidery on a swing-needle machine, using the zigzag stitch, set up the machine in exactly the same way, but use the stitch width lever. This will give a much thicker free embroidery style, either as zigzag or as satin stitch.

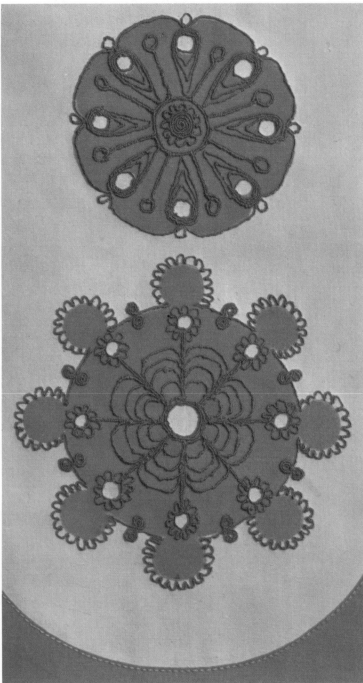

A close view of the embroidery shows how the use of simple whip stitch (see next machine embroidery chapter) can transform a plain dress

The close view shows how spots have been used as a base on which to plan a most attractive design to follow the yoke shaping of the dress

Interesting stitches and effects can be achieved by altering tension and by using thicker yarns or metallic yarns. These are explained more fully in the next chapter on machine embroidery.

Preparing the fabric for embroidery

Stretch the fabric to be embroidered tightly across the frame and then tighten the screw as far as it will go, so that there is no possibility of the material slipping while it is being worked. This is important because without the presser foot on the machine, stitches will be missed if the fabric is at all slack.

The method of working

After mounting the fabric in the frame, place the fabric under the needle and bring the spool cotton to the top of the work so that both threads are on the surface of the fabric. Lower the lever which would normally lower the foot because this lever also controls the top tension.

Hold both threads in the left hand and start the machine, moving the fabric until two or three stitches have been machined. The threads have now been locked together and the loose ends can be cut off. You can now move the frame and fabric under the needle and stitch in every direction, quite freely.

Keep the elbows down and hold the frame with the thumb and little finger of each hand, with the remaining fingers lying just inside the frame (see diagram opposite). Take great care not to let the fingers slip under the needle. Finger protectors, which can be fitted to any make of machine, are available.

After completing embroidery, remove the frame, with the threads, from the machine very carefully, remembering that the needle is unprotected.

Chapter 49

Experiments in free machine embroidery

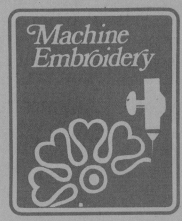

There is a great variety of stitches and techniques used to obtain effects in free machine embroidery, and this chapter gives detailed instructions on how to set up the sewing machine to achieve these effects. The illustrations opposite show the results of using these methods of free machine work and give an idea of the different textural patterns involved.

The dress and bolero shown in this chapter are an exclusive design, but you could adapt the idea to make a perfect going-away outfit. Choose commercial paper patterns for the dress and bolero which you can adapt and use the chart given overleaf as a guide to the embroidery.

Once the basic running and zigzag stitches are mastered, more advanced free machine embroidery stitches can be tried. These are made by altering machine tension, using thicker or metallic threads on the spool, or by catching threads too thick to use on the machine to the background fabric.

Whip stitch

Tightly stretch the fabric to be embroidered into a circular frame. Remove the presser foot, lower the feed teeth, and set the machine for running stitch. Loosen the spool tension from normal and tighten the top tension. This brings the bottom thread to the top of the work, making a beady corded stitch much thicker than the basic running stitch.

To produce a good neat stitch, move the hoop smoothly and slowly so that the little loops are close to one another. The top thread should not be seen. If the tensions are altered even more (by loosening the spool and tightening the top tension still further) a very exaggerated, spiky stitch results because the top thread is so tight. This stitch is best worked into circular shapes because it can then lie flat on the background fabric. A slightly thicker thread used on the bobbin gives an even more pronounced effect.

The choice of thread must be determined by the weave of the background fabric because thick threads will not easily pull through a tightly woven cloth.

When altering tensions, either on top of the machine or in the spool, make the alteration gradually, trying out the effect between each change.

Working in thicker threads

Begin by setting the machine for running stitch. Thicker threads such as pearl cotton No. 5 and 8, stranded cotton, thin wool and metallic threads are wound on to the spool by hand as described in Machine Embroidery Chapter 47

Machine embroidery cotton, or mercerised sewing cotton such as Sylko, is used on top of the machine. The work is machined face downwards because the interesting thread is in the spool. Spool tension should be loose and top tension either normal or slightly tight for working with these types of thread. If the speed of the

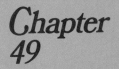

needle is kept steady and the fabric moved smoothly a cording effect will result. For really thick threads, keep the spool tension quite loose or it will pull too much on the background cloth.

Towelling stitch

With pearl cotton, stranded cotton or thin wool on the spool, a more loopy effect can be obtained by loosening the spool tension even more and tightening the top tension. By pushing the frame slowly under the needle, the loops have time to build up.

For a greater looped effect using a thick wool, such as double knitting wool, completely remove the tension

screw on the spool case. The free or darning foot is used so that larger areas of fabric can be covered at any one time without using a frame.

Always remember to lower the presser foot lever whether the foot is on the machine or not, as this engages the top tension.

Metal threads

Only metal threads which are specifically made for machine embroidery will stitch through fabric. Other kinds break and should be wound on to the spool by hand and worked from the wrong side.

Providing the fabric is not too tightly woven, lurex thread can be used for whip stitch. In this case, the Sylko thread

A striking example of the use of machine embroidery for fashion

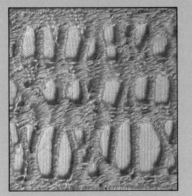

Drawn threads worked with zigzag

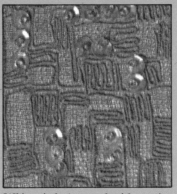

Embroidery on a printed organza

Whip stitch decorated with sequins

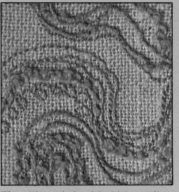

Towelling stitch with thick wool

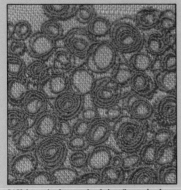

Whip stitch worked in fine circles

Thicker threads couched with zigzag

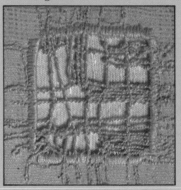

Flower design in fine whip stitch

Whip stitch decorated square hole

Satin stitch with metal thread

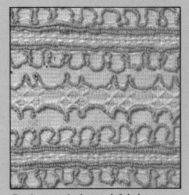

Design worked round fabric weave

Whip stitch in gold with beads

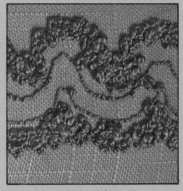

Towelling stitch with pearl cotton

on top must not show. When using metal threads, work very smoothly and at a slightly slower speed than with other kinds of threads. This is because a sudden jerk will snap the metal thread.

If you are working zigzag or straight stitch, the tension of the metal thread needs to be slightly looser than the Sylko thread. The Sylko remains on the wrong side of the work and the metal thread is smooth and the work completely metallic on the right side. If the metal thread is of a type which can be used on top of the machine, a larger needle should be used. Metallic threads look especially rich and decorative when used in zigzag stitch.

Fabric with unusual weaves

Zigzag stitch can be used most successfully on soft and open weave fabrics. A pulled fabric effect results on open weave fabrics, such as linen scrim, open furnishing nets etc., by working with machine embroidery cotton with both tensions slightly tighter than normal. The zigzag stitch pulls the open weave threads together and small motifs can be worked leaving large areas of the background fabric unworked. Alternatively, cover the fabric completely with hundreds of zigzag stitches touching each other so that the finished result is rich and textured. The best results with this technique are obtained with the fabric held

in a frame.

For drawn thread work and machine embroidery choose loose weave fabrics such as scrim, hessian or linen, and pull out the warp or weft threads (or both) using different widths of zigzag stitches. The effect is particularly interesting where the fabric is made up of two colours and the threads pulled out in either direction so that one colour remains.

Embroidering holes

Lacy effects are worked by using zigzag stitches round a shape in the design and then cutting the inside fabric away, leaving a hole. For a spider's web effect, for example, work

running stitch across the hole and then strengthen the stitches with a small zigzag stitch. To achieve this, the fabric must be in a frame and the tension of top and bottom threads exactly equal so that they twist round each other when worked across the space.

Very thick textured threads

Any thread which is too thick to be wound on to the spool, or too textured to pull through, can be caught to the fabric with a running or zigzag stitch. This method of couching by machine using the ordinary or free foot can be worked using knitting wool, weaving wool, string, raffia, ribbons, tapes or braids.

165

Free fashion embroidery

To make a bolero like the one illustrated, which was made up in a washable Courtelle fabric, first choose a commercial paper pattern and mark the outline of the garment on to the fabric. Some of the stitches described in this chapter have been incorporated into the bolero. The embroidery design is not repetitive but we give guide lines to trace for one front plus a large flower motif, which the more experienced embroiderer could adapt for the left front of the garment. Use a frame and either follow the guide accurately or improvise with your own ideas.

Do not cut out the pattern pieces until the embroidered design has been worked. Once the embroidery is finished, make up the bolero according to the pattern instructions.

Trace the outline of the design on these pages and use as a guide for free machine embroidery

Chapter 50

Introduction to canvas work

From the time that someone called the famous Bayeux panel a tapestry, people have been confused about what is embroidery, what is tapestry and what is canvas work.

In fact, the Bayeux panel is an example of early English embroidery, worked in wools on a linen fabric. Tapestry is always woven, in patterns and pictures, on a loom, with small sections woven individually, then stitched together by hand. When next you visit a museum, look carefully at the tapestries and you'll see how small some sections are.

Canvas work is embroidery on canvas. It was very popular in England and Europe from the early sixteenth century until the mid-eighteenth century, but then it marked time, until it was recently revived.

Now the lovely variety of traditional canvas work stitches, which have for so long been neglected, are enjoying a new importance. They are being used in fabulous modern designs, often with unusual new yarns which were not formerly associated with embroidery.

Today, canvas work is an adventure in the use of stitches, yarns, and abstract designs which lend themselves to the square formation of the stitches.

Colourful, textured and tough

The attraction of canvas work today, apart from the fact that it is hand-made and not mass produced, is that all-over embroidery on canvas makes objects and decorations which are really tough and hard-wearing.

It is simple to do, and you have only to visit the yarn counter of any shop to be inspired. Brilliant silks, metallic threads, stranded shiny cottons, soft matt cottons, new knobbly-textured wools and bright plastic raffia all come in a myriad of beautiful colours.

As well as the colour, the success of all canvas embroidery depends upon the texture of the stitches and the threads.

Canvas size

The canvas must be firm, supple, and evenly woven, and the number of threads per centimetre can vary from 48 per 5cm for fine work, to 6 per 5cm for very coarse work.

There are two types, single thread canvas and double thread canvas. You can also use evenly woven fabrics such as Aida cloth, or Hardanger, and even-weave linens or woollen fabrics.

Single thread canvas is measured by the number of threads to 5cm and double thread canvas is measured to the number of double threads to 5cm. Single weave canvas is the best to use since it is possible to embroider a wide variety of stitches on it, whereas double weave is restricted to four or five only.

Needles

Use tapestry needles with large eyes and blunt points. They are available in a variety of sizes, of which sizes 18-21 are the most popular, but size 14 is better for very coarse material.

Frames

Canvas work should be worked in a slate frame. This helps you to maintain the correct shape of the work while it is being embroidered. Small items which you can easily hold in your hand need not be framed. See Embroidery Chapter 13.

Yarns

In canvas work the stitches must completely cover the canvas. Threads are available in differing thicknesses and some are made up of several individual strands which are twisted together but can be separated as required. To cover the canvas you need to use the correct thickness of thread. If, however, the thread coverage looks thin and mean, you should pad it out with the technique known as tramming to fill the space. Never use too long a yarn as it will wear thin and your work will look uneven and tired. If you find the yarn becoming thin or fluffy, start a new length of yarn at once. It is usually quicker to use a short length—which is a yarn about 30 to 36cm long.

A modern cushion, designed by Joan Nicholson for Penelope's Simpler Range, with abstract pattern repeats, and clear bright colours

The right yarn for the canvas

1. Double thread canvas
12 double threads to 5cm
Yarns: tapestry wool, crewel wool, 4-ply knitting yarns, Pearl cotton, stranded cotton, linen embroidery thread, metallic yarns, stranded pure silk

2. Double thread canvas
20 double threads to 5cm
Yarns as for No.1 plus double knitting yarns, plastic raffia

3. Coin net
24 threads to 2·5cm
Yarns as for No.1

4. Single weave canvas
36 threads to 5cm
Yarns as for No.1 and No.2 plus knitting yarns in a variety of textures such as mohair, tweed, metallic and wool mixtures, soft embroidery cotton, carpet thrums, Rya rug wool, applied braids and cords, spinning yarns

5. Single weave
20 threads to 5cm
Yarns as for No.1 and No.2 and No.4 using more than one thickness of yarn where necessary plus fine ribbons, strings

Check off your canvas information against the picture on the right ▶

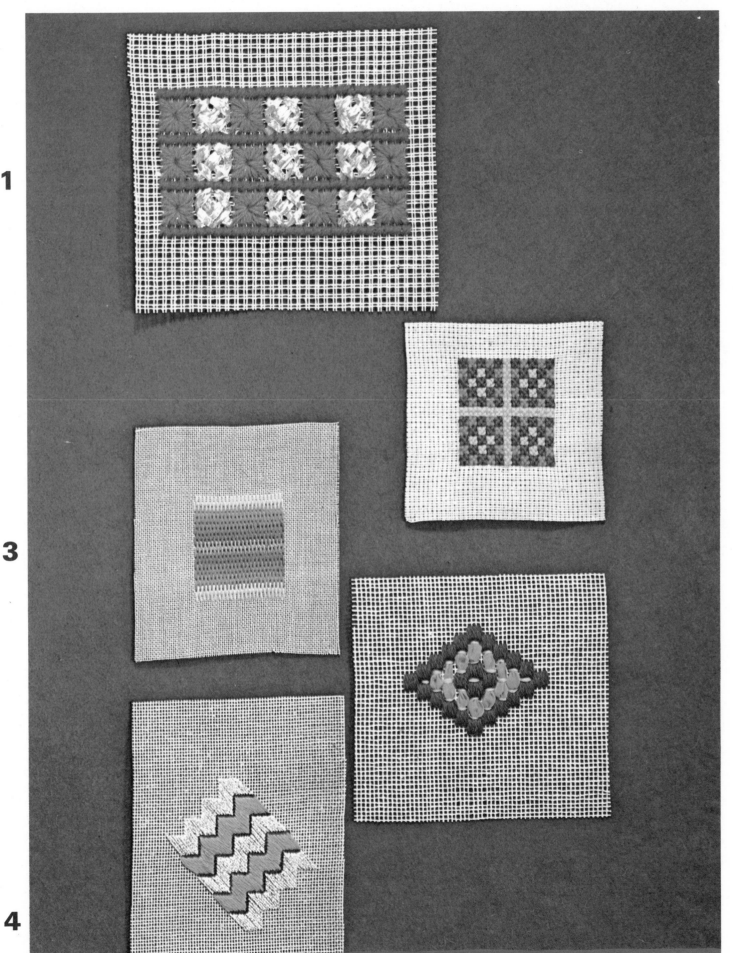

1

2

3

4

5

Chapter 51

Introduction to half cross stitch

Half cross stitch is hard-wearing—smooth, flat and ideal for things which need to be tough, like stool and chair seats. But because it is so simple to do, it is one of the best stitches to use for any small scale patterns. In this chapter we explain how to work half cross stitch and also tramming, which serves as a padding stitch. Incorporate both these methods of stitching into making the buttons illustrated on the opposite page.

Half cross stitch

This stitch is worked as shown, from left to right. Up through the canvas from bottom left, down through the next 'hole' on top right. This makes a diagonal stitch on the front and a short straight stitch on the back.
Fasten off at the end of each patch of colour and begin again so that you do not leave long lengths of thread at the back.

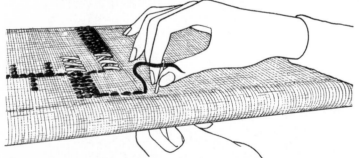

The drawing shows the method used when working in a frame.

Tramming

Tramming is a padding stitch which is used when the thread is not thick enough to cover the canvas completely.
The tramming wool runs along each horizontal single canvas thread, or pairs of thread (called 'tramlines') as shown in the illustration right. Bring the thread up through these tramlines, leaving a short tail at the back. Work in overlapping tramming stitches, not more than about 12·5cm long, for the length of your working area. Then take the thread down through the tramlines again. Work the stitch over the tramming thread, binding in the tramming tails as you go.

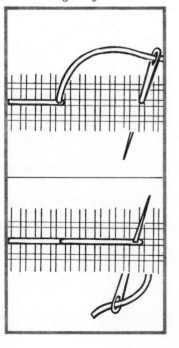

▲ *Half cross stitch.*
▼ *The stitch worked over tramming*

How to make the buttons

Use do-it-yourself buttons which come in four sizes from most haberdashery departments. Here are five designs to start with, plus a chart to show you the right fabric and thread to use for each size of button. Always use an even-weave cloth.
The chart gives the turning allowance which will take the worked material safely over the edge to the back of the button. Simply draw a circle round the button, allowing enough for the turnings as well, and you are ready to start stitching.

N.B. The snap-together buttons are simple to make and come with easy-to-follow instructions on the packet, but if you prefer, your local Singer shop will turn the finished work into buttons. Use half cross stitch, trammed, or untrammed, as you find it necessary. (The background could be worked in long-legged cross stitch for a more exciting textural effect). Follow the exact number of stitches shown in the picture. To work out your own patterns, plot them out first on squared graph paper with coloured pencils.

The yarns used here are Anchor Stranded Cotton, Anchor Pearl Cotton, Anchor Tapisserie Wool and Appletons Crewel Wool

170

Trim button size + turning	Fabric threads to 2·5cm	Suggested threads
2cm +3mm turning	28	3 strands of stranded cotton 2 strands of crewel wool Pearl cotton
2·3cm +3mm turning	25	4 strands of stranded cotton
2·8cm +6mm turning	18	6 strands of stranded cotton
4cm +6mm turning	14 Aida cloth (14 blocks of thread to 2·5cm)	6 strands of stranded cotton tapestry wool raffia 4-ply knitting

How to start

1. Find the centre of the piece of canvas by folding it in half twice; mark the centre lightly with a coloured crayon or thread. Start in the centre, but instead of using a knot, draw the needle up through the canvas, leaving a tail about 1·3cm long at the back.

2. Hold this thread close to the canvas and work over it, binding it in with the first few stitches (which are seen here from the back).

To finish off

Darn the thread into the stitches at the back of your work to secure it. To continue with a new thread, darn its tail into back of the previous row.
Never allow any of these threads to accumulate in one place as this results in unsightly bumps.

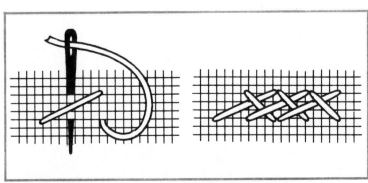

▲ *Long-legged cross stitch, a simple but effective variation*

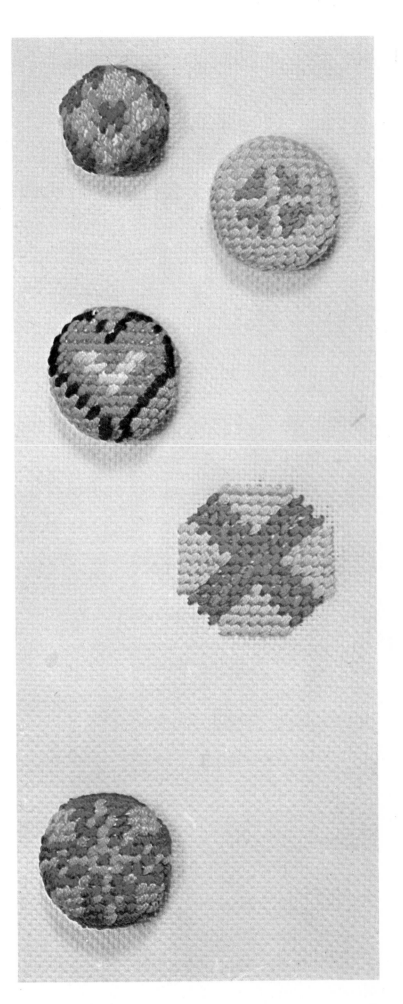

Chapter 52

Designs in half cross stitch

Adapted from a tile patterned wallpaper, this striking design in chunky yarns is quick to work. The stitch used here is half cross stitch (see Canvas Work Chapter 60) but other stitches can be used to create more textured effects. Several exciting ideas for using the design are illustrated and similar designs can be lifted from pottery tiles.

To work the panel measuring 45cm square you will need:
- ☐ Piece of single weave canvas 61cm square with 21 threads to 5cm
- ☐ Piece of lining fabric measuring 51cm square
- ☐ Piece of ply wood cut to measure 45cm square for mounting
- ☐ Tapestry needle size 18
- ☐ DMC Art 313 Embroidery Wool in the following colours and amounts: 7 skeins blue 7317; 6 skeins blue 7313; 5 skeins blue 7314; 1 skein blue 7307; 4 skeins green 7351; 2 skeins green 7346; 1 skein green 7428; 5 skeins white

To work the panel
Work the panel in half cross stitch over one thread of the canvas. Stretch completed work and mount the panel over the wood. Finish the edges with a finger knotted cord and four large tassels. Make a further length of finger knotted cord to hang the panel.

▼ *This chart shows $\frac{1}{4}$ of the design. Each square = 1 stitch*

Chapter 53

A bolero in half cross stitch

This beautiful bolero is specially designed for Golden Hands, with two colour schemes to choose from. On this page is the graph for the pattern—turn over for embroidery chart

What you will need to make the bolero:

- ☐ 70cm double weave canvas with 20 double threads to 5cm
- ☐ 60cm corduroy or velvet 90cm wide for back of bolero
- ☐ 1·20m lining 90cm wide
- ☐ 3·2m folded braid
- ☐ Sewing cotton
- ☐ Anchor Tapisserie Wools
- ☐ Soft lead pencil
- ☐ Graph paper

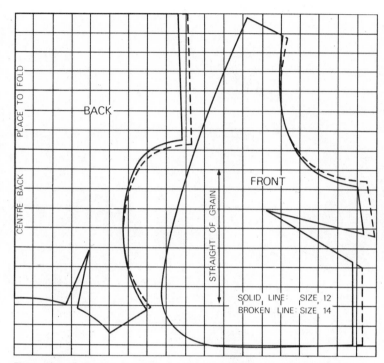

Pattern graph for Front and Back of bolero. Each sq = 2·5cm. Solid line = 87cm bust, broken line = 92cm bust. Pattern is without seam allowance

The pattern

Simply copy the pattern for your size from the graph on this page on to squared paper. Cut out the pattern. The graph pattern is given in 87cm and 92cm bust sizes only, but you can, if you need to, use a commercial bolero pattern in a larger size. Simply extend background stitching over the extra canvas. For larger sizes remember to check yardage and background yarn amounts.

Transfer the outline for the bolero Fronts on to the canvas by tacking the pattern in place, then drawing round the edge and into the darts accurately with a soft pencil. Now work the design on to both sections (full design details on next page). Complete the stitching before cutting out the Fronts, as you need the rectangle of canvas to enable you to set the work up in a slate or rectangular frame. (It is essential to frame work this size, to keep it in shape.)

Stitching the design

The original design was worked in half cross stitch with the centres of some of the flowers in slanting Gobelin stitch (see Canvas Work Chapter 59) and cross stitch. You can add more texture stitches if you wish, but be careful not to use too many or you may detract from the design itself. Alternatively, if you prefer, you can use tent stitch throughout (see Canvas Work Chapter 59). Work the stitching right up to the traced edges and just over the dart line, so that no canvas shows when the darts are closed.

Cutting out

When the design is completed, stretch and trim the canvas as described in Canvas Work Chapter 64 leaving 1·6cm turnings on shoulder and side-seams only. Trim the canvas as close to all other edges as possible without cutting into the stitching. Cut out the back of the bolero from the corduroy and then cut out lining to match both the Back and the Fronts, allowing 1·6cm seam allowance on the side- and shoulder-seams.

Making up

Stitch the darts on the bolero Fronts either by machine or with a firm back stitch. Slash up the centre of the dart and press it open with a slightly damp cloth and a medium hot iron. Trim away canvas to 1·6cm, tapering off to point of dart. Stitch darts on back of bolero and stitch side- and shoulder-seams. Press seams open. Stitch the lining in the same way and then place bolero and lining together, wrong sides facing. Tack round edge of bolero and round armholes, matching up seams of lining to those of bolero. Work a line of machining or back stitch 6mm in from all edges and then cover with braiding as follows.

Turn under 1·6cm at one end of the braid and start pinning it to the right side of the bolero from a side-seam. Stretch the braid slightly as you pin so that it lies smoothly round the curves. Neaten the end of the braid by turning in 1·6cm and stitching it to join at the seam. Stitch the braid on the right side with a small, neat hem stitch and then hem braid to lining. Use thread the colour of the braid.

Below: one Front worked in the alternative colourway Right: the bolero

Simply work the design from this chart. Each square represents one
half cross stitch.

Normally it is usual to start working a charted design from the
centre, but in this case it is vitally important to commence working
from the point of the dart, to ensure accurate placing of the design
so that it will fit into the shaping of the bolero.

Wool quantities

The numbers in the charts below refer to Anchor Tapisserie Wool
colours.

Area		Blue/Green Colourway Wool Number	Red/Olive Colourway Wool Number	Skein Quantities
Background	☐	lime 0279	olive 0422	7
Leaves	◼	blue 0133	red 065	4
Leaves	◣	green 0229	orange 0334	4
Leaves	⊞	grey 0398	pink 0894	2
Flowers	⊙	blue 0168	blue 0105	3
Flowers and Flower Centres	⊡	mauve 0106	pink 085	2
Flowers	⊙	pink 0893	orange 0314	2
Flowers	▼	purple 0107	magenta 089	2
Large Flower Centres	▷	slate blue 0849	dark pink 0429	1
Flower Centres	⊠	blue 0170	mauve 0122	2
Flower Centres	⊠	green 0280	pale green 0842	2
Flower Centres	▣	dusty pink 0339	salmon pink 0337	1

176

Chapter 54

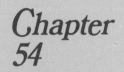

Buckles and watchstraps in cross stitch

▲▼ Vibrant pink and red design as a belt buckle

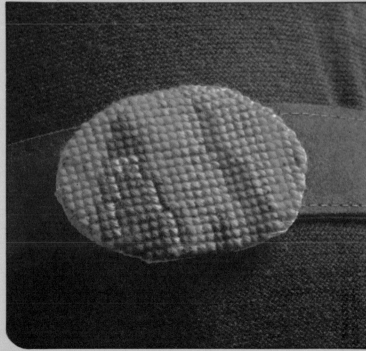

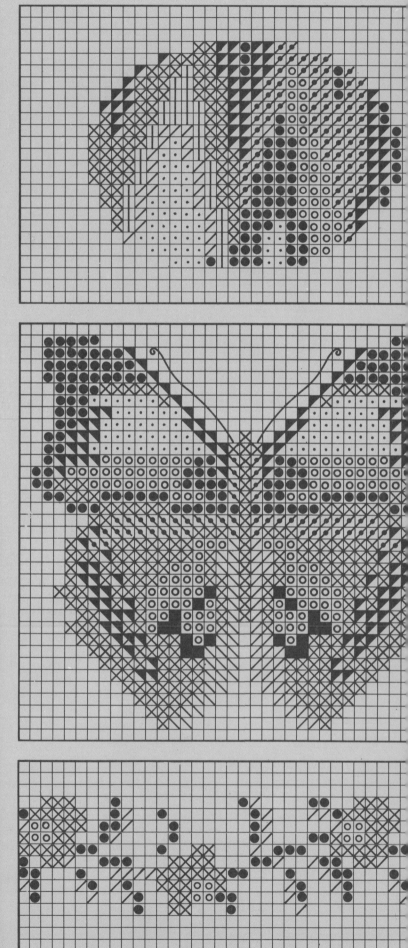

Quick-to-make canvas accessories to make you feel special or to work for a friend. Two charming motifs to wear as belt or shoe buckles and two watchstrap designs, one striped and one patterned with rose-buds.

Stitches used

All the designs given in this chapter are worked in cross stitch (Embroidery Chapter 34) on fine mesh canvas. Colour key working charts are given for the two buckles and for the rosebud watchstrap. Work the striped watch by using the illustration as a guide.

Oval buckle

To make the oval buckle measuring about 7cm by 5cm you will need:
☐ Canvas with 20 double threads to 5cm, 15cm square
☐ Anchor Tapisserie Wool in the following colours (1 skein of each): cerise 063; orange 0335; dark red 013; brownish red 0897; dark pink 085; pink 037; oxblood red 019; lilac 0106
☐ Small piece strong cardboard
☐ Small piece foam plastic 6mm thick
☐ Small piece lining fabric
☐ Tapestry needle No. 18

To make

Work the design in cross stitch from the chart and complete the buckle in the same way as instructed for the butterfly buckle.

Butterfly shoe buckle

To make the butterfly buckle, measuring about 7cm by 6cm, you will need:
☐ Double weave canvas with 28 double threads to 5cm, 15cm square
☐ Small piece strong cardboard
☐ Small piece foam plastic 6 mm thick
☐ Small piece lining fabric
☐ Tapestry needle No.24
☐ Anchor Stranded Cotton 1 skein each in the following colours: dark red 020; orange 010; dark brown 0360; light brown 0369; blue 0119; pink 074; lilac 0107; deep pink 063; background worked in off white 0390

To make

Using four strands of cotton in the needle work the design in cross stitch from the chart. When the work is completed, stretch the canvas. Cut a piece of cardboard slightly smaller than the area of worked canvas. Glue a piece of foam plastic to the card and trim it to the shape of the card. Stretch the canvas work centrally over the cardboard and lace firmly in place using strong cotton. Cover the back of the buckle neatly with a piece of lining cut to the same shape as the buckle with edges turned in.

Watchstraps

To make the watchstraps you will need:
For Rosebud strap:
☐ Single weave canvas with 36 threads to 5cm
☐ Anchor Stranded Cotton—one skein each in the following colours: light green 0264; olive green 0889; light pink 060; cerise 064; the background is bright green 0267
For striped strap:
☐ Canvas with 20 double threads to 5cm
☐ Anchor Tapisserie Wool—one skein each in the following colours: dark red 019; deep pink 063; and light pink 085
For both straps:
☐ Ribbon or lining fabric to neaten back of strap
☐ Velcro fastening or buckle

To make

Work from the chart, finish off and sew on buckle or velcro fastening.

▼ *Butterfly buckle motif for a pretty shoe*

▼ *Watchstraps, striped and patterned with rosebuds*

Chapter 55

Flowered wall panels in cross stitch

These delightful Art Deco flowers bring a modern look to canvas work and are something you could design yourself. By changing the colour scheme you can completely change the mood of the panel, using bright, clear colours for summer flowers, as in the summer flowers panel on the opposite page, or rusty yellows and oranges for the autumn ones below.

▼ *This wall panel depicts flowers in the mellow tones of autumn*

Apart from single and double weave canvas you can also use many canvas work stitches on softer cotton or jute cloths with Aida weaves. True Aida cloth is a cotton embroidery fabric woven in blocks of threads. It has a slightly starched finish which launders out once the embroidery is completed. This cloth is too fine for standard canvas work wools but the jute canvas with Aida weave, which comes in one size only, gives twelve cross stitches per 5cm. This produces quick results and these bold wall panels can be worked in just a few hours. Alternatively, use Binca cloth which is similar.

Summer flowers panel

Materials you will need
☐ 50cm Aida weave jute canvas (finished size about 38cm square)
☐ Tapestry needle size 18
☐ Hardboard or softboard 38cm square
☐ 1 skein white, 3 skeins orange, 3 skeins blue, 1 skein brown, 9 skeins pink, 2 skeins yellow, 6 skeins green, 12 skeins turquoise (background)

NB You can use either soft embroidery cotton or tapisserie wool. The amounts given above are for tapisserie wool which has 13·7m to the skein, whereas soft embroidery cotton skeins contain 9·5m Allowing for an equivalent length, in some cases more skeins of soft embroidery cotton will be required. Use one strand throughout.

To work the picture
First find the centre of the canvas by working two lines of tacking, one from side to side and one from top to bottom as indicated by the arrows (see Canvas Work Chapter 60). Work the design by counting out from the centre of the chart, outlining the shapes in back stitch first then fill in the design with cross stitch (see Embroidery Chapter 34). Each cross stitch is worked following the weave of the canvas, which is divided into squares.

To mount the finished work
When the design is completed, stretch the canvas as described in Canvas Work Chapter 64. Trim the board to the exact finished size of the panel. Lay the board centrally over the back of the work and lace the canvas with fine string, picking up the fabric well in from the edge. Take the lacing across the back from side to side and then repeat the process from top to bottom. Pull the lacing firmly so that the work is evenly stretched without puckering. Secure the ends of the string by knotting them several times.
If you want to hang the panel unframed, make the work neat by sewing unbleached calico or holland over the back to conceal the lacing.

Autumn flowers panel

Designing your own picture
To design a flower picture such as the one shown here, working on stiff paper, simply draw round drinking glasses to form the flower shapes. Cut out several flowers in varying sizes and then arrange them, overlapping, until you achieve a pleasing effect. Trace the outline of the design on to the canvas and work in cross stitch as for the summer flowers.

Larger scale canvas work
To work to an even larger scale use rug wools or two strands of double knitting wool on continental jute, which is made for rugs and has a similar weave to Aida cloth, which will give 8 cross stitches to 5cm. Worked on this larger scale canvas, the summer flowers panel will measure about 56cm square.

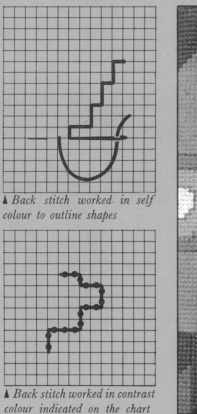

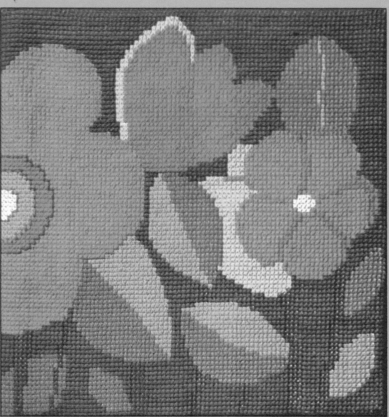

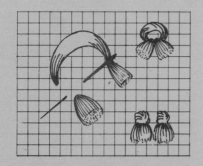

▲ *Back stitch worked in self colour to outline shapes*

▲ *Back stitch worked in contrast colour indicated on the chart*

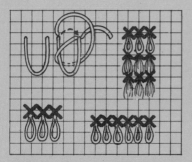

▲ CENTRE

Stitch Library

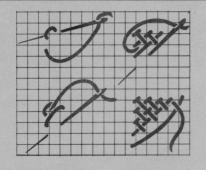

Single or tufted stitch
The stitches are worked between each other in alternate rows and imitate carpet knotting

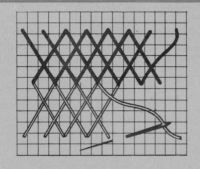

Velvet or astrakhan stitch
All the stitches should be worked before any of the loops are cut

Web stitch
Web stitch gives a woven effect and is useful as a filling for small areas

Plaited Algerian stitch
This is worked in the same way as closed herringbone stitch

Chapter 56

A cushion and rug in cross stitch

This cross stitched design of pink roses, syringa blossom and burnished autumn leaves looks just as beautiful whether worked on a rug or adapted to a cushion or framed picture. The design chart and colour key are on the following pages.

Cross stitched cushion

You will need:
☐ 60cm 90cm single thread canvas (28 threads to 5cm)
☐ Tapisserie or crewel yarns (see colour and quantity key)
☐ 60cm 90cm material for backing (e.g. velvet or corduroy)
☐ Tapestry needle size 19
☐ 50cm zip to match backing material
☐ Cushion pad 40·5cm deep by 61cm wide
☐ Sewing cotton
(Finished size of cushion 44·5cm deep by 62cm wide)

Stitching the design
Binding the raw edges with 2·5cm wide tape to prevent fraying, find the centre of the canvas and mark it with a pencil or a line of tacking thread. Using cross stitch worked over two threads of canvas (see Embroidery Chapter 34), work the design from the centre outwards.

Yarns and colour schemes
Although tapisserie and crewel yarns are fairly easily obtainable, alternative types of wool can be used to give a wider choice of colours and texture. Double and 4 ply knitting wools and Shetland wools are all suitable for single weave canvas.
The background colour of the cushion shown here is a very light grey, and the rug border is deep olive green, which will tone in with most room colour schemes, but it is quite simple to adapt a charted design to match different colour combinations. Select your alternative colours and indicate them beside the symbols on the colour key, covering the original colours to avoid confusion.

Making up and finishing
When you have finished stitching the design, stretch the canvas (see Canvas Work Chapter 64) and trim away excess fabric, leaving 1·6cm canvas all round for seam allowance. Overcast the edges to prevent fraying. Lay and pin the finished canvas work on the backing material and cut the cushion back to the same size as the front. With right sides facing, pin and tack the canvas work and the back together, along the seam allowance. Working as close to the cross stitches as possible, machine stitch or back stitch round three sides and each end of the fourth, long, side leaving 50cm unstitched for inserting the zip. Trim each corner diagonally and oversew the trimmed edge.
Turn the cushion cover to the right side and gently poke out the corners using a blunt pencil. (Don't push too hard or the fabric

Pink roses in cross stitch add welcoming colour to a couch

may split.) Still working from the right side, tack the seam allowance of the zip opening back against the inside of the cushion cover. Keeping the zip closed, pin and tack the zip into position along one side of the opening. Open the zip carefully and pin and tack the other side. Stitch the zip by hand using a half back stitch (similar to back stitch but a tiny stitch is taken up on the surface and a longer stitch underneath). The zipped fastening enables the cushion pad to be removed so that the cushion cover can be cleaned (canvas work should never be washed) but if the cover is not going to be cleaned, it is possible to close the cushion by oversewing the fourth side.

The cross stitched rug

You will need:
☐ 70cm of 90cm wide canvas (20 double threads to 5cm)
☐ Tapestry needle size 14
☐ Tapisserie wool or carpet thrums
(142g of yarn for 30cm square of canvas approximately)

The rose, syringa and leaf design in a rug with a classic border

The cross stitch cushion

The cross stitch rug

Carpet thrums are the ends cut from the loom when carpet weaving is finished and provide excellent material for rugs as regards both colours and wearing qualities.

It is worth remembering however that a considerable quantity of one colour is required for the border of the rug and the background. It is advisable therefore to buy sufficient thrums at one time as colours are inclined to vary each time they are purchased from different dye lots.

Making the rug

Using both sections of the chart, the centre design (used for the cushion) and the border design, work from the centre outwards in cross stitch over one double thread each way (see Embroidery Chapter 34).

Finishing

When you have finished stitching the design, stretch the canvas and trim away excess fabric, leaving 4cm of canvas all round. Oversew to prevent fraying and turn the 4cm edge under to the wrong side. Pin and tack the turned hem, finishing the rug with hem stitching all round, using strong cotton.

185

CENTRE

CENTRE

CENTRE

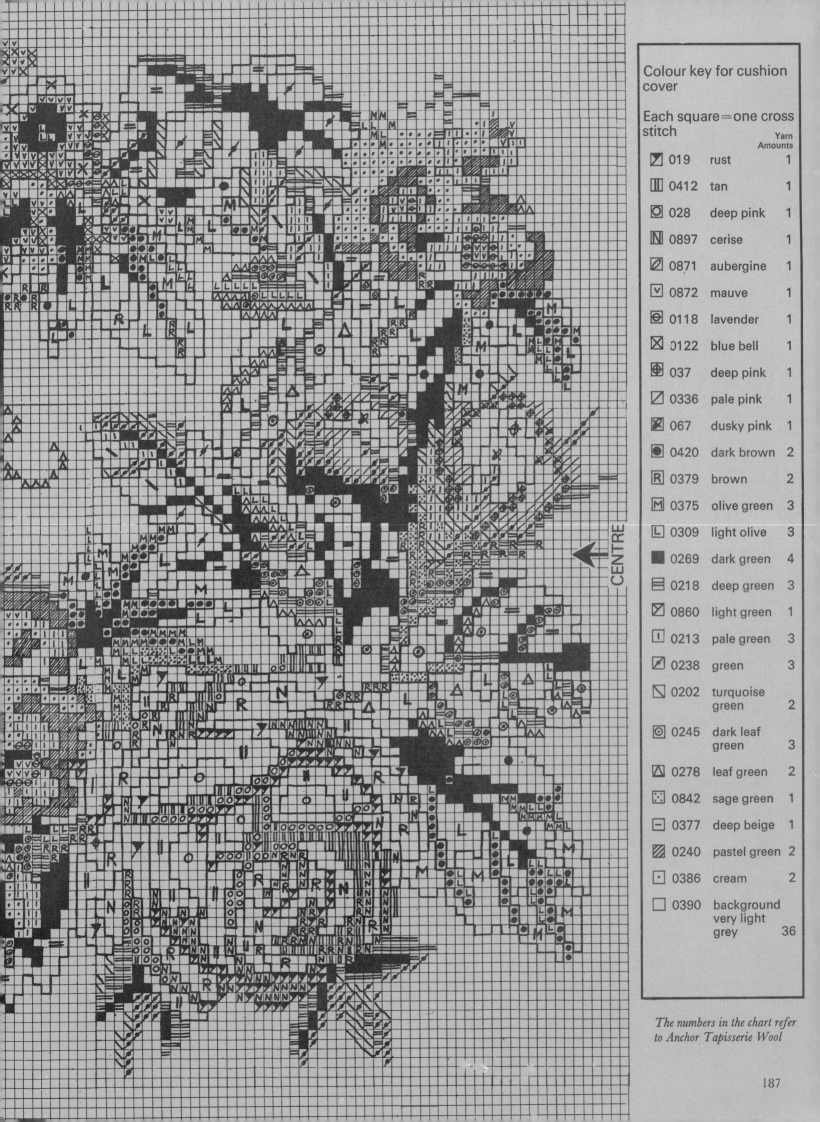

CENTRE

187

CENTRE

Chart for the cross stitched rug border

One quarter of the rug border is shown. Use the cushion cover chart for centre of rug, extending design with the border.

188   *Diagram shows how to fit the four quarters of the rug border together with the rug centre design (used for the cushion)*

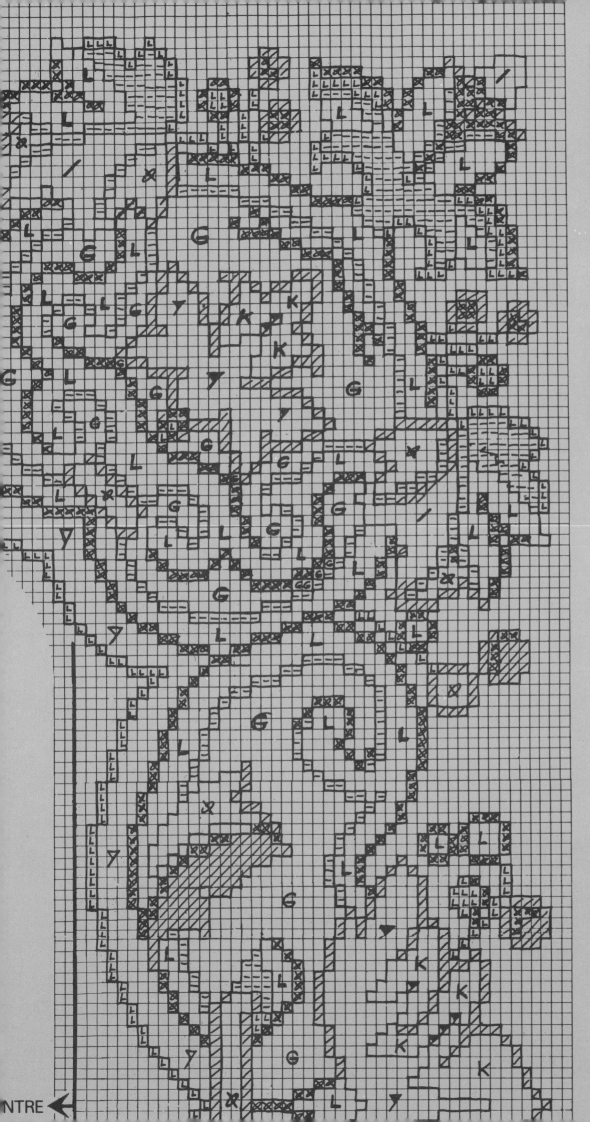

Colour key for rug border

Each square = one cross stitch

			Yarn Amounts
⊠	019	rust	6
⊠	0337	salmon pink	8
⊠	0860	light green	12
L	0309	light olive	24
G	0376	beige	24
K	013	red	4
−	0377	deep beige	12
⧄	0336	pale pink	12
□	0375	background to rug edge olive green	48

The numbers in the chart refer to Anchor Tapisserie Wool

NTRE

Chapter 57

Panel using a variety of stitches

This dragon design, in a dramatic range of reds and pinks, is shown on a chart so that you can make it in practically any size you wish by choosing a larger or smaller mesh canvas and coarser or finer yarns to correspond.

Work a small dragon to guard your jewels on the lid of a jewel box or a larger one for a picture or wall-hanging. The magnificence of this design would be impressive on a headboard, cushion cover, rug or firescreen, too.

The small dragon is worked completely in stranded cotton but the larger one is worked on heavier canvas using some stranded cotton together with tapisserie wool and soft embroidery cotton. Using a mixture of yarns will give you experience in variations of texture and show how the planning of different stitches and yarns can add enormously to the finished effect of the work.

Materials you will need
Small dragon (below)
- [ ] Single weave canvas 30·5cm by 23cm with 40 or 44 threads to 5cm: finished size 18cm by 12·5cm
- [ ] One skein each of Anchor Stranded Cotton No.09, 010, 011, 013, 019, 031, 039, 043, 044, 057, 065, 066, 069, 072 and two skeins of 045
- [ ] Tapestry needle size 22

Large dragon (right)
- [ ] Single weave canvas 51cm by 45·5cm with 26 threads to 5cm: finished size 41cm by 28cm
- [ ] One skein each of Stranded Cotton No.039, 057, 043, 044, 013; Soft Embroidery Cotton No.031, 011, 078, 028, 044, 019; Tapisserie Wool No.09, 010, 013, 019, 0897, 065, 0895; two skeins Soft Embroidery Cotton No.043, three skeins of No. 076; twelve skeins Tapisserie Wool No.045
- [ ] Tapestry needle size 18

How to use the stitch and design charts

For the small dragon, follow the chart using each square as one stitch. For a larger dragon, one square on the chart represents four squares of canvas. The boldly drawn black lines separate different parts of the dragon's body, described on the stitch chart here and small chart, bottom right. The numbers on the stitch chart refer to Anchor yarns.

Part of Dragon	Stitch Reference	Symbol	SMALL DRAGON Stranded Cotton	LARGE DRAGON Stranded Cotton (12 strands)	Soft Embroidery Cotton (2 strands)	Tapisserie Wool (2 strands)
Eye	Detached eyelet		031 (3 strands)			
Eye surround	1 row long-legged cross stitch		039 (6)	039	031	
Nose	Work 1 rice stitch		09 (6)			09
Upper and lower jaws	Work in cross stitch see Embroidery Chapter 41		013 (9), 043, 019, 039, 010, 09	013, 043, 039	043, 028	013, 019, 010, 09
Ears	Slanted Gobelin / Long-legged cross stitch		065 (4), 069, 043 (6), 039		078, 043, 028	065
Mane	In three shades work short bands in padded satin stitch. Work long bands in long-legged cross stitch		013 (6), 043, 039, 066			0895
Band down back	Work slanted Gobelin stitch over number of threads indicated by chart see Canvas Work Chapter 68		065 (4), 043, 013, 011, 019	043		065, 013
Top of head and neck	Use upright oblong cross-stitch, filling in odd corners with cross stitch. Work back stitch (3 strands) between the rows		043 (9), 065, 039, 057, 066		043	065
Tail —textured bands	Upright oblong cross stitch filling corners with cross stitch		031 (9), 057, 039, 065	039	031, 076	065
—satin bands	Slanted Gobelin over number of threads indicated by chart		069 (4), 010, 013, 039, 043, 019	039, 043	078	010, 013, 019
Blocks at base of tail	Rice stitch		069 (6), 065		078	065

LARGE DRAGON

Part of Dragon	Stitch Reference	Symbol	SMALL DRAGON Stranded Cotton	Stranded Cotton (12 strands)	LARGE DRAGON Soft Embroidery Cotton (2 strands)	Tapisserie Wool (2 strands)
Tail tip	Long-legged cross stitch		039 (6), 057, 043		028, 076, 043	
Chest	Alternate diagonal rows of: Algerian eye stitch, Rice stitch		057 (4), 039 (6), 019, 031, 011		076, 028	019
Bands across front legs	Slanted Gobelin in rows over number of threads indicated by chart		043 (4), 065, 057		043, 076	065
Rest of legs, front and back	Italian cross stitch		065 (6), 057, 066, 039, 043, 013, 011		076, 028, 043, 011	0895, 013
Claws	Padded satin stitch		011 (6), 013, 019, 039, 057, 066		011	013, 019, 0895
Hips	Cushion stitch squares, alternating direction. Work back stitch (2 strands) between squares		043 (4), 019, 039, 013, 010, 011	039, 057	043, 028, 011	043, 019, 010, 09
Flowers	Make a cross as indicated by heavy lines using straight stitches. Work four blocks of satin stitch over arms of cross		044 (6), 043, 011, 039, 031, 057, 065	044	043, 011, 028, 031, 076	065, 019, 0897
Stalk	Long-legged cross stitch		044 (6)		044	045
Background	Work 1 row tent stitch round dragon and fill background with alternating tent stitch for small dragon, bricking for large dragon. Use tent stitch between paws and round tail tip. Alternatively speckle by using 1 thread of darker shade with 4 of main		045 (5), 072 (1)			0897

Stitch Library

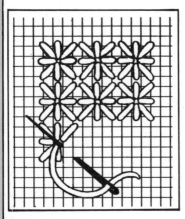

Star stitch
Work clockwise round the star in diagonal rows, until all eight points are completed. (Algerian eye stitch is worked in the same way but sew round the star twice for a more cushioned effect.)

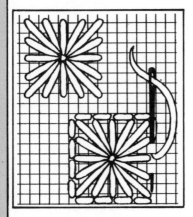

Detached eyelets
Work stitches radiating outwards from the central point. Take a backstitch over two threads round the outside of the eyelet. The eyelet shown in the diagram is worked with eight stitches over four threads of single weave canvas but if a larger one is required work over three or four threads of the canvas for each stitch.

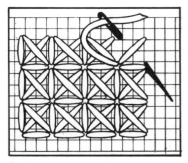

Italian cross stitch
Work in two stages. In the first stage vertical, diagonal and horizontal stitches are worked over three or four threads repeated along the row from left to right. From right to left work the second stage of cross stitch over the first diagonal.

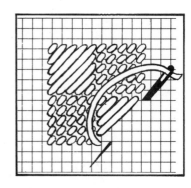

Leaf stitch
Work stitches round the leaf shape bringing the needle inwards to the centre from the outside edge.

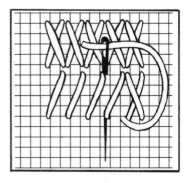

Padded satin stitch
Work satin stitch over a line of horizontal stitches to give a more padded effect.

Rice stitch
Rice stitch consists of ordinary cross stitch with the arms crossed by bars of cross stitch in the same or different coloured thread.

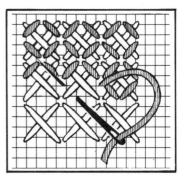

Chequer stitch
Work alternate blocks of tent stitch and cushion stitch.

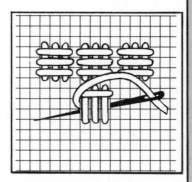

Oblong cross stitch
Work cross stitch inserting the needle four holes down, two holes across and so on.

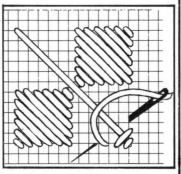

Cushion stitch
Work diagonal stitches into the shape of a square. The diagonal stitch through the centre shows the method for padding this gap.

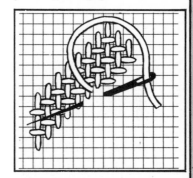

Tile stitch
Work upright cross stitch so that the upper stitch is alternately vertical and horizontal.

Blocked satin stitch
Cover three vertical satin stitches by three horizontal satin stitches.

Yarn key for dragons

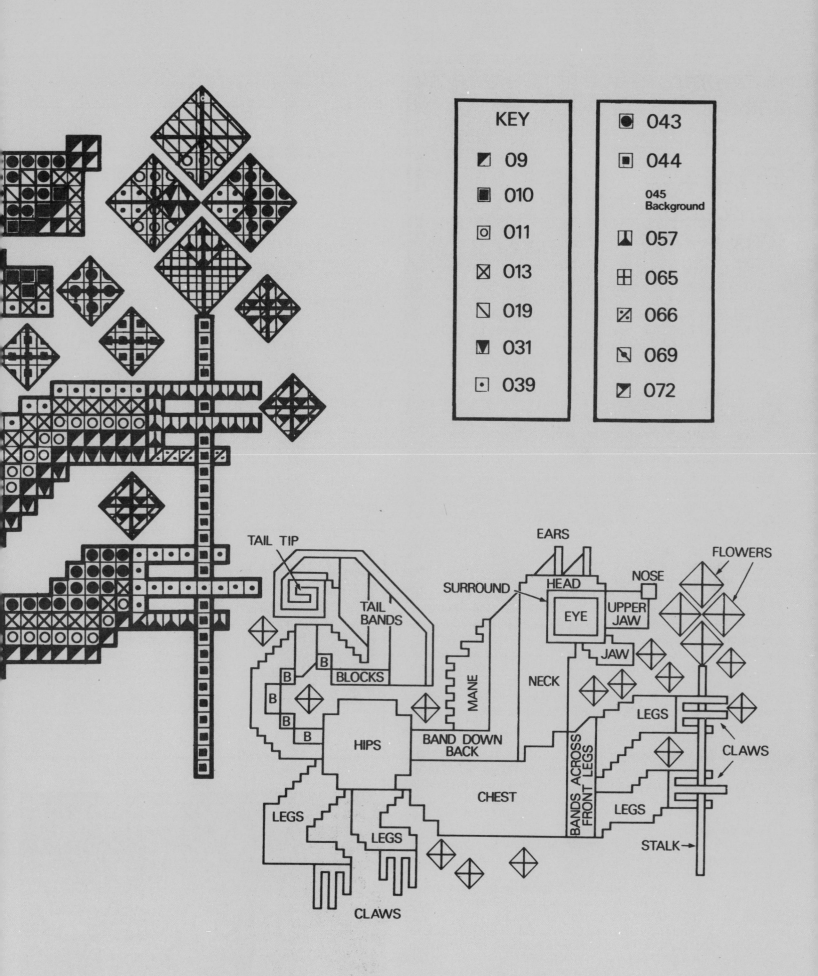

KEY

◪	09
◼	010
◉	011
⊠	013
◹	019
◢	031
⊡	039

◉	043
◼	044
	045 Background
◭	057
⊞	065
◪	066
◣	069
◪	072

TAIL TIP

TAIL BANDS

EARS

SURROUND

HEAD

NOSE

EYE

UPPER JAW

JAW

FLOWERS

B

B

BLOCKS

B

B

B

NECK

MANE

LEGS

CLAWS

HIPS

BAND DOWN BACK

BANDS ACROSS FRONT LEGS

CHEST

LEGS

LEGS

LEGS

STALK→

CLAWS

195

Chapter 58

A tote bag in double cross stitch

Canvas work is ideal for making all kinds of bags, from elegant evening purses worked in fine silk to casual hold-alls in colourful wool. By following the chart overleaf you can make this richly decorated tote bag, which is worked in tapisserie wool with touches of plastic raffia.

Tote bag

Materials you will need to work both sides of the bag
- ☐ 50cm single weave canvas 90cm wide, 36 threads to 5cm
- ☐ 50cm lining material, 90cm wide
- ☐ Two skeins each of Anchor Tapisserie Wool in dark blue No. 0148, blue No. 0168, green No. 0239, pink No. 085, turquoise No. 0203, lime green No. 0290; four skeins pale blue No. 0167; twenty skeins purple No. 0107
- ☐ Two skeins purple plastic raffia
- ☐ Tapestry needle No.18

To use the pattern
Draw the outline of the bag from the chart on to strong paper and cut out. Tack the pattern on to the canvas, leaving plenty of space round the shape for 1·6cm seam allowance and stretching. Also make sure that the grain line on the pattern follows the grain of the canvas.

Draw round the outline of the pattern using a felt-tipped pen, or mark with tacking stitches. Remove the pattern and repeat the process for the other side of the bag.

Alternatively, you could work only one side of the bag in canvas, using for the second side a textured fabric such as tweed, halving the amounts of yarn required.

To work the embroidery
Mark the centre of each side with lines of tacking (see Canvas Work Chapter 60) and plan the design out from the centre. Using the chart, work the design on each side of the bag.

To make up
When the work is complete stretch and trim the canvas (see Canvas Work Chapter 64) and cut out the two pieces of lining to the shape of the trimmed canvas.

Pin and tack the two sides of the bag together, right sides facing, stitch from A to B (see diagram) using one of the seaming methods given then stitch seam of the handle (see diagram).

Snip into the seam allowance on curves, and turning the bag to the right side, fold back the seam allowance round the upper edge of the bag and handle edges and tack down.

Sew the pieces of lining together in the same way as for the bag, folding the seam allowance round the top and along the handle to the back, and tack. Slip the lining into the bag, matching seams to

those of the bag. Pin, tack, and slip stitch into place, taking care to bring the lining right up to the edge of the embroidery so that no canvas is visible on the finished bag.

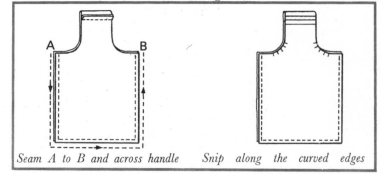

Seam A to B and across handle   Snip along the curved edges

Seam methods
For canvas work items which receive hard wear, a good strong method of seaming is needed.

After stretching the finished work (see Canvas Work Chapter 64) trim away excess canvas leaving not less than 1·6cm seam allowance all round. Place the work with right sides together and pin, matching the patterns carefully, and then tack. Back stitch by hand using either yarn of the background colour or matching linen thread. If you prefer to machine stitch the seam, use a strong linen thread matched to the background colour. Stitches should be placed as close as possible to the edge of the embroidery.

Oversew the raw edges of canvas to prevent fraying and trim back the corners. Turn the work to the right side and if any canvas shows along the seams, work a slip stitch, picking up one stitch of embroidery from each side of the seam to draw the stitches together over the canvas.

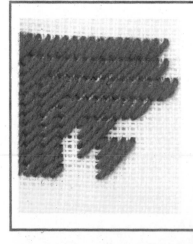

Slanted Gobelin
Blocked rows of slanted Gobelin show the method used for turning a corner (Canvas Work Chapter 59). Finally, here is one more stitch to add to your canvas work repertoire. This stitch produces a damask-like texture which will add richness to your work. It can be used either to highlight areas of a design or as a background stitch.

▼ *Close-up of textured stitches used on tote bag pictured opposite*

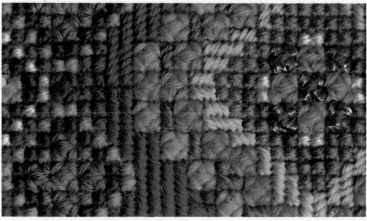

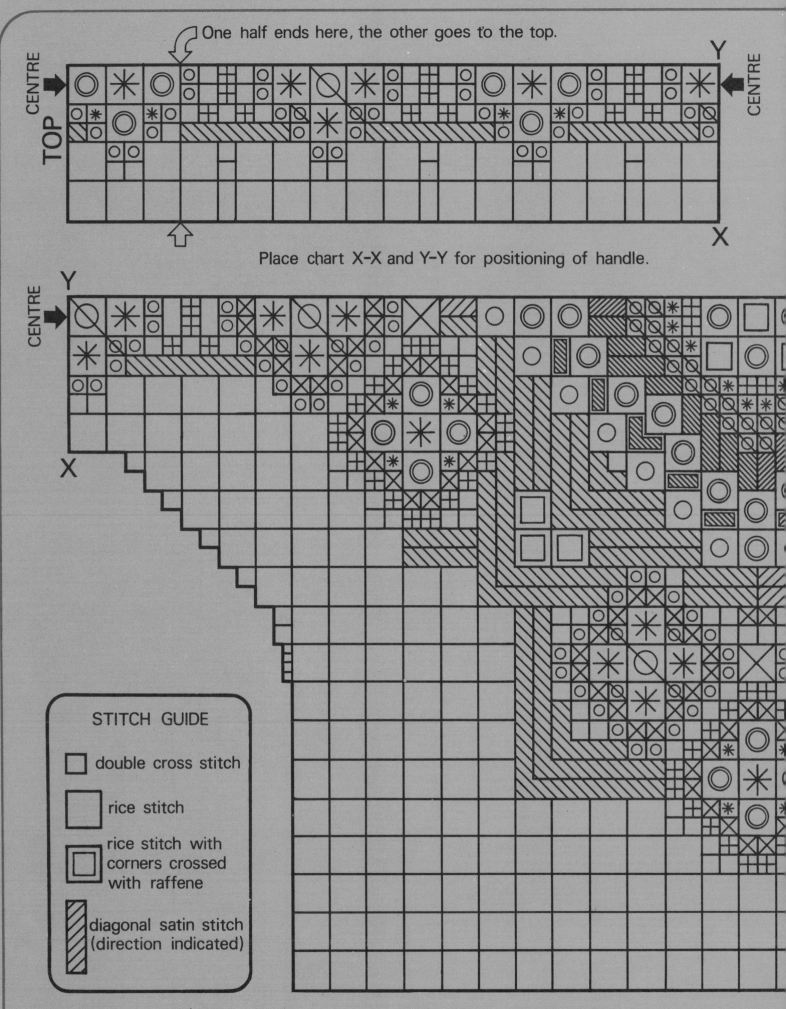

One half ends here, the other goes to the top.

Place chart X–X and Y–Y for positioning of handle.

STITCH GUIDE

- □ double cross stitch
- ▢ rice stitch
- ▣ rice stitch with corners crossed with raffene
- ▨ diagonal satin stitch (direction indicated)

Working chart for the tote bag

ANCHOR TAPISSERIE WOOL COLOUR CHART

◎ = pink _____ 085

⊠ = dark blue _____ 0148

◎ = blue _____ 0168

⊘ = turquoise _____ 0203

▨ ✳ = green _____ 0239

⊞ = pale blue _____ 0167

▨ = lime _____ 0290

□ = purple _____ 0107

purple raffene (Atlas) colour No.20

Double cross stitch worked over 2 threads each way.
Other stitches worked in proportion to this stitch.

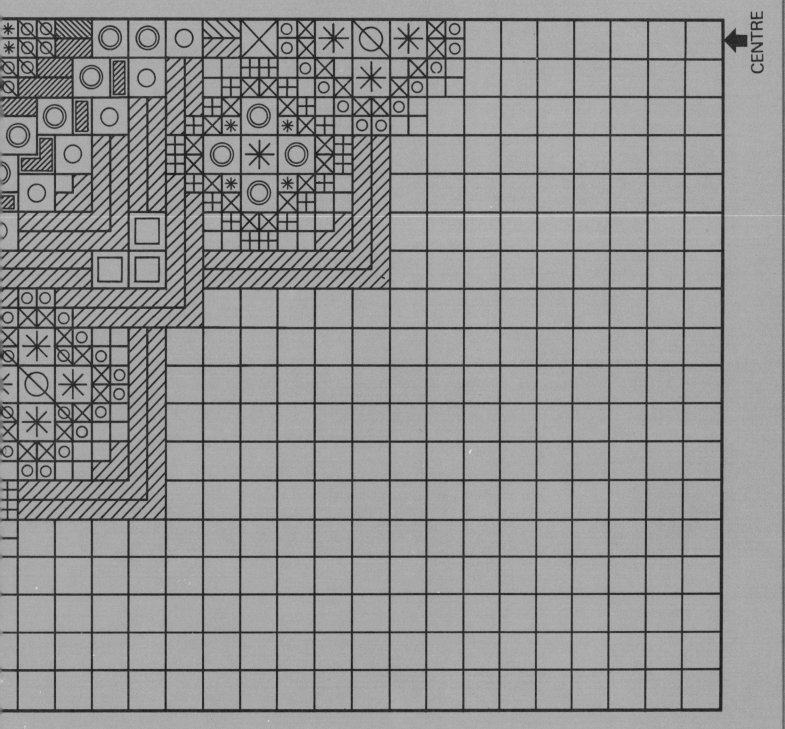

CENTRE

Chapter 59

Introduction to tent stitch

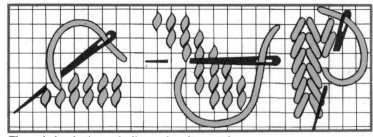

Tent stitch—horizontal, diagonal and reversed

Here are some easy and attractive stitches which can be used as groundings or fillings. They also form lovely patterns on their own when worked in two colours or two tones of one colour. Try tramming them with a contrast yarn or colour so that the contrast shade peeps through.

Tent stitch or petit point

Bring the needle through to the right side and then take it back and down one thread further on. Continue to the end of the row and then work backwards and forwards until the area is filled. If the work is spread over a large area it is advisable to work the stitch diagonally to prevent the canvas being pulled out of shape. Take the needle back over 1 thread and forward 2 threads, making a longer thread on the back of the work than the front. The stitch can also be worked in vertical or horizontal lines in alternate directions, that is, with the stitches sloping from left to right in one row and right to left in the next. When this method is used, it is called reverse tent stitch.

A bird panel worked in tent stitch

Upright Gobelin

This is worked with straight up-and-down stitches, usually over four horizontal threads of canvas.

Slanted Gobelin

This is similar to upright Gobelin, but worked over 2 vertical and 4 horizontal threads.

Bricking

This upright stitch is worked in interlocking rows.
1st row. Work alternate stitches over 4 horizontal threads.
2nd row. Start 2 threads lower and work a row of stitches over 4 threads, between the stitches of the first row.

Slanted bricking

This stitch is also worked in interlocking rows, but over 2 vertical and 4 horizontal threads which gives a smooth, slanted texture.

Parisian stitch

This is a small, close, filling stitch worked in interlocking rows over 1 and then over 3 horizontal threads.

Hungarian stitch

Again, this stitch is worked in interlocking rows, over 2 and then over 4 horizontal threads.

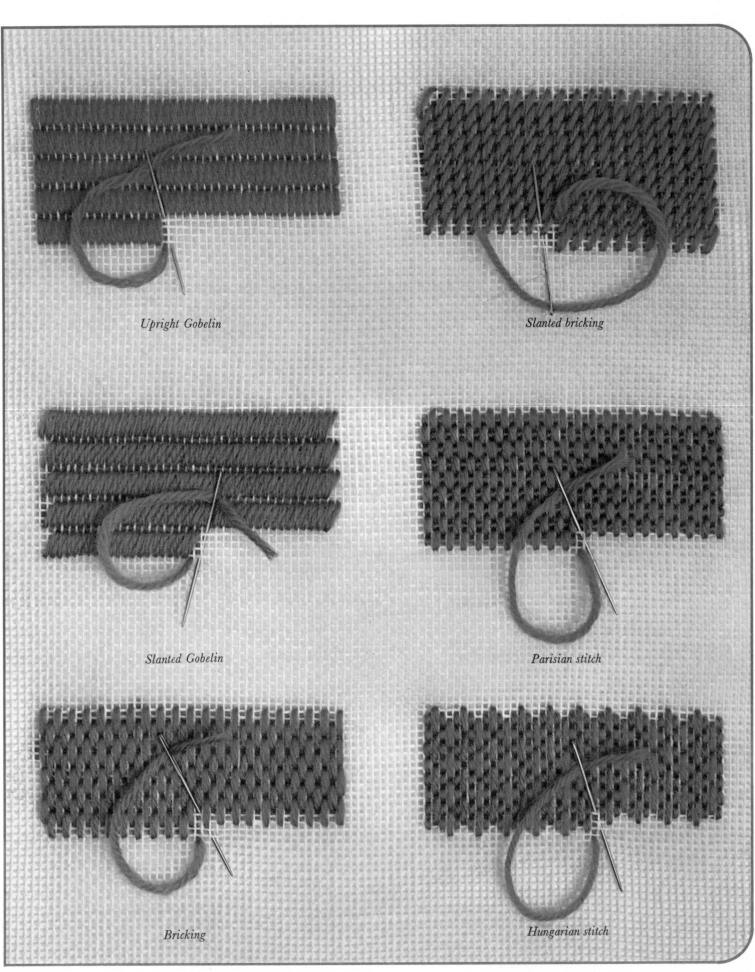

Upright Gobelin

Slanted bricking

Slanted Gobelin

Parisian stitch

Bricking

Hungarian stitch

Chapter 60

A pincushion in tent stitch

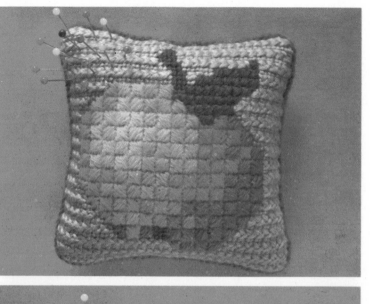

A pincushion is a good way to begin working from a charted picture. This is less expensive than choosing a painted or trammed canvas, which will confine you to the most commercially available designs, while a charted picture gives you the opportunity of picking your own colours and building up your own designs. For instance, you can repeat the apple motif given opposite at random all over a cushion, or turn it into a yellow Golden Delicious or a green Granny Smith.

Using a chart

A chart demands a little concentration when it comes to plotting the outlines, but once these are worked out the rest is easy. Start by finding the centre of the chart. In this case you need to find the centre of the apple motif, so count the number of squares from top to bottom and from side to side, divide each total by half and mark the centre. Then fold the canvas in half both ways and mark its centre with a pencil or lines of tacking. Start counting and stitching, from the centre. Each square on the chart corresponds to one thread intersection on the canvas.

If there are large areas of colour to be filled in, mark the outline and the smaller areas first, and then fill in the larger areas.

Two pincushions to work: one from the chart opposite, one row by row

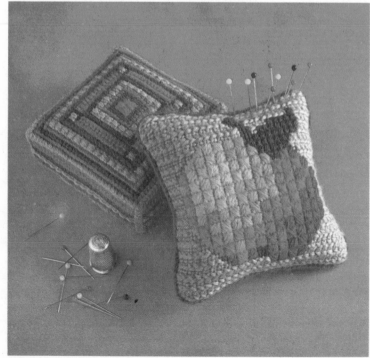

The right stitch for the right texture

Any design loses impact if all areas are worked in the same texture, that is, all rough or all smooth. For the most pleasing effect, it is important to separate areas of the design into smooth, medium and rough textures. (Tent, Gobelin, straight and satin stitches are all smooth. Cross, rice and star stitches are semi-rough. Double cross, oblong and tufted stitches are very rough.) Some stitches lend themselves to particular textures and shapes. For instance, slanted bricking (see Canvas Work Chapter 59) has a good texture for walls and brickwork, while fishbone stitch (see Canvas Work Chapter 66) interprets water very well. Tent and Gobelin stitches (see Canvas Work Chapter 59) clarify the line of design and for any form of intricate, realistic shading, nothing is quite as effective as tent stitch.

Strong texture often looks most effective when it is used sparingly. For example, you could work just the mane and tail of a horse in a rough textured stitch, or use different stitches for flower centres and leaves, or the underside of a fish.

Apple pincushion

This plump apple pincushion uses lustrous cushion stitch (see Canvas Work Chapter 57) to interpret the shiny apple, cross stitch for the gnarled leaf, and precise tent stitch for the neat shape of the stalk and eye.

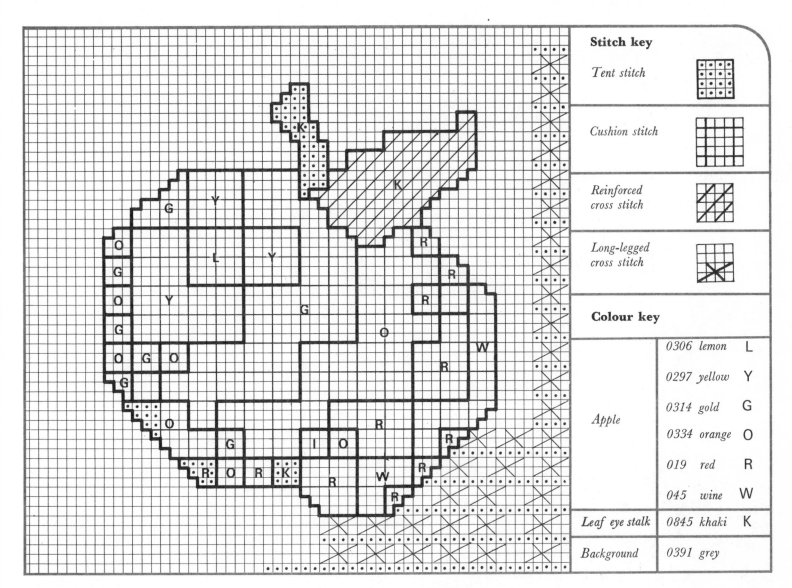

Stitch key

Tent stitch	
Cushion stitch	
Reinforced cross stitch	
Long-legged cross stitch	

Colour key

	0306	*lemon*	L
	0297	*yellow*	Y
	0314	*gold*	G
Apple	0334	*orange*	O
	019	*red*	R
	045	*wine*	W
Leaf eye stalk	0845	*khaki*	K
Background	0391	*grey*	

You will need

☐ Single weave canvas 25·5cm square, 28 threads to 5cm. (Finished size about 10cm square.)
☐ No.20 tapestry needle and a sharp needle for sewing up.
☐ Velvet or other backing material, 15cm square.
☐ One skein each of Anchor Tapisserie Wools 0306, 0297, 0314, 0334, 019, 045, 0845, 0314; and two skeins of 0391.
☐ 40·5cm of cord for trimming.
☐ For filling, bran from the corn merchant, or sawdust.

To work apple

Prevent the canvas from fraying by cutting strips of brown paper and tacking them over the edges. On the chart each square represents 1 canvas thread crossing which is to be covered by a single tent stitch.

Apple: work in cushion stitch in groups of four, over 3 threads.
Eye and stalk: work in tent stitch over 1 thread.
Leaf: work in reinforced cross stitch (ie, cross stitch worked twice over) over 2 threads. This ensures that there is a good coverage of the canvas.
Background: work in alternate rows of long-legged cross stitch worked over 2 threads, and tent stitch worked over 1 thread.

Stretching the canvas back into shape

When the design is completed stretch the canvas (see Canvas Work Chapter 64 and trim off excess canvas allowing 1·6cm turnings.

Finishing off

To back the cushion, cut a square of velvet to the size of the trimmed canvas. Tack the turnings to the wrong side to make a neat, accurate square. Tack canvas turnings to back of work, pin velvet to canvas, wrong sides together, and hem the velvet firmly into place, stitching into the outer row of canvas work stitches. Leave half of one side open for stuffing.
Bran is the stuffing which best allows pins to be pushed in easily. Pack it in very tightly—a teaspoon will help. Close the opening with pins and hem tightly when fully stuffed. Brush off any bran left lying on the pincushion. Neaten by sewing cord all round the edge, covering the seam.

Square pincushion

The square pincushion is worked in delightful, bright, rich colours in a simple geometric design using a variety of lovely stitches. Work it outwards from a centre block of 4 cushion stitches in rows as follows: 2 rows tent stitch, 1 row cross stitch, 1 row double cross stitch, 1 row satin stitch, 1 row oblong cross stitch with bars, 1 row long-legged cross stitch, 1 row double cross stitch, 1 row satin stitch, 1 row cross stitch. For the sides work 1 row oblong cross stitch with bars, 1 row long-legged cross stitch, 1 row double cross stitch, 1 row long-legged cross stitch, 1 row oblong cross stitch with bars. Work long-legged cross stitching for seams.

Chapter 61

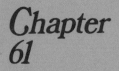

Fashion accessories in tent stitch

Canvas work has recently been updated by working it in brilliant colours for fashion accessories. The belts and bands given here are worked on double thread canvas with 20 double threads to 5cm. Tent stitch is used throughout. All colours and numbers refer to Patons Beehive Tapestry Wool.

▼ *Chart for matching wristband, neckband and fringed girdle*

▼ *Chart for the leather thonged belt on the right*

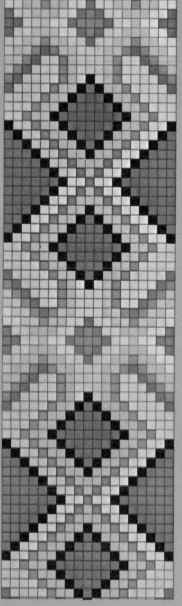

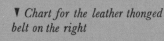

Neckband

Measurements
Finished size—5cm deep by neck measurement

Materials
☐ Canvas 15cm by 56cm
☐ 50cm ribbon, 5cm wide
☐ 61cm leather thonging
☐ 2 hanks each of red No. 2502, purple No.2522, lilac No.2524, black No.2622, orange No.2592, yellow No. 2580

Method
Work the design from the chart for the required length. Stretch and trim the canvas (see Canvas Work Chapter 64). Turn the raw canvas on the long sides to the back of the work and catch them down with herringbone stitch. To make the channel through which the thonging slots, turn the raw canvas on the two ends to the back of the work and back stitch them down 1cm from the edge. Line the band with ribbon using slip stitches and working through only one thickness of canvas at the ends so that the thonging channel is left open. Slot the thonging upwards through one channel and downwards through the other (see illustration).

Fringed girdle

Measurements
Finished size—8·5cm deep by the waist measurement, taken loosely, plus 16cm overlap

Materials
☐ Canvas 18cm by 1m
☐ Lining 10cm by 1m
☐ 6 hanks each of red No. 2511, lilac No.2524; 3 hanks each of purple No. 2526, yellow No.2579; 2 hanks each of black No. 2622, orange No.2592
☐ Piece of card 8·5cm by 15cm
☐ Large press studs

Method
Work the design from the chart for the required length. Stretch and trim the canvas (see Canvas Work Chapter 64), fold

under the raw canvas and herringbone stitch into place. To make the fringe, wind wool for 7·5cm along the card. Carefully sew one end of the loops to the canvas 6mm in from the end of the girdle, making sure that every strand is included. Slide the card out and work a row of back stitches to secure the fringe. Complete work by lining the girdle, enclosing the ends of the fringe. Use press studs for fastening, laying one end of the girdle over the other (see illustration).

Thonged belt

Measurements
Finished size—6·5cm deep by the waist measurement, loosely taken.

Materials
☐ Canvas 16cm by 1m
☐ Lining 10cm by 1m
☐ 1·15m leather thonging
☐ 10 eyelets and eyelet tool
☐ 4 hanks orange No.2591; 3 hanks red No.2594; 7 hanks lilac No.2521

Method
Work the design from the chart for the required length. Stretch and trim the canvas (see Canvas Work Chapter 64). Fold under the raw canvas and herringbone stitch into place. Line the belt and then insert five eyelets vertically, evenly spaced on each end of the belt. Lace the thonging through and tie.

Wristband

Measurements
Finished size—5cm deep by wrist measurement

Materials
☐ Canvas 15cm by 25·5cm
☐ 23cm ribbon, 5cm wide
☐ 61cm leather thonging
☐ 1 hank each of the colours given for neckband

Method
Work in the same way and to the same design as for the neckband.

▲ *The neckband with leather thonging tie*
▼ *Wristband to match neckband and girdle*

A fringed girdle to wear with a simple dress ►
▼ *A belt with leather thonging laces and detail of thonging*

Chapter 62

Director's chair in tent stitch

Directors' style chairs are easy to cover and look marvellous in brilliant embroidery. The stylised flower design in this chapter is simple to copy and looks best in a modern setting.

The modern canvas chair can vary in styling detail. In this chapter you will find two basic methods of making covers and one or other will adapt to most variations.

Pop-on cover (photographs)

This type of cover simply fits over the original back and seat sections and is easily removed for cleaning purposes.

Materials you will need
- [ ] Canvas with 20 double threads to 5cm
- [ ] Tapisserie wools
- [ ] Sateen lining
- [ ] Press stud tape for attaching cover
- [ ] Plastic foam 2·5cm thick (optional)

Canvas Work

To make a pattern
Pin a sheet of strong paper over and around the fabric back and another over the seat of the chair. With a pencil, mark the edges of the shape onto the paper. Remove the paper and even up the shape before cutting out. Once the pieces are cut out, check them against the back and seat to make sure that they fit well.

Pin the pieces onto canvas, following the grain lines of the canvas. Mark the outline onto the canvas with a felt tipped pen, leaving sufficient canvas all round for seam allowances and stretching.

Completing the embroidery
Plan the flower design as described in Canvas Work Chapter 55 using the chart on the following pages as a guide if you wish. Work the design in tent stitch or cross stitch. When it is completed, stretch and trim the canvas as described in Canvas Work Chapter 64, leaving 1·5cm turnings.

Padding
For additional comfort, pad between the canvas and the lining with 2·5cm thick plastic foam.

To make up
Cut the lining to the size of the stitched and trimmed canvas. Turn seam allowances to the back and tack. Turn all canvas raw edges to the back of the work and herringbone stitch in place. Line the shapes with sateen lining. Stitch lengths of press stud tape to each end of the canvas work back and seat sections and then on to the corresponding areas on the actual chair.

Slip cover (drawings)

This type of cover has tube openings at each end of the back section to slip over the back supports, and also at each side of the seat section to slide on rods which are held in place by the structure of the chair. This cover replaces the original back and seat covers on the chair.

Materials you will need
- [ ] Canvas with 20 double threads to 5cm
- [ ] Tapisserie wools
- [ ] Dull finish cotton such as sail cloth for lining back of the cover
- [ ] Canvas or hessian (optional) for lining seat

To make up
As the original sections are removed from the chair first, they can be used as a pattern guide. Cut out the pattern and work the embroidery as for the pop-on cover.
Line the back section as for the pop-on cover with sail cloth. The seat of the chair must be reinforced either by backing it with strong canvas or hessian or by using the original seat section.
Once the backing has been stitched to the canvas work, turn under the ends as on the original sections and stitch. Slide into place on the chair frame.

▲ *The director's chair folded*
▼ *The back and seat sections*

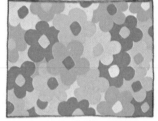

▲ *Slip on back and seat of chair*
▼ *The director's chair complete*

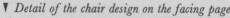
▼ *Detail of the chair design on the facing page*

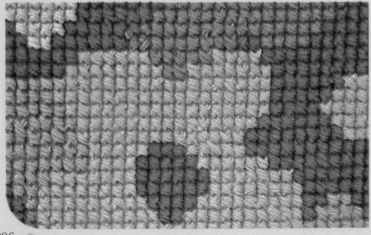

The working chart for the chair cover

Each square on the chart = 1 stitch

Use one horizontal section of the chart for the chair back and as much as you need of the complete chart for the seat (the chart does not give exactly the same repeats as the photograph).

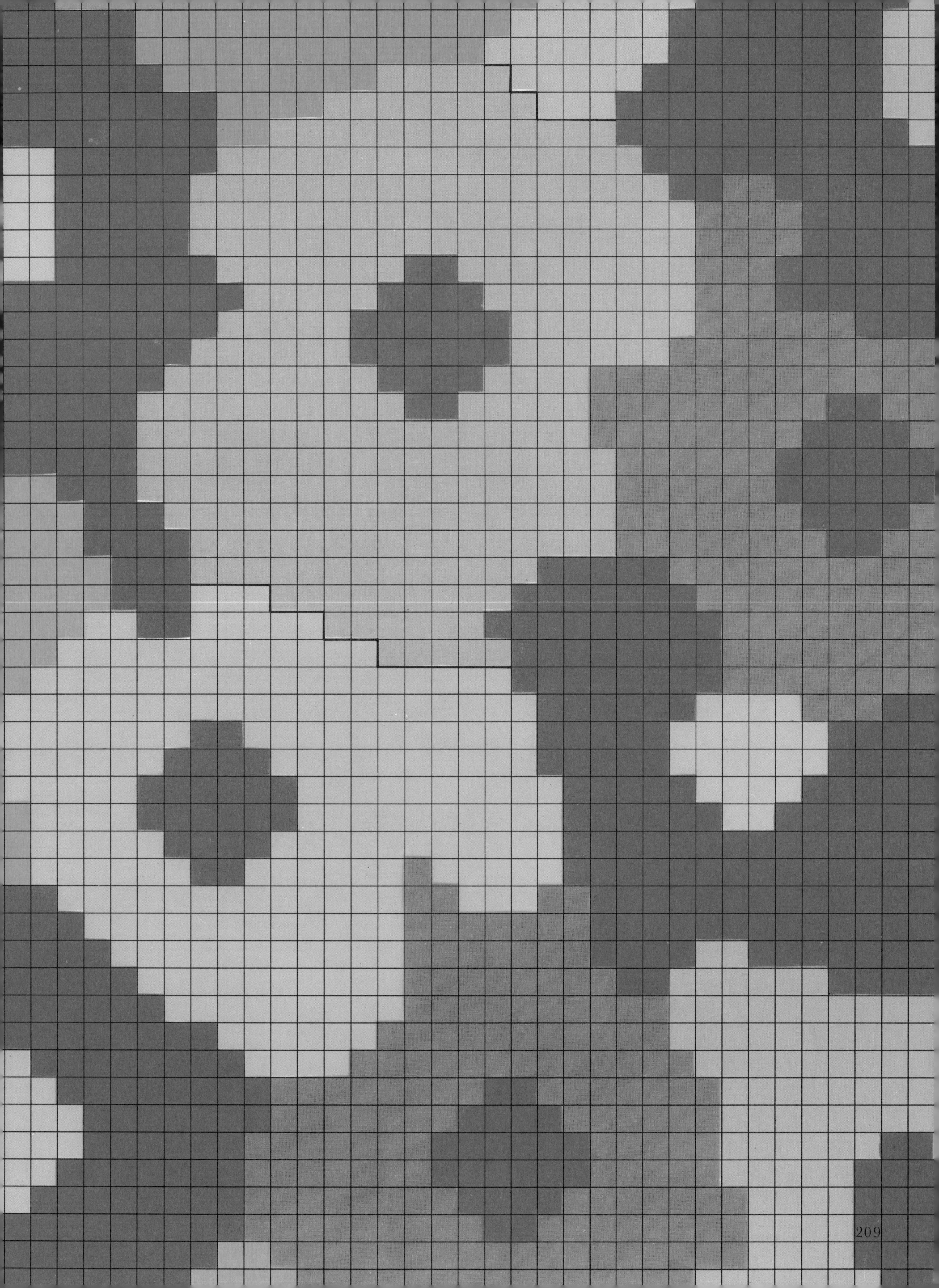

Chapter 63

A handbag worked in tent stitch

This chapter gives detailed instructions for making up a canvas work handbag and mounting it onto a metal handbag frame. It also gives some extremely useful hints on the planning of your own designs for handbags.

Designs for canvas work bags

The traditional floral design worked in tent stitch illustrated in this chapter is always popular, and similar designs can be found either in the form of working charts or painted onto canvas. These are several points to be considered when planning an original design for a bag. The design should fit happily into shape of the bag and should be of neither too large nor too small a scale in relation to the size and shape. For example, one tiny motif in the centre of the bag might look insignificant, whereas a very large motif overspilling the size of the bag might look clumsy. Over-all patterns should be designed in a proportionate scale to that of the size of the bag. The placing and planning of a design for the gusset of the bag also requires careful thought. It should neither detract attention away from the main design by being too complex, nor should it appear as a trivial afterthought. If an all-over geometric pattern is used, care must be taken to ensure that the lines of the design match accurately on the gusset and the sides of the bag.

To make a canvas work bag you will need:
- [ ] Canvas 81·5cm by 51cm
- [ ] 50cm lining fabric
- [ ] 50cm hessian
- [ ] Yarns
- [ ] Tapestry needle
- [ ] Crewel needle
- [ ] Strong sewing thread (for making up bag)
- [ ] 1·40m piping cord
- [ ] 1·40m 2·5cm wide bias cut fabric or piece of fine leather for piping
- [ ] Bag frame measuring 20·5 cm across top between mounting isles

To cut bag pattern

Draw the pattern for the bag onto 2·5cm squared paper. Cut the pattern out and pin it onto the canvas, matching the grain lines of the pattern with the grain of the canvas. Mark the outline of the pattern pieces onto the canvas using a felt tipped pen. Leave at least 10cm space between each pattern section to allow for stretching and seam allowances. Mark the centre of each side of the bag and the gusset with vertical and horizontal lines of tacking stitches. Using the centre guide tacks, plan and work the design of your choice on the bag sections.

▼ *The trace-off pattern for the bag and gusset*

NO SEAM ALLOWANCE SHOWN

HALF GUSSET LENGTH

◁ LINE OF GRAIN FOR GUSSET ▷

CENTRE

↕ LINE OF GRAIN

EACH SQUARE = 2·5cm

To make up bag

When all stitching has been completed, stretch the canvas as described in Canvas Work Chapter 64. Trim the excess canvas away leaving 1·6cm on all edges for seam allowance.

Cut out the hessian interfacing and lining to match the trimmed bag sections. Pin and tack the hessian sections to each of the canvas work sections and make up as one.

Make two lengths of piping by covering piping cord with either 2·5cm wide bias cut fabric or strips of leather and pin and tack this round the edge of each side section of the bag.

Match up the centre mark on the gusset to one side of the bag, pin and tack the gusset in position, cutting notches on the curves where necessary. Stitch by machine as close to the piping as possible, using the piping foot, or by hand using a strong back stitch starting and finishing at the points of the gusset. Repeat the process for the second side of the bag. Turn and tack the seam allowance round the top of the bag and gusset to the back of the work. Position the bag top on the bag frame, and hold in place with tie tacks through the holes on both sides of the frame at the corners. Stitch firmly in position using sewing silk threaded double in the needle, sliding the needle through the fold along the top of the bag until it is level with a hole in the frame. Bring needle out and make two or three oversewing stitches through the hole and into the wrong side of the canvas.

Sew the lining pieces together and pin into position inside the bag, turning in the edges to fit the inside of the bag frame. Slip stitch firmly into position. If a mirror pocket is desired inside the bag, this should be stitched to the lining before it is sewn together.

▼ *The piping stitched to the bag*

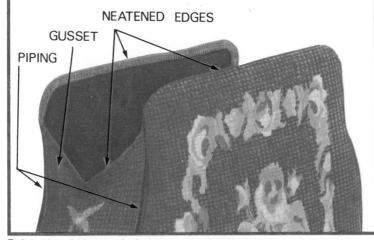

▼ *Stitching the bag to the frame*

▲ ▼ *Two views of the completed bag*

Chapter 64

Stem stitch and mosaic stitch

If you are not yet very experienced at canvas work you will find that a lighter case or spectacle case are both quick, fun and easy to make. You can try out your favourite stitch to work all-over, rich textured patterns, or you can use any of the other stitches shown here.

Stem stitch. Work from the bottom upwards over 2 horizontal and 2 vertical threads. The spaces between the rows are filled with back stitches in a yarn of contrasting colour.

Mosaic stitch. This is worked in diagonal rows from top left to bottom right of the canvas in groups of 3 stitches; over 1,2, and 1 threads of canvas.

Mosaic diamond stitch. This is worked in rows from left to right over 1, 3, 5, 3, and 1 threads of canvas.

Instructions for making up canvas work

Sometimes canvas work, which takes quite a time to complete, can be ruined by hurried making up, so in order not to spoil your careful work follow these instructions.

Stretching

It is essential to allow for stretching purposes at least 5cm of canvas all round the finished size of the work. The excess canvas is trimmed away to the required seam width after stretching. Canvas work should never be pressed with an iron, as this flattens the textured stitches and ruins the appearance. Most stitches distort the canvas because of their diagonal pull and the best way to restore the canvas to its original shape is as follows.

Dampen the back of the work with cold water. Cover a drawing board, or old work table with several sheets of white blotting paper. Place the work face down on the board and pin out, using drawing pins at one inch intervals. Pull the work gently into shape, adjusting the drawing pins. Dampen the work again thoroughly and leave for at least 24 hours, away from heat, until it is dry. When the work is completely dry, check for any missed stitches and fill them in at this stage.

How to make a seam

There are several seam methods suitable for canvas work and this one is particularly good for small items which cannot be turned through to the right side after being seamed. The usual seam allowance is 1·6cm, but for smaller items, such as a lighter case, 1cm is sufficient. As canvas frays easily it is a good idea to oversew the raw edges before making up. With imaginative use of yarn and stitches, the seams can form a complementary and decorative feature to the piece of work.

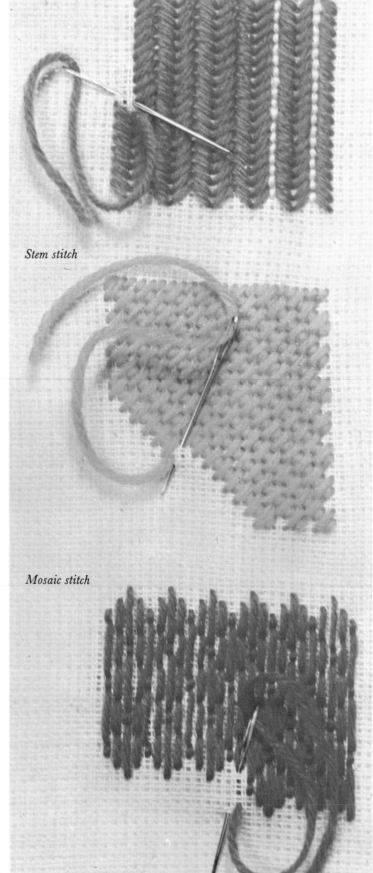

Stem stitch

Mosaic stitch

Mosaic diamond stitch

Method

Trim the canvas work ready to seam and fold all turnings to the wrong side of the work. Trim and neaten the corners and tack the seam allowance in place. Pin the two seam edges with the wrong sides together, matching up the pattern. Work whip stitch, cross stitch or oblong cross stitch along the seam on the right side, picking up opposite threads of the canvas from each side as you work. The seam when completed becomes part of the canvas work.

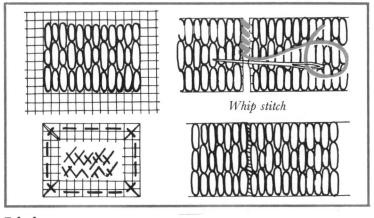

Whip stitch

Linings

The choice of lining is most important since it should not draw attention away from the stitching, either in colour or texture. It is best to choose a firm, dull-surface fabric in a plain toning colour. Pick the darkest tone used in the design because this will give strength to the design, whereas a light colour will draw more attention to the lining than to the canvas work. Lining seams can either be machined or hand sewn with back stitch.

Spectacle case

You will need: ☐ canvas ☐ yarn ☐ 10cm length of cord ☐ lining.
Cut the canvas to measure 47cm x 17·5cm, and cover an area which measures 37cm x 7·5cm with stitches.
Stretch and trim the canvas, then cut a piece of lining material to the trimmed size.
To prepare the canvas work for seaming, fold lengthwise leaving a 6·5cm flap, right sides facing. Stitch the piece of cord securely to the seam allowance on the wrong side, 2·5cm down from the opening. Tack edges and seam.
With right sides of the lining together, turn up 14·8cm leaving a 7·5cm flap. Stitch the side seams from the fold to within 1cm of the opening. Fold the seam allowance round the flap and across the opening to the wrong side of the lining, tack and press. Slip the lining into the case, using a blunt pencil to push it right down into the corners. Pin the lining round the edges of the opening and flap, matching the seams of the lining to the seams of the case, and tack them together and slip stitch neatly into place. Remove tacking. Fold over the 6·5cm flap and tuck it under the cord.

Lighter case

You will need: ☐ canvas ☐ yarn ☐ lining.
For an average size lighter case, cut the canvas to measure 17cm x 25·5cm and embroider an area measuring 7cm x 15·5cm. Stretch the canvas and prepare it for seaming. With the right side of the work facing you, fold it in half and stitch the side seams, finishing as described for the spectacle case, omitting the flap and cord.

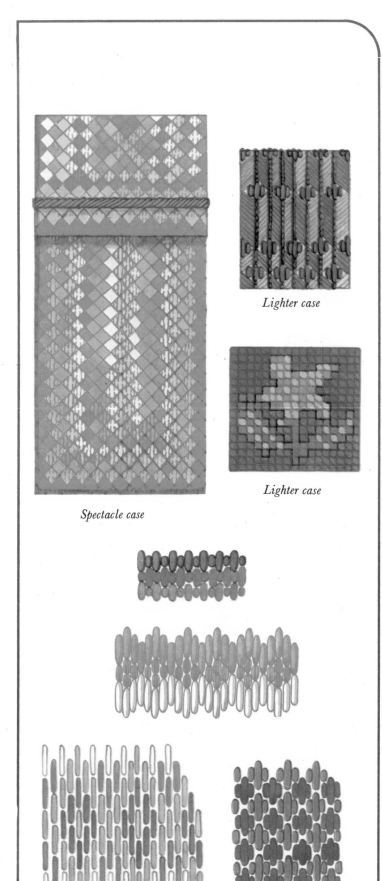

Lighter case

Lighter case

Spectacle case

Some ideas for colour and stitch combinations

Chapter 65

Stylised panel in a variety of stitches

Once you have built up a repertoire of canvas work stitches it is fascinating to combine them into a project. This panel incorporates many stitches which are built up into a cityscape of buildings seen by the light of the moon. Norwich stitch, recently discovered on a piece of work in the Norwich museum, is used at the base of the fountain.

Special effects

Each stitch has been chosen for the special effect it creates. Particular examples are the leaf stitch effect on the trees in the square, the paving stones represented in cushion stitch and the blue blocks of satin stitch for a tiled roof (see Canvas Work Chapter 57). Under the arches the areas of shadow are created by using a mixture of pink and grey-pink yarns in the needle.

As well as an imaginative use of stitches, the colours and yarn textures contribute to the atmosphere of the picture. The town hall at the lower right-hand corner and nearly all the houses are in darkness, but a light shines from two windows, one in pink, the other giving a warm red glow. Other windows reflect the moonlight in plastic raffia, and in the square the spray of a fountain sparkles in silver beads. The soft warm tones of the colours are evocative of a hot summer night.

Materials you will need

- ☐ 51cm by 56cm single weave white canvas with 28 threads to 5cm (finished size 29cm by 40cm)
- ☐ Tapestry needle size 18
- ☐ Hardboard 29cm by 40cm
- ☐ Fine string
- ☐ Slate frame
- ☐ 5 skeins Anchor Soft Embroidery Cotton 0167; 7 skeins 0103
- ☐ 1 skein each Anchor Stranded Cotton 0103, 0872, 0112
- ☐ 1 skein each Anchor Tapisserie Wool 0987, 089, 0168, 0417, 0388
- ☐ 2 skeins each Anchor Tapisserie Wool 0132, 063, 087, 0504; 3 skeins 0125; 12 skeins 0118
- ☐ Small quantities purple wooden beads, small silver beads, dark blue plastic raffia

Working the panel

Work with the canvas in a slate frame, using the illustration as a chart. Begin by working the left-hand building first, then out and across the other buildings, filling in the background as you progress. If the background areas are left until the buildings are all completed, the worked stitches will have spread the threads of the canvas, thus pulling the remaining canvas threads too close together for easy stitching. Complete the panel by working the outer background on all four edges to the required depth.

Stretch the work (see Canvas Work Chapter 64) and mount over the piece of hardboard (see Canvas Work Chapter 55). The panel can be hung framed or unframed.

Stitch guide

1. Blocked satin stitch	11. Parisian stitch
2. Detached eyelets	12. Tile stitch
3. Tent stitch	13. Plaited Algerian stitch
4. Rice stitch	14. Mosaic stitch
5. Norwich stitch	15. Satin stitch
6. French knots	16. Double cross stitch
7. Leaf stitch	17. Raised chain band and
8. Encroaching Gobelin stitch	darning worked on a
9. Cushion stitch	foundation of encroaching
10. Chequer stitch	Gobelin stitch

Norwich stitch worked over odd number of threads, in numbered sequence, in directions indicated

Raised chain band edged with darning stitch over a base of encroaching Gobelin stitch

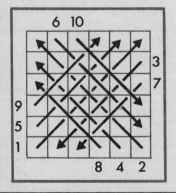

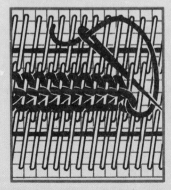

Chapter 66

Introduction to chevron stitches

Here are four more textured stitches for covering large areas of canvas or for working interesting textured backgrounds to designs. Work them in grouped areas of strongly contrasting colours for the brilliant effects shown on the doorstop.

Rep stitch
A stitch worked in vertical rows on double weave canvas.

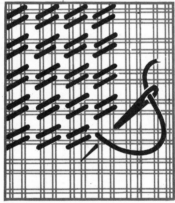

Worked in a thick yarn which completely covers the canvas, the stitch resembles the fabric from which it takes its name.

Basket filling stitch
This is a surface filling stitch usually worked on counted threads, but it makes an ideal

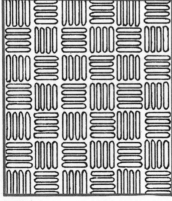

canvas work stitch, giving a lovely texture for a background. Interesting effects can be achieved by using two tones of one colour.

Fishbone stitch
This stitch is worked over three horizontal and three vertical threads of double thread canvas. Each long stitch is caught down with a short stitch across one double thread of canvas. It is worked in alternate rows from top to bottom and from the bottom upwards. The stitch makes a good grounding stitch and can be equally successful when worked on single weave canvas.

Knitting stitch
This stitch resembles chain stitch but it is worked in a similar way as stem stitch in

vertical rows. It is used only on double thread canvas. Bring the needle out at the top and insert it two holes down and across to the left. Bring the needle out two holes across and one hole up to the right and continue to the end of the row. The second row is worked in reverse from bottom to top.

Knitting stitch worked on double thread canvas

Fishbone stitch in a single colour

Fishbone stitch in four colours

To make a brick door stop you will need

☐ 50cm of double or single weave canvas about 61cm wide

☐ A small piece of hessian or felt for backing

☐ One brick

☐ Yarns

☐ Tapestry needle and a crewel needle for sewing up

Making the pattern

Lay the brick on a sheet of paper and draw all round the base. Tip the brick onto a long side, keeping the edge exactly along the longest edge of the line already drawn, and draw round this side. Tip the brick onto a short end and draw again. A pattern will result shaped like the diagram. Cut the shape out. Tack the shape to the canvas, making sure that the edges run exactly in line with the thread of the canvas, and outline it with a felt tipped pen. Remove the paper pattern and mark the centre of the pattern with two lines of tacking. Also mark the edges of the top area of the brick so that you can plan the design centrally.

Work the pattern shape with a stitched design. Stretch and trim away the excess canvas allowing 1·6cm turnings of raw canvas (see Canvas Work Chapter 64). Slash into the corners to within 6mm of the stitching and cut across the outer corners diagonally to within 6mm of the point of stitching. Fold all the seam allowances to the back of the work, mitre the corners and tack. With the right side of the work facing you, bring A and B together and seam, using the seam method given in Canvas Work Chapter 64. Seam the remaining three corners in the same way. Now cut a piece of hessian or felt for the base of the brick (if using felt, no turnings are required). Fold turnings to the wrong side of fabric, tack and press carefully.

Slip the canvas work over the brick, pin the piece of hessian or felt to the base and oversew it firmly to the canvas.

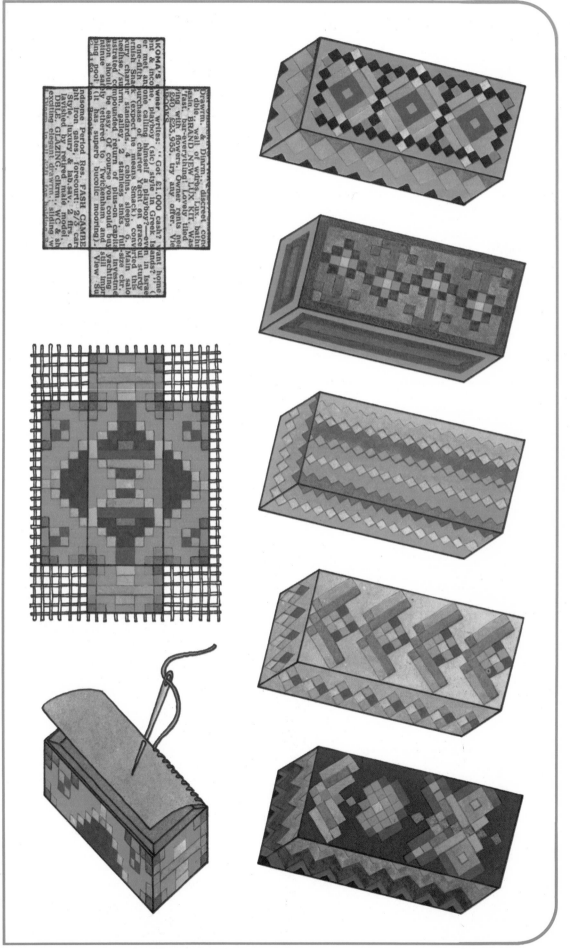

Collector's Piece

Florentine from the New World

Popular with embroiderers all over Europe, including England, it was inevitable that the technique of Florentine should have been carried across the Atlantic to the American colonies. The beautiful examples shown here, all from American collections, are dated from before 1800, yet the colours of the yarns are only slightly faded. The group of purses, which are dated between 1750 and 1800, feature the carnation, strawberry and flickering flame patterns. The brilliantly coloured purse which is worked with the name of the owner, Hendrick Rutgers, is also worked with the date of its execution—1761. The Queen Anne type wing chair, dated 1725 and now in the Metropolitan Museum of Art, New York, is a curiosity. The front of the chair, as seen, is worked in Florentine stitch. The back of the chair is rather surprisingly adorned with a magnificent panel, freely worked in crewel wools, showing various aspects of hunting—running deer, pursuing hounds, birds in flight, ducks on a pond, all against an undulating landscape.

Four purses from the Boston Museum of Fine Arts; Hendrick Rutgers purse from the Museum of the City of New York; part of a carnation pole screen from the collection of Ginsberg and Levy; Queen Anne type chair from Metropolitan Museum of Art, New York, a gift from Mrs J. Insley Blair

Chapter 67

Introduction to Florentine

Florentine, also known as Bargello and Hungarian embroidery, is made up of flat stitches worked in a range of different, coloured threads. Rarely out of fashion, it had a great vogue during the early 18th century when bed hangings, chairs and other household furnishings were worked in Florentine. It was ideal for bed curtains as the wavering designs, creating an illusion of movement, looked handsome whether the curtains were open or closed. Flame stitch, yet another name for this embroidery, aptly describes it.

In its simplest form it is very quick and relaxing work and also adapts to experimentation in both design and colour. The samples opposite illustrate this point. Notice the different pattern structures and the way in which the colours alternately blend together and contrast sharply.

Method of working Florentine

The simple, flat stitch is taken over four threads of single weave canvas and back two (diagrams 1 and 2). The stitches are worked so that only a small amount of thread shows on the back of the canvas (diagram 3). From this beginning lines of zigzag stitching are worked across the canvas and the pattern is repeated above and below the basic line.

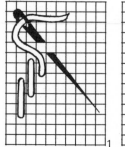

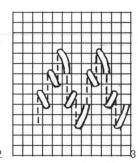

Pattern and colour experiments

Try working the samples illustrated opposite by following the design lines from the photographs. Begin with the bright contrast colours and follow the sequence of colours above and below it.

Materials you will need

☐ Single weave canvas 36 threads to 5cm
☐ Tapestry needle size 18
☐ Anchor Tapisserie Wool in the following colours:
☐ Pattern A: 1 skein yellow/green range of tones 0306; 0290; 0265; 0268; 0269; 1 skein yellow/brown range of tones 0308; 0358; 0359; 0360

☐ Pattern B: 1 skein red range of tones 0893; 0894; 0895; 0896; 0430; 1 skein pink 063
☐ Pattern C: 1 skein cyclamen 086; 1 skein blue range of tones 0106; 0107; 0125; 0850; 0851
☐ Pattern D: 1 skein pink 063: 1 skein cyclamen 086; 1 skein blue range of tones 0107; 0125; 0851

Suggestion for using these patterns

Any of the samples opposite can be worked on cushions, chair pads, stools or wall hangings. Try combining several for the most decorative effect on a wall hanging or work them on a smaller scale using stranded cotton on even-weave linen. They could also be used as border patterns on table linen, or decorations on belts.

Florentine cushions

Work Florentine using the samples opposite as a guide. You might experiment using different colours and so vary your design.

Materials you will need

☐ 51cm by 40·5cm single weave canvas with 36 threads to 5cm: finished size 40·5cm by 30·5cm
☐ Anchor Tapisserie Wool: 3 skeins of each colour for patterns B to D and 4 skeins of each for pattern A
☐ Lining 45·5cm by 35·5cm
☐ Cushion pad to fit
☐ 35cm zip

Making the cushion

Mark the centre of the canvas and the outline of the finished size. Begin at the middle point of the centre line from a high point in the pattern and stitch outwards. (If you are working pattern A, begin at the centre of the green oval). Continue working in rows across the canvas below this line, until the marked area is filled. When you reach the outline it will be necessary to fill in with half stitches to form a straight line. Stretch the finished work as shown in Canvas Work Chapter 64 and make up cushion as shown in Embroidery Chapter 15.

Two panels in Florentine

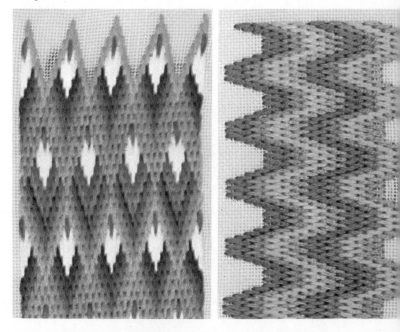

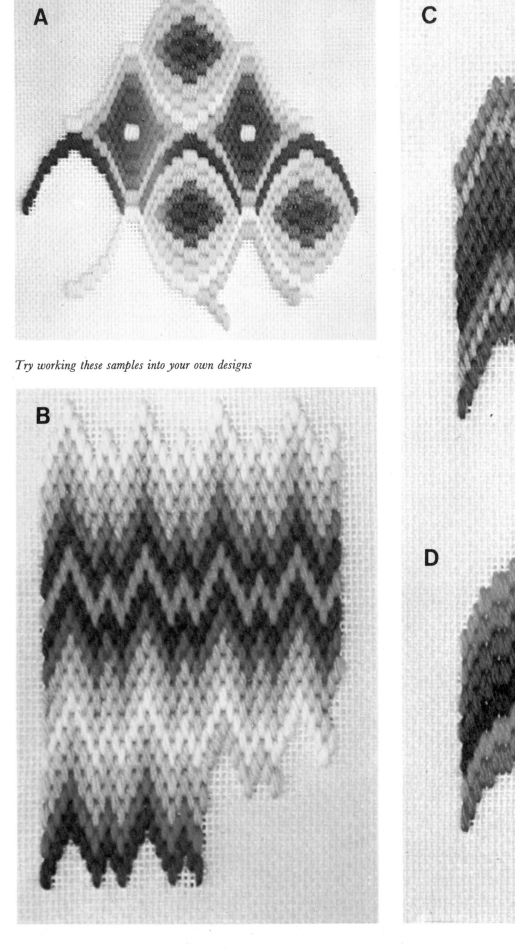

Try working these samples into your own designs

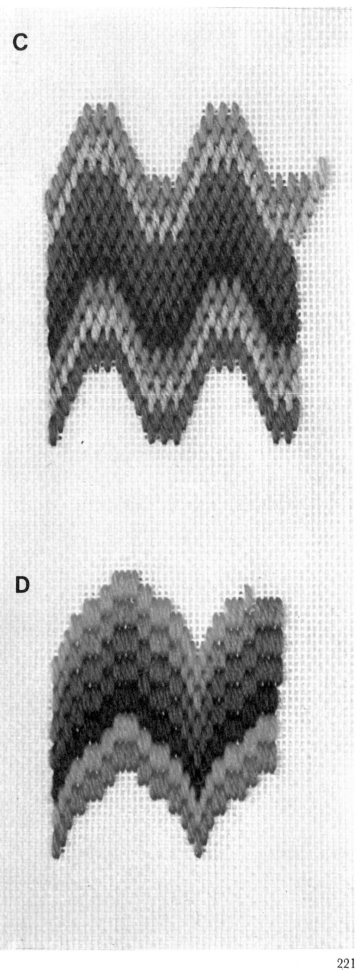

INDEX